Arthur Leared

Marocco and the Moors

Being an Account of Travels, with a General Description of the Country and its

People. Second Edition

Arthur Leared

Marocco and the Moors
Being an Account of Travels, with a General Description of the Country and its People. Second Edition

ISBN/EAN: 9783337207434

Printed in Europe, USA, Canada, Australia, Japan

Cover: Foto ©Andreas Hilbeck / pixelio.de

More available books at **www.hansebooks.com**

MAROCCO AND THE MOORS:

BEING

ACCOUNT OF TRAVELS, WITH A GENERAL DESCRIPTION
OF THE COUNTRY AND ITS PEOPLE.

BY

ARTHUR LEARED, M.D. Oxon., F.R.C.P.,

FELLOW OF THE ROYAL GEOGRAPHICAL SOCIETY, MEMBER OF THE ROYAL IRISH ACADEMY,
AND OF THE ICELANDIC LITERARY SOCIETY, COPENHAGEN, ETC.

SECOND EDITION,

REVISED AND EDITED BY

SIR RICHARD BURTON, K.C.M.G.

WITH ILLUSTRATIONS.

London:

SAMPSON LOW, MARSTON, SEARLE, & RIVINGTON,
LIMITED,
ST. DUNSTAN'S HOUSE, FETTER LANE, E.C.

NEW YORK: SCRIBNER & WELFORD.

1891.

[*All rights reserved.*]

PREFACE.

I ENDEAVOUR in the work thus presented to the public to give an account of what I saw and heard in a country almost as little known as any in the world. It was my habit while travelling in Marocco to note down everything that seemed worth recording. But in order to make up for length of personal observation, I supplemented this with information derived from residents in the country. In this respect I am especially indebted to Horace White, Esq., H.B.M. Consul, and to M. Lambert, at Tangier; to Charles Murdoch and George Hunot, H.B.M. Vice-Consul, Esqs., at Saffi; and to M. Beaumier, Consul of France, and Thomas Yule, George Broom, and Judah Yuly, Esqs., at Mogador.

I own to being one of those who prefer a plain narrative, such as is found in the works of the older travellers, to those of more modern style, and even plead guilty to a desire to be instructive. While, therefore, every effort has been made to insure accuracy of statement, no one will, I hope, be disappointed at finding an entire absence of smart writing.

One thing held in view has been to bring into notice, as much as possible, the incomparable climates to be found in Marocco for persons suffering from affections of the chest.

The difficulty of travelling in Marocco accounts for the few books which have appeared on the subject in modern times. The work of Gerhard Rohlfs, "Adventures in Morocco," admirably, but anonymously, translated into English, is mainly taken up with what its name imports. It contains, however, much valuable information, and, even after allowing for the difficulty of arriving at truth in that country, some strange inaccuracies.

A. L.

Nov. 1, 1875.

INTRODUCTION.

AFTER a lapse of fifteen years—years so changeful and prolific of progress to England, so languorous and monotonous to Marocco—a reprint of the work by my late friend, Dr. ARTHUR LEARED, is required by the public; and Mrs. Leared has honoured me with a request for a few lines expressing my opinion of the author's travel-tale.

"Marocco and the Moors" is the work of a learned physician, a skilled practitioner, an observer of no common powers, and a genial, liberal, travelled man, well known in Iceland and in westernmost Mauritania — Maghribu 'l-Aksa. The object of the book is by no means literary, nor does the author attempt to rival

M. Tissot in geographical or antiquarian research, to emulate Herr Gerhardt Rohlfs in romantic and perilous adventure, or to draw admirable word-pictures like Signor Edmondo de Amicis. His style is not "smart," as he confesses in his preface; but it suits right well his main object, to portray, soberly and correctly, the scenes and places which meet the traveller's eye. His specialty, viz., philanthropic professional studies, had convinced him that the Sanitaria of Southern Europe offer but few advantages to the large class of invalids in whom he had ever taken peculiar interest; and he presently came honestly to the conclusion that Mediterranean Tangier, like remote Mogador, has a climate of sovereign efficacy for those suffering from pulmonary affections.

In early September, 1872, Dr. Leared first touched ground at Tangier, now an open roadstead, once a fine artificial and well-fortified harbour. Here the traveller is first introduced to Maroccan town-life. The Customhouse shed on the foul Marina (strand) is exceedingly primitive, a *hangar* tenanted by turbaned and long-bearded Malignants who let the rich pass scot-free and who miserably plunder the poor. A wretched ramp leads up to the mass of the settlement, the venerable Tingis of the Classics and Tanjah of the Moslems, showing all the stagnation of dirty and decrepit old age. The streets, made for camels not for carriages, are rock-paved alleys like torrent-beds, which serve mainly for drains, sewers, cesspools: here every kind of festering offal offends eye and nostril, from poultry-feathers and kitchen-slops to corpse of rat and cat—dead baby not being wholly unknown. The tenements are the normal mixture of huge white-washed palace, dingy pauper hovel and tumble-down ruin; the shops are holes in the walls; the mosque doorways are screened lest Káfir glance pollute these holy barns, and the Súks, or market-places, are alternately sheets of mud, viscid and ankle-deep, and dust-heaps, fit dwellings for microbes and playgrounds for the winds. And this mass of impurities is girt by fortifications, walls and bastions, built to resist six-pounders.

Yet close behind and north of such abominations is a breezy upland of natural turf, crowning the cliffs and stretching about a mile in length by half that breadth. Upon the sandstone rock-face, here and there dotted with oblong hollows, locally called "Phœnician graves," the pure Mediterranean wave ever breaks, and there is a constant alternation of winds, now a zephyr, then a gale, between the Atlantic Ocean and the Midland Sea. My daily constitutionals, mostly in this direction, supplied me with a prophylactic against the heat and fumes of the fetid town. Here the late Lord St. Maur built a villa, now occupied by the Sherif and Sherifah of Wázán, and here Dr. Leared secured a piece of land sufficient for his intended Sanitarium.

Tangier, now a replica of Egyptian Suez during the barbarous days before the Overland Transit, has a manifest destiny in the near future. She is the only terminus of the railway which presently must connect the seaboard with the sundry capitals of the "Shereefian Empire," and which will subdue the refractory and rebellious tribes of Southern Sús and of the furthermost interior. Under two generations of Hays—father and son—this threshold of a luxuriant desert was reduced to the humble *rôle* of supplying the garrison of "Gib" with its daily ration of beef: the idea was suggested by Nelson, and has been carried out by systematically fostering native barbarism. Even the telephone concessions lay for years in the obscurity of the concessionnaire's pocket or pigeon-hole. Naturally enough, this do-nothing policy, this "masterly inactivity," found huge favour with the Moors, a savage people, sharp-witted withal, who have studied and duly appreciated the wild and reckless havock which "Civilisation," *versus* Native Rule, has wrought and still works in the Nile Valley. But these "Barbari" are fighting a losing fight. The time is coming when France and Spain, the Powers most interested in the matter will, by perpetual pressure, get the better of some softer-headed "Caliph of our lord Mohammed, enthroned by Allah his will;" and the steam-whistle on the Tangier-Fez railroad shall destroy not only "feudalism," but fanaticism and privacy, lethargy and independence. Nor will the European occupant, after the danger and damage of defeating a nation of *fous furieux*, of fanatics brave to desperation, find great difficulty of securing his conquests. The invader has only to follow the frontier-policy of ancient Rome, ably imitated by the modern Briton. He will buy Maroccans to fight Maroccans; pay them liberally, officer them ably, and arm them efficiently. Wild races always and everywhere prove how greatly gold downweighs patriotism. You can always rule the Moslem by telling him the truth, by dealing with him honestly, and by respecting his women and his religion.

Dr. Leared's first travel in Marocco was by sea, and steamer-trips led him from Tangier down coast. He broke the voyage, however, by sundry excursions inland, especially from Mogador to the capital, returning by the Safí or northern line. He saw the city of the Sheríf without seeing the Sheríf, and he and his companion incurred no little risk—the party out of power, the opposition, would have made capital by the Kafírs' death. On a subsequent occasion, in 1877, he was more fortunate.

He also visited (A.D. 1877) Al-Kasru 'l-Kabír, or "Great Palace," the Portuguese Alcacerquivir, where Dom Sebastiam lost his army and his life; and he described the ruins of the famous Tingitano-Roman city Volubilis, a name which had almost dropped out of history. I have strongly advised that those pages be introduced into the Appendix of the Second Edition.

The Maroccan interior is no longer "far less known than such remote countries as China and Japan." Every year opens up new regions, and brings us fresh information. A single Athenæum (No. 3232) reviews one book ("La Martinière's"), and announces another by the late Mr. Richard Wake, of Tangier. Yet the public will not readily forget its old and trustworthy sources of information, and as such I can conscientiously recommend to them Dr. Leared's "Marocco and the Moors."

RICHARD F. BURTON.

TRIESTE,
October 1, 1890.

CONTENTS.

CHAPTER I.
Voyage—Tangier 1

CHAPTER II.
An Excursion from Tangier 10

CHAPTER III.
Casa Blanca 51

CHAPTER IV.
Mazagan 59

CHAPTER V.
Mogador 66

CHAPTER VI.
Excursions from Mogador 80

CHAPTER VII.

Journey to the City of Marocco . . . 97

CHAPTER VIII.

Residence in the City of Marocco . 119

CHAPTER IX.

The City and its Neighbourhood . 154

CHAPTER X.

Marocco to Saffi 182

CHAPTER XI.

Saffi . . 192

CHAPTER XII.

Azamoor, and a Ride at Night 202

CHAPTER XIII.

The Country and the People . . 208

CHAPTER XIV.

Government, Law, and Military Power . 239

CHAPTER XV.

Education, Religion, Superstitions, the Healing Art 261

CHAPTER XVI.

Agriculture, Domestic Animals, Manufactures, Money . 279

CHAPTER XVII.

Natural History and Sport 297

APPENDICES.

A.

The Site of the Roman City Volubilis 321

B.

The Sultan's Passport . - 330

C.

The Drugs in use amongst the Moors . . 333

LIST OF ILLUSTRATIONS.

	PAGE
The Sultan going to Mosque	*Frontispiece*
Map of Marocco showing Author's Route	*To face page* 1
Tangier, the Landing-place.	3
Old Map of Country about Tangier	7
Village of Conical-shaped Huts	63
Plan of the Town of Mogador	68
Mogador from the Sea	70
Tattoo Mark	91
Moorish Costume—full dress	132
City of Marocco	140
Snake-charmer	142
Map of the City of Marocco	155
Cabalistic Charm against Scorpions	173
Tail-piece, with Camels	181
Our Halting-place on the Tensift	182
Diagram to show the Growth of an Olive-tree	199
Moors on a Journey	215
Tail-piece, with Tower	238
Ruins of Roman City of Volubilis	322, 323
Fac-simile of Sultan's Passport	331
Copper Vessel for Holding Flower Water	349

MAROCCO AND THE MOORS.

CHAPTER I.

TANGIER.

If going by sea, it is hardly necessary at the present day to say how one arrived at any particular place. Steam has made the shores of most countries easy of access, and in this respect Marocco—a country comparatively near England—forms no exception. But the circumstance which calls for remark is the fact, that far less is known of the interior of Marocco than of such remote countries as China and Japan.

I left Southampton in the "Mongolia," and reached Gibraltar on the fifth day afterwards. It was a fair voyage, and, by the aid of agreeable society, passed pleasantly away. A word may be said here of the maligned Bay of Biscay. Its waters are often smoother than those of the Channel. Poets and ballad-mongers have done it injustice, and "Biscay's sleepless bay" is more frequently tranquil than is commonly supposed.

It is not my intention to say anything about the famous rock so often described, which I left on the day after my arrival. Communication is maintained with Tangier by means of Messrs. Blands' boats, the "Hercules" and "Gibeltaric," which, weather permitting, go daily. The Transatlantic Company's boats come every Monday most punctually, and many others. The "Jackal," belonging to Cowan & Co., in which I embarked, was a small but strongly-built steamboat, well adapted for the tumbling water of the Straits. The mountains of the African coast, which were in view when leaving Gibraltar, stood out in bolder outline as we approached them. But the first clearly-defined object was the ruin of a Roman bridge [1] close to the shore, and a short distance eastward lay the quaint old town. To do Tangier justice it should be viewed only from the sea— to put one's foot within the walls is to dispel an illusion. Its mosques and flat-roofed houses, batteries, and castellated walls give it a compact and even formidable appearance; but it is formidable only to the wild hordes of the country.[2]

---

[1] This bridge has almost all fallen now. The Duke of Westminster has a fine painting of it, taken some years before I saw it, in his mansion in Park Lane.

[2] It has been much fortified of late, even with Armstrongs.

THE LANDING PLACE, TANGIER.

[*To face page 3.*

There is no harbour at Tangier; the mole built by the English more than two centuries ago was destroyed by them when they abandoned the place. But the anchorage in the open roadstead is good. The coast is, however, subject to heavy surf, which is a drawback to all the southern ports.

Our steamer anchored at a considerable distance from the shore, and Marocco being advanced enough to value health, the first thing that approached was the quarantine boat, in which sat a quasi-medical officer, an aquatic-looking Spaniard, who, without coming on board, soon despatched the formalities of his office. Other boats followed, into which the passengers transferred themselves, and were rowed as far as the shoaling water permitted. As soon as these grounded, a crew of yelling Jews rushed to meet us, up to their waists in water, and then commenced the fiercest competition for business possible to conceive. Unhappily, being a stranger, I became the centre of the tumult. It was almost as useless to resist as it was to remonstrate. All wanted to carry me ashore, but as only one could effect this, it almost seemed as though I should be torn limb from limb by the eager crowd. At last, having selected a lusty fellow, and got astride his shoulders, I was landed on the beach.[3]

The landing-place, called the Marina, consisted

---

[3] Now this is all changed; there is a small pier, so passengers have not all this inconvenience.

of a smooth portion of the sandy shore enclosed within walls. Here we were met by the captain of the port, a fine-looking Moor of commanding presence. We were then conducted to the Custom-house, a mere shed, under which the turbaned officials sat upon their mats. The scrutiny of our baggage, although rather exact, was effected with politeness.

The competition commenced in the water was equally keen on land. A different, but no less eager, set of porters seized and squabbled over the luggage: added to this there was the same persecution from the touting tribe with which all travellers are familiar. To these gentry, who spoke a little of many languages, was entrusted the recommendation of the various hotels; and, as usual, each represented the establishment to which he belonged to be the best in the world, and consequently greatly superior to that of any of its neighbours. Among these worthies there was a Moor, conspicuous by his jacket of cherry-coloured cloth as well as by his confident bearing. This was the redoubtable Hadj-Kaddúr, who must be known to every one who visits Tangier. He afterwards for some time followed my fortunes. Finding that he represented the Victoria Hotel, to which I had been recommended, I placed myself under his guidance.[1] A stay of some weeks at

---

[1] This hotel is now done away with, and its place has been taken by the Printemps, which is doing a good business.

this house afforded ample opportunity for observing the town and neighbourhood, and these I shall now describe.

In several respects there is an analogy between Dover and Calais, Gibraltar and Tangier. The respective places are separated by narrow straits almost of the same breadth. In both cases, when the narrow seas are crossed, the traveller finds himself in a country very unlike that he has recently left, the people being wholly different in language, habits, and mode of life. But if this is the case in the north, the difference is tenfold in the south. He crosses from what may be termed a bit of England on outpost duty to the land of the Moor. No transformation effected by a fairy wand could well be more complete. Tangier, known to the Romans as Tingis, was the capital of their province Mauritania Tingitana. It afterwards passed successively into the hands of the Goths and the Saracens, and thus came into possession of the mixed race known to us as the Moors. It was taken, in 1471, by Alphonso, King of Portugal, after a severe struggle. King Edward, the father of Alphonso, had previously besieged the town, but had been compelled to beat a hasty retreat, and to leave his brother Ferdinand in the hands of the Moors as a security that Ceuta should be delivered up.

England had at one time a great interest in the place. It formed part of the dowry of Catherine, the Infanta of Portugal, who married Charles II. But the gift, like the proverbial white elephant, caused more trouble than it was worth. It is probable that the Portuguese were only too glad to get rid of so worthless a possession, for only just before parting with it they met with a serious rebuff. The matter is thus described in Lord Sandwich's Journal, 1662:—

"*Sunday, January* 12*th*, 1662.—This morning the Portuguese, 140 horse in Tangier, made a sally into the country for booty, whereof they had possessed about 400 cattle, thirty camels, and some horse, and thirty-five women and girls, and being six miles distant from Tangier, were intercepted by 100 Moors, with harquebusses, who in the first charge killed the Aïdill with a shot in the head, whereupon the rest of the Portuguese ran, and in the pursuit fifty-one were slain, whereof were eleven of the Knights besides the Aïdill. The horses of the fifty-one were also taken by the Moors, and all the booty relieved.

"*Tuesday, January* 14*th*.—This morning, Mr. Mules came to me from the Governor for the assistance of some of our men into the castle.

"*Thursday, January* 16*th*.—About eighty men out of my own ship and the 'Princess' went into Tangier, into the lower castle, about four of the clock in the afternoon.

"*Friday, January* 17*th*.—In the morning by eight o'clock the 'Martyn' came in from Cales

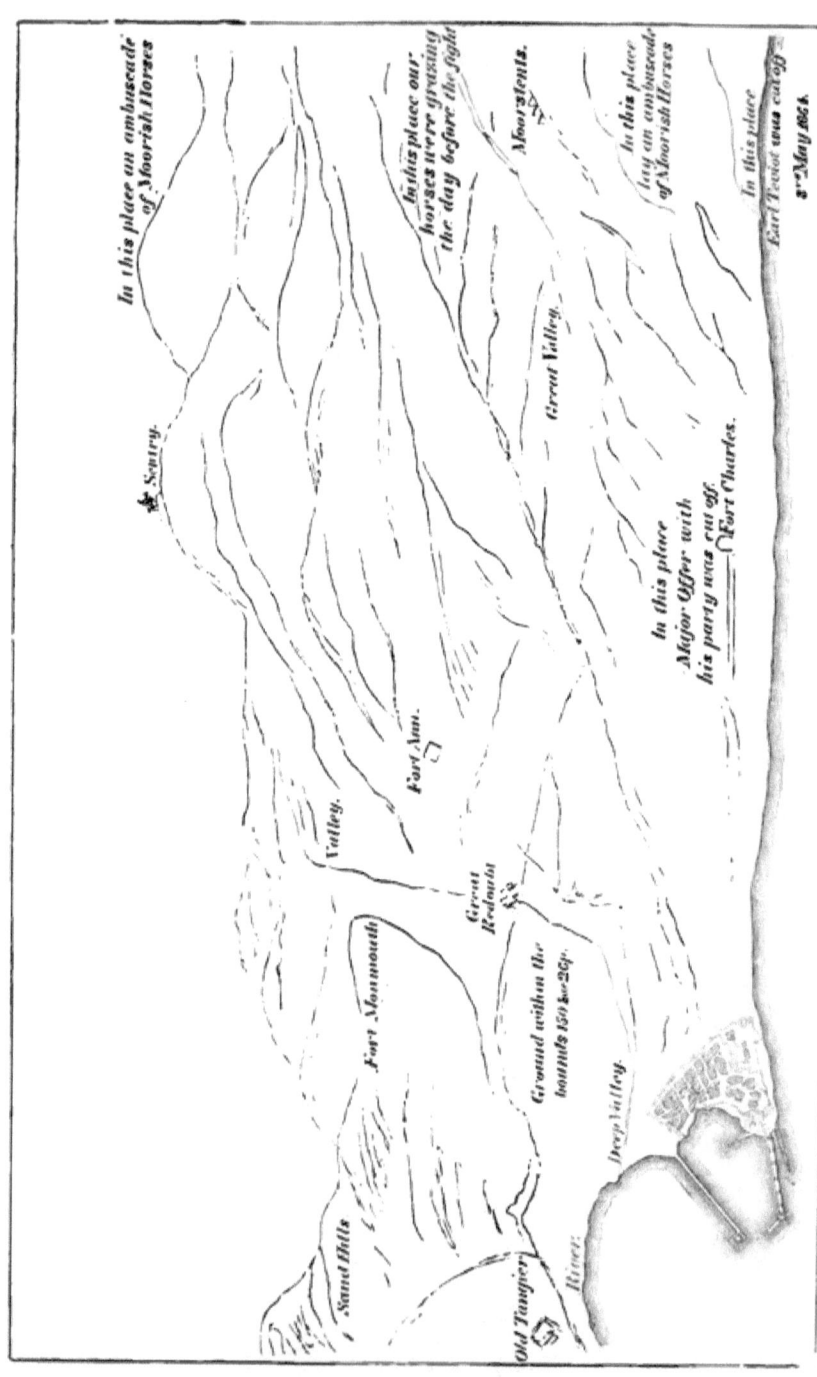

(Cadiz) with provisions, and about ten o'clock I sent Sir Richard Stayner with 120 men, besides officers, to the assistance of the Governor into Tangier."

One hundred more men were sent from the fleet into Tangier on the 23rd; and meanwhile, Lord Peterborough and the garrison having arrived from England, Tangier was handed over to him by the Portuguese, January 30th, 1662. Next day Sir Richard Stayner and the sailors embarked.

Great expectations were formed about Tangier, and it engaged, to a large extent, the attention of the Government of that period. Pepys, in his Diary, makes frequent mention of the place. A commission, presided over by the Duke of York, sat weekly to manage its affairs, and of this commission Pepys himself was treasurer. Large sums of money were voted by Parliament for the garrison of horse and foot soldiers, and for strengthening the fortifications. A mole, which extended nearly 2,000 feet into the sea, was also constructed. This was strongly fortified with batteries, and a harbour was formed capable of containing the largest vessels. Old maps of this period show that it must have been a secure harbour.

The English, like the Portuguese, suffered severely at the hands of their wily enemies the Moors. The garrison lived in a state of perpetual warfare, and were constantly harassed by ambuscades. Lord Peterborough being recalled in 1663, the Earl of Teviot was sent to replace him. This unfortunate nobleman was attacked by a noted Riff chieftain, named Guyland, at the head of a wild horde, and lost his life together with nineteen officers and a large number of men. This event is thus quaintly described by Pepys under date of June 2nd, 1664:—

"It seems my Lord Teviott's design was to go a mile and a half out of the town, to cut down a wood in which the enemy did use to lie in ambush. He had sent several spyes; but all brought word that the way was clear, and so might be, for anybody's discovery of an enemy before you are upon them. There they were all snapt, he and all his officers, and about 200 men, as they say; there being now left in the garrison but four captains. This happened the 3rd of May last, being not before that day twelvemonth of his entering into his government there; but at his going out in the morning he said to some of his officers, 'Gentlemen, let us look to ourselves, for it was this day three years that so many brave Englishmen were knocked on the head by the Moors, when Fines made his sally out.'"

Many other losses were subsequently incurred. Although the place was strengthened by redoubts erected on the neighbouring hills, the town was constantly besieged by the Moors; and notwithstanding a lavish expenditure, it was found that the place was kept in bad condition owing to jobbery and a misapplication of funds.

At length, in relation to Tangier, the nation became impatient of the constant drain upon its resources. Under date of April 9th, 1667, Pepys writes that he told Sir W. Coventry, "It is plain that we do overspend our revenue; it is of no more profit to the King than it was the first day, nor in itself of better credit, no more people of condition willing to live there, nor anything like a place likely to turn his Majesty to account; that it hath been hitherto, and for ought I see, likely only to be used as a job to do a kindness to some Lord, or he that can get to be Governor."

But worse than expense and loss of life was the impression which soon prevailed in the House of Commons, that the garrison of Tangier was fast becoming the nucleus of a Popish army. This was a death-blow to the place as an English colony. Lord Dartmouth was despatched to bring home the troops, and to destroy the work of the engineers. In a letter to Mr. Pepys, dated January 11th, 1683-4, his lordship says, "You will easily imagine the condition we have beene in, by the ill weather you have beene witness of where you have beene, but God be thanked we have struggled in it so farr that the mole is totally destroyed; nay much more than you will imagine, till you see it."

Thus the place was given up after an occupation

of twenty-two years, and as there was no disposition to assist the Moors in their piratical expeditions the unfinished harbour was destroyed. When the tide is out the foundations of the mole can still be seen, and show the substantial nature of the structure. It was intended to have made a splendid harbour, with depth of water between the pier-heads capable of floating a seventy-gun ship of the period. Since the evacuation by the English, Tangier has remained in possession of the Moors. Pepys says, " A fine map of Tangier was done by one Captain Beckman, a Swede." Many curious views of the place were made by Hollar, and some of them were engraved by him and still exist.

Lord Nelson declared the possession of Tangier would be necessary to England in case she was at war with a maritime power. This was because Gibraltar depends for subsistence as much upon Marocco as it does upon Spain, which latter country might be hostile, or else be prevented from affording supplies.

Like Tangier, the island of Bombay formed part of the dowry of the Infanta of Portugal, wife of Charles II. Who could then foresee the subsequent value of that small possession, or what a focus for the extension of British power it has since become? And although, through mismanagement, Tangier proved to be a worse than useless possession, it is not improbable that had it been retained it also would have become a centre endowed with a like vitality and with a similar power of growth. In that case a land far more accessible than India, with a soil and climate among the most favoured in the world, would now be yielding rich returns. Immense tracts which at present lie waste would be used for the growth of cotton; and a strong but just government would exist in place of an uncertain and grinding tyranny.

The rise of tide at Gibraltar, just outside the tideless Mediterranean, is four feet; at Tangier it reaches a height of six feet.

The town is built on the sloping side of a promontory, which, with its fellow four or five miles to the eastward, forms the bay. The town is sheltered on the north and west by the hills under which it lies, and on the east by a range of low hills, while behind these and far inland the range of the Lower Atlas, which is visible from the Kasba, protects it from the scorching desert winds.

The town nestles under a cliff. At the summit of the cliff is a flat surface of about a mile in length, and a varying breadth not exceeding a few hundred yards. The side of the promontory farthest from the town is very precipitous, and overhangs the sea. There are here some curious excavations in the solid rock, supposed to be Phœnician graves.

Wherever the Mohammedan dwells, the rigid jealousy with which women are guarded influences the style of his architecture. The houses have their backs turned to the streets, and, as there are no windows, the blank walls and flat roofs present a cheerless and monotonous appearance. A gateway leads into the square or *patio*. Around this the house is built. The enclosure sometimes contains a fountain, and a fig-tree generally affords pleasant shade from the glaring rays of the sun.

As seen from the sea, the houses of Tangier appear to stand one above the other like steps. As might therefore be expected, many of the streets are very steep, and all, with the exception of the main street, are mere winding lanes, so narrow that in some of them the inhabitants could shake hands from the opposite windows provided these existed. The pavement consists of rough stones, placed purposely, one would think, to make walking over them as difficult as possible. Blondin, who visited the place, left a memorial in the visitors' book of one of the hotels to the effect that it was needless for him to test his balancing powers here, "because he was able to say that he had walked both up and down the main street of Tangier and had not fallen." The drainage, although imperfect, is better than might be expected, and an attempt at keeping the streets clean has been made by the Consuls. Dust-bins are things unknown to the natives of Marocco, and animal and vegetable offal of all kinds is thrown into the streets; but this *débris* is now removed on the backs of donkeys, though there still remains much room for improvement. There are no bazaars on the scale usual in the East; but the shops for various wares are for the most part mixed together. The "shop" is a small square cavity in the dead wall of the street, the floor being about two feet from the ground. Pigeon-holed in these recesses sit cross-legged, grave-looking men surrounded by their wares. The same floor also serves the customers for a seat, though their legs dangle in the street. In a few instances the introduction of European customs may be observed in larger premises and glass windows.

The principal street runs up the hill from the water-side to the Sók or market-place, just outside the walls. The upper part of this street is used by the female sellers of bread, milk, vegetables, and fruit, who stand or sit ranged on each side. It is difficult for a stranger to find his way through the mazes of the smaller streets. But rich Moors and Jews possess good houses in these confined situations. There is no Jewish quarter in Tangier as there is in most Moorish towns, but the Israelites live peaceably amongst the general population. Some of the consulates are good houses, and the residence of the British Plenipotentiary has some fine apartments.

The batteries facing the sea were once formidable. I went over one of these in company with Colonel Mathews. The buildings are in fair repair, but the absence of sentries and the lounging attitude of the few artillerymen in charge looked anything but war-like. I counted twelve iron thirty-six pounders and twelve smaller guns; most of the latter were bronze, of English make. One of the bronze guns was a long thirty-two pounder Spanish gun, bearing the date of 1780. It had also a name, "Lastimoso" (the Pitiful), engraved on it. The Spaniards had a practice of naming their guns; but why this particular epithet should be given to such a destructive implement is not obvious. The iron guns were in wretched condition, and the carriages of all were rickety affairs of rotting wood.[5]

The Kasba, or citadel, is situated on a height commanding the whole of Tangier, just as at Boulogne the upper town overlooks the lower one. A considerable space is enclosed by high walls, and in this are a large mosque, the harem of the Bashaw, the prison, and the treasury. I visited the prison, and obtained leave to inspect the prisoners through an aperture in their den, from which issued an effluvium that made a long inspection undesirable. Not having then seen prisoners in other parts of Marocco, I thought this damp, dark chamber as dreary and dreadful a place of confinement as could well be conceived. The prison for women is a separate, but adjoining building. The view of the town from the gate of

[5] There are now six Armstrong twenty-ton guns.

the Kasba is remarkably fine. The white glistening houses, interspersed here and there with the green of the graceful palms, are thrown into the fullest relief by the intense blue of the contiguous sea.

The Continental Hotel overlooks the sea and Custom-house; and its proprietor, Mr. Ansaldo, does all in his power to make every one welcome and comfortable. There is an excellent table d'hôte; charges from 10s. a day, according to the requirements of visitors.

The Villa de France, on the top of the Sók, another large hotel, is also considered very good; charges about the same. There are various smaller hotels.

A sign of the progress of the place is that scarcely more than twenty years ago there was but a single hotel in the town.

A great event in the history of Tangier, and of the whole state of Marocco, took place in March, 1873. A post-office, which is a branch of the Gibraltar office, was then opened. Tangier is now, therefore, regularly *en rapport* with the rest of the world.[6]

Spanish is the European language best known in Marocco. The geographical position of Spain partly accounts for this, though the intimate connexion long existing between the two countries

---

[6] There is now from Gibraltar a daily Postal Service, and from England three times a week *via* Cadiz.

has had still more influence. Most of the Moors, as well as the Jews, know Spanish more or less. English is only spoken by the *commissionnaires* attached to the hotels, and a few others.

Markets are held on Thursdays and Sundays, and on these days the town is filled with a motley crowd, who come long distances from the surrounding country. Conspicuous among the number are the men of the wild Riff tribes, who inhabit the mountains to the north of Tangier. They are a fine race, and are known by the long lock of hair left unshaven on one side of the head. On some occasions as many as a hundred camels, with half that number of tents and a numerous throng of horses and asses, may be counted in the Sók. It was a strange sight to see so many kneeling camels massed together, their huge saddles projecting from their backs. All kinds of country produce were retailed in this market, water-melons being a conspicuous article. To ward off the fierce glare of the sun, some of the vendors were under temporary shades of palm leaves. Muffled women crouching over their wares, and showing but one eye to their customers, seemed stifled with heat, and itinerant sellers of water and of sweetmeats vociferously cried their goods.

In the evening, when the sun gets low, the Sók is the resort of story-tellers and jugglers of various kinds, in whose tales and feats the Moors take great delight. There was one old fellow to whom it was always a pleasure to listen, although I never obtained more than a faint outline of his stories through an interpreter. With some of his tales we are familiar in the Arabian Nights' Entertainments; others were fables, in which the lower animals bore a leading part. A crowd of men and boys seated in a semicircle was in front of him, while the old man, with the utmost vivacity and great skill, suited his voice and movements to his stirring narratives. It was curious to observe the riveted attention, and hear the bursts of laughter of the swarthy audience. Copper coins were thrown to him pretty freely as a reward for his exertions. Snake-charmers also exhibited their feats, but these were inferior to what I afterwards witnessed in the southern capital.

The shadow of Europe under which Tangier lies has exerted its influence so far that, unlike what happens in the interior of Marocco, Christians are free from insult and annoyance. One may wander unmolested everywhere about the town and vicinity, provided only that the prejudices of the people are respected, and especially that their holy places are not too curiously inspected. For, unlike his co-religionist in Turkey, the Mussulman here has not relaxed sufficiently the fervour of his faith even to allow the Kaffir—the name by which the

Christian infidel is known—to set foot within the precincts of a mosque. A screen is always placed before the open door to prevent profane eyes from peering too closely into the building.

As might be expected, remains of antiquity are found in Tangier and its neighbourhood. In the *patio* of the Victoria Hotel there is a capital of an Ionic marble column, now hollowed out so as to form a cistern. Many such fragments have been found. About three miles from the town, on the shore of the bay, are some ruins supposed to be Roman. This place is called Tanja Bælea, or Old Tangier, and here was situated the Tingis of the Romans. Some fragments of the walls are of great thickness. At a short distance from the ruins the sands are crossed by a small river, once spanned by a fine bridge. One arch, unquestionably of Roman work, is all that now remains. But the ruin is highly picturesque, and affords an interesting subject for the artist. This bridge, it is supposed, connected the old city with the naval fort close at hand. The entrance for the galleys, built of stone, can be seen yet.[7]

---

[7] Marocco is almost unexplored ground for the antiquary. The northern division of the country contains many ruins. In the *Athenæum* for September 18th and October 30th, 1875, Mr. Trovey Blackmore has given a very interesting description of certain fourteenth-century tombs of the Sultans, in the deserted town of Shella, close to Rabat. The inscriptions on the tombs serve to verify historical dates.

There are several fine gardens outside the walls of Tangier. The most remarkable is that called the Swedish garden, from its having formerly belonged to the Swedish Consulate. It is of considerable size, and commands some fine views. The town, close at hand, lies spread out as if on a map; while looking far across the water the rock of Gibraltar may be distinctly seen. The garden contains some fine trees, and a splendid specimen of the dragons'-blood-tree deserves special notice. The Dutch garden and vineyard are about four acres in extent, and being well supplied with water, were formerly noted for the luxuriance, beauty, and variety of the shrubs and flowers. But its glories have departed, and it is now overrun with weeds. Some splendid trees are all that remains. Nearly all the gardeners are Riff mountaineers, who, notwithstanding their wild habits when at home, make excellent and faithful servants.

The manufactures of the town are inconsiderable. There are some tanneries, one of them adjoining the Victoria Hotel, from the windows of which the whole process of making leather can be seen, though it is not the sort intimately associated with the name of the country. The principal trade is in bullocks for the supply of the garrison of Gibraltar. But even this is limited, as only a certain number of animals are allowed to be exported. Fowls, vegetables, and fruits in considerable quantities are also sent across the strait. With the exception of canary seed, which is grown largely in the neighbourhood, the export of grain is small.

There are some Moorish coffee-houses in Tangier, and I visited one with my guide. It was a moonless night, and travelling over the uneven streets was difficult and even risky. At last, after groping our way through many winding and narrow lanes, we came to a spot where a portion of the street was covered in by a roof of interlaced boughs. Beneath this a number of men were lying about, some singing, others asleep; they were an unprepossessing set to meet in the dark. At first we could only distinguish their white turbans and teeth, but gradually their dark and stalwart forms became visible. Entering a door close at hand we found ourselves in a small room with white-washed walls and matted floor. Men were squatting about smoking cigarettes and drinking black coffee mixed with the grounds as in Turkey. There was the customary charcoal stove for boiling coffee; and the place, dimly lighted by an oil lamp, had a sufficiently lugubrious appearance.

I could not learn that the Tangerines indulge to any great extent in the use of hashish, although it is known to them. It is to be regretted that the people are learning the use of alcoholic drinks from their neighbours. There are some drinking-houses kept by Christians and Jews, where bad brandy and other stimulants are retailed ; and, notwithstanding the injunctions of the Koran, the Moors are fond of indulging in them whenever a chance presents itself.

The cost of living is moderate at Tangier. The hotel charges have been already mentioned. Beef, though not of English quality, can be had for $2\frac{1}{2}$d. a pound; mutton of fair quality at the same price; ducks at 1s., fowls at $9\frac{1}{2}$d., hares at 5d., and rabbits $2\frac{1}{2}$d. each. Wages have increased considerably within the last few years. The present hire of a labourer is from $7\frac{1}{2}$d. to $9\frac{1}{2}$d. a day, or if a female 4d. to $5\frac{1}{2}$d. Masons and carpenters are paid from 2s. to 3s. a day. All these things have more than doubled at the present day.[*]

For the space it occupies Tangier is a populous town. The population in November, 1872, was estimated at 14,600, in the proportion of 9,000 Moors, 5,000 Jews, and 600 Christians. The number of Christians is greater than in any other town of the empire. There are two Roman Catholic churches, a large monastery, and a school; the principal church being allowed the use of bells. There is no place for Protestant worship; but when a clergyman happens to be in the town service is conducted at the

[*] It is curious to observe how the recent decline in the value of gold is felt in remote corners of the world. Thus, in Iceland, a country with which I am familiar, prices have fully doubled between my first visit to the island (1862) and my last (1874).

Legation." The Jews are allowed to have public synagogues, but they are unpretentious buildings. There are several Moslem schools for boys.

The foreign officials at Tangier are numerous enough to form a society among themselves. These consist of five Ministers Plenipotentiary—Great Britain, France, Italy, Portugal, and Spain; Ministers Resident—Belgium, Germany, and Austria; Consuls-General — Sweden and Norway; Consuls—Great Britain, United States of America. On Sundays and *fête* days the flags of the different nations give the town a gay appearance.

The climate of Tangier is so very equable and pleasant that I have formed a high opinion of its suitability for invalids suffering from chest affections. Its maritime position and the protection of mountain ranges on the south secure it against the scorching heat to which the inland parts of Marocco are exposed. The desert winds, which are so objectionable in Algiers and other places on the Mediterranean littoral, are here almost unknown. The ordinary summer temperature ranges between 78° Fahr. and 82° Fahr., and the latter is rarely exceeded. The summer heat is maintained until the autumnal

---

" The Sultan has recently given a piece of land on which an iron church has been erected, and divine service is performed on Sundays and saints' days.

rains are established. As an example of the steadiness of temperature, it may be stated that of twenty-three observations made by myself at almost every hour of the day and night between September 15th and 23rd, inclusive, the thermometer in my bedroom ranged between 72° Fahr. and 78° Fahr., while the mean was 74·2° Fahr. During this time the weather had broken up, and on one day there was heavy rain. The mean temperature of winter is about 56° Fahr., and fires are sometimes acceptable at night. Frost never occurs; and in addition to the indigenous palms and other trees and shrubs of warm climates, many tropical plants, such as the banana, flourish throughout the year in the open air.

The first rain falls about the middle of September, and lasts from two to three days. This is succeeded by bright, exhilarating weather, the enjoyment of which is heightened by the change which the country now undergoes. Brown hills, that seemed hopelessly arid, are suddenly clothed with verdure, and the landscape is changed as if in an hour from death to life. All through October the weather is just what the invalid desires; but in November there is generally heavy rain, at times for some days. After this the weather both of winter and spring —the latter lasting till May—is mild and genial. Now and then a rainy day may occur; but even in the wettest winter weather it is very unusual not to be able to get out during some part of the day. The south-west wind sets in with the autumn rain, and prevails in winter. Thunderstorms are unfrequent, and rarely happen with the first rain. The climate is moist, as shown by the facility with which iron rusts. But it is less moist than that of Madeira, between which and that of Algiers it holds, in this respect, an intermediate place. The advantages of climate possessed by Tangier over Gibraltar are freely acknowledged by the inhabitants of the Rock. They are constantly in the habit of crossing the strait in search of better air.

Although, as already said, the sanitary arrangements are very imperfect, Tangier is a healthy place. Intermittent fevers sometimes occur, but they are not of a severe type.

I received much kindness from Colonel Mathews, the American Consul. Accompanied by this gentleman and Mr. Martin, I visited the Grand Cherif of the Empire, Hadj Abd es Salem, Prince of Wazan. The object of the visit was to obtain a letter of recommendation to the Sultan, then on his way to his southern capital, where he had not been previously for five years. As I had resolved to visit the city of Marocco, the expected arrival of the Sultan there was regarded as a most fortunate circumstance. I had a long conversation, through the medium of Colonel Mathews, with the Cherif. He asked particularly if I would wait at Marocco for the Sultan, in case he had not arrived when I got there, to which I replied in the affirmative. Through the favourable representations of my friends, the Cherif gave me a kind and valuable letter addressed to Muley Hassan, the Sultan's son and heir.[10] The translation of the address on it was, "*Caliph of our Lord enthroned, by the will of God, our Lord Hassan.*" What became of this letter, as well as what befell me in my attempt to deliver it, will be afterwards related.

The Cherif is regarded, next to the Sultan himself, as the most powerful man in the empire, and as he had never before given a letter of the kind to a European, I was considered most fortunate. The prince was about thirty-five years of age, of middle height, but rather too fat for active habits. The expression of his face was pleasant, and showed that he wished to be agreeable. He wore a fez, and was dressed in a suit of cherry-coloured cloth. As the hereditary head of the great religious sect of the Manley Taib, and a lineal descendant of the Prophet, he is a great power in the Church, and therefore in the State, which in Mohammedan countries are inseparable. His influence not only extends throughout Marocco, but over Algiers, where it is acknowledged by the French authorities. But the sect of which

---

[10] Since raised to the throne by the death of his father.

he is the head, and which is said to rival in subtlety and ambition that of the Order of Jesus, extends still further to the east, and has its ramifications even in Bombay. The Cherif is known to the Spaniards as *El Santo,* the Saint. He made great personal efforts in the war of 1859-60 to rouse the fanaticism of the Moors against the Spaniards. In one particular action, at which he was present, he so excited the soldiers that they charged with an impetuous, although fruitless valour, that excited the admiration of their enemies. The Cherif's duties are, ordinarily speaking, not onerous. It is enough that he is of the Prophet's blood. To obtain his blessing is considered worth money, and no inconsiderable part of his income arises from this source. He is regarded with superstitious awe; and when he goes abroad in the country the people kiss the hem of his garment. This prince was said to possess large estates at Wazaan, and to be altogether very wealthy. He is fond of shooting, and also, as people said, "of good living." It was also stated that he showed his preference for the English nation by his desire, above all things, to have an English wife.

The Cherif has a small marine residence at Tangier. The room in which he received us was furnished much in European style, for which he evidently showed a decided preference. We sat upon chairs—a great innovation. There was a grand piano in the room and a handsome buhl table. But he was waited upon by a female black slave, and there were other indications that the European surroundings were exotic.

Nevertheless it is a significant and hopeful fact that this high-class Mussulman has imbibed, from contact with Europeans, so much liberality and spirit of progress as to adopt, to a great extent, their habits; and this in spite of prejudices, and the possible ill-will of his fellow-countrymen. He no longer eats in the Moorish manner, and is very polite at table. He takes great interest in the affairs of Europe, and the English illustrated papers afford him much amusement. He is very fond of all mechanical contrivances. In his family his rule is absolute. Seventeen female servants, some of whom are slaves, obey his slightest wish. At the present time there are four generations of one family living in his house. All the servants are clothed and fed at his expense, but receive no wages; the temporal honour, and possibly the eternal advantage, of serving this undoubted descendant of the Prophet, are considered sufficient payment. Children are sometimes dedicated to him at their birth, and these when old enough enter his service.

While I was at Tangier news arrived from the Sultan that he had been victorious in his southern progress over the rebellious tribe of Anchi Haskid. Report said, that taking advantage of harvest time, when the tribe, having left the mountains, are engaged in the plains, he attacked it with a large army. At first the mountaineers had the best of the fight, but being subsequently defeated, a great number of prisoners were taken and beheaded. Proclamation of the victory was made by a public crier, and great rejoicings were ordered. The Victoria Hotel shook with the report of the old guns which were fired off just beneath it.

The Moors are fond of burning powder, and *Lab Elbaroud*, or powder-play, is a diversion in which they particularly delight. I went to the open space in the Kasba to see the performance, and a wilder sight could scarcely be witnessed. Several men stood opposite each other, a dozen yards or so apart, as if about to dance a quadrille. They carried long guns, and with their loose dresses and turbaned heads looked gallant warriors. To stimulate their martial ardour a band of twelve blacks played on outlandish instruments, in addition to a couple of drums and some timbrels; the whole producing a most amazing din and crash of sounds. It seemed, as I have said, as though the turbaned soldiers were about to dance a quadrille; but their evolutions were much more complicated. One man throughout acted as master of the ceremonies. The whole advanced, retreated, followed, threatened. Now a warrior who, with the sword of his adversary pointed at his heart, seemed about to be slain, would extricate himself from his dangerous position by a contortion of the body as wonderful as it was rapid. Next they fired at each other individually, then *en masse*. Nothing could exceed the savage gallantry of the whole affair. In European judgment the Moorish soldier is undisciplined; but much training must be requisite to arrive at perfection in this mad species of mimic warfare. Our riflemen would be puzzled by some of the shooting postures; for the men discharged their long unhandy weapons while in every conceivable position, such as supported on an elbow, or on the soles of the feet, and while lying on the back, the side, or the face. In loading the guns the powder was never measured, but poured from the pouch into the hand. Neither was wadding used. The safety of the guns was perhaps due to this cause; but the report they made was remarkably loud. Another exercise consisted in throwing the gun with a whirling motion high in the air, and catching it with great dexterity while descending. In the performance of these various exercises there seemed to be the greatest rivalry between the tribes. The Riffians, easily distinguished by the long tuft of hair on the side of the head, and by some peculiarities of dress, displayed great dash. The men of Sus were also conspicuous. At the conclusion of this wild pastime all present fired several almost deafening volleys, of which the firing was executed well together.

There is much marrying and giving in marriage at Tangier. The weddings take place at night, and are made known by the usual expressions of rejoicing—firing off guns, and monotonous music played on drums and a kind of flageolet. I followed one of the marriage processions closely, and as far as was prudent. There was no marriage ceremony, but the bride was conveyed to the house of her husband in a kind of box placed on the back of a mule. This box was supported on either side by men, and the lady's sash was tied around it as an indication of her presence within. Behind the mule came a band, and also a number of men carrying lanterns. The gunners went in front and kept perpetually firing. With these demonstrations the bride was paraded through several streets, and was then taken to the bridegroom's house.

One of the accessible sights of Tangier is a Jewish wedding. The Jews have no objection to the presence of strangers, and thus a good opportunity is afforded of seeing the ladies in all their glory. But many of the Jewish women of Tangier really require nothing to enhance their great beauty. It is, however, a beauty of the languid, voluptuous, and unintellectual type. According to English ideas the ladies are too fat, but then fatness is at a premium in Marocco.

I had a good opportunity of witnessing a

wedding of the better class. It was attended by some of the Consuls, as the bridegroom was an *employé* at one of the consulates. The ceremonies and festivities which attend a Jewish wedding in Marocco are protracted and expensive. Happy the man who goes well through all without a sense of fatigue, and a purse not unduly lightened. Several hundred pounds are often expended, and dowries are not uncommon.

In this matter, as in others, coming events cast their shadows before, and on the Thursday a fortnight previous to the actual wedding ceremony is performed *Tesere el-Gumleh*. This consists in breaking a jar full of corn at the bride's chamber door, by which the wish is symbolically expressed that she may be fruitful.

On the following Thursday the wedding festivities (*Nadr Azmung*) commence. The bridegroom attends early service at the synagogue of which he happens to be a member, and all the congregation, as well as his own and the bride's relatives, afterwards breakfast with him. All again assemble at one p.m., and arrange themselves for a spectacle on the galleries which surround the *patio* of the bridegroom's house. In the space below a bull is then sacrificed by the priest cutting its throat. This is done amid an astounding din of music, accompanied by a peculiar mark of rejoicing practised by the elder women, both Moors and Jews. It is called *taghareet*, and consists of a sharp, continuous squealing sound, produced while the tongue is rapidly moved from side to side. Meanwhile the visitors, in succession, throw down money from the galleries, for the priest and attendants, into a cloth placed over the body of the bull. Then follows a method of encouraging generosity which recalls to mind that pursued at a charity dinner, where applause is proportioned to the subscriptions announced. The name of each person is shouted out by those below as he throws down his offering, accompanied by the words *Allah ma' Tazar flá bus flá* ("God is with the merchant So-and-so"), or Mr. So-and-so, as the case may be, and the more he gives the more is he considered to have done honour to the happy couple.

At the conclusion of this ceremony the bridegroom takes a bit of cotton wool, dipped in a mixture of honey and henna, and places it, together with a piece of silver money, upon the bride's head, as an omen of their future prosperity.

On Saturday, the Jewish Sabbath, a great gathering takes place at the house of the bride. This is called *Abraz*, and is an important ceremony for the unmarried ladies, who attend arrayed in all their finery, and with a general intention to captivate beholders. The bride is seated on a daïs at the end of a large room, while the spinsters sit ranged around the wall on each side of her. In the meantime the bridegroom, having first attended at the synagogue, entertains a large company at breakfast, during which hymns and sacred songs are sung. The single men of the party then accompany the bridegroom to the bride's chamber, where, as already said, the single ladies are "on view." It is upon these occasions that the young men select the fair ones to whom fancy directs them. In such cases the next step is to despatch a relative to the parents or guardians of his choice, and if the suit is accepted, presents are sent to her, and then he proceeds, accompanied by his friends, to the lady's house, and is formally engaged. After this—will any Englishman believe it?—according to the usual etiquette, the couple never see each other until the marriage ceremonies commence. As may be supposed, the girl herself has seldom any voice in the matter at all; she has only to obey what has been decided upon by her friends.

After the young ladies have been sufficiently stared at, the bachelors commonly amuse themselves with a strange game. It is called *Tai egrét Arras*, and is a kind of judge-and-jury trial. The bridegroom is accused by some one present of some crime, and is condemned to receive a number of lashes, for the infliction of which many in the company are provided with stout silken cords. The culprit then demands to be ransomed by his bride, who divests herself of all her jewels and trinkets, and hands them over for his redemption. The accusation and the ransom also apply to young men of the company who are supposed to have an eye upon ladies present. In any case, if the ransom is declared insufficient, or if the lady refuses to pay it, the accused is raised upon the back of some strong fellow, while the others belabour him soundly.

When this horse-play is over, and the jewellery has been returned to its owner, the young men disperse; but they return, accompanied by the bridegroom, in the evening, when this long-suffering individual, mounted on the backs of two men, is danced up and down before his bride, and then, amidst a great tumult of music and shouting, is at length allowed to take his seat beside her. A mixture containing leaven, *khamir*, is now set before them, in which both dip their hands, in token of their future thrift and attention to domestic duties. After this a grand supper is given, at which the bride and bridegroom are seated side by side on a sort of throne. This supper, in the case of the wealthy, is often a sumptuous feast, but a rigid etiquette forbids the bride to take anything except water, which a little girl, who sits beside and fans her, now and then raises to her lips. For all this time the poor bride's eyes are firmly closed, and she sits amidst the revelry as immovable as a statue. The musicians now play their loudest and merriest tunes, and, like the priest and his followers, are rewarded by the guests. The donors' names are cried out in the same manner as before, and also that the gifts are presented in honour of the bride and bridegroom and the assembled company.

A ceremony takes place on the succeeding Tuesday evening, from which it is called *Lal-l Henna* ("the Henna Night"). The bridegroom goes, as before, with a crowd of followers to the bride's house, and, seating himself beside her, applies henna to her hands, by the reddish stain of which their beauty is supposed to be enhanced. He now also removes a ring from her finger, or a bracelet from her arm, and wears the one or the other until after the nuptials have been finally celebrated. Another grand supper, with the usual uproar, follows.

On the following day, Wednesday, the real wedding at last takes place. The bride is then conducted after dark to her future home, accompanied by a crowd of relatives and lookers-on. Men bearing huge wax candles and lanterns give light to the procession. This is preceded by musicians and dancing women, playing and singing hymns of joy, and also by the elderly ladies, who keep up the *taghareet* with great vehemence. As for the bride herself, she is led with closed eyes along the rough street by two relatives, each having hold of one of her hands. Such, indeed, is the regard paid to propriety on this solemn occasion, that the bride's head is held in its proper position by a female relative who walks behind her. This precaution is taken, perhaps, on account of the tiara decorating her head, and which, ending in a high point, has a gauze veil drooping gracefully therefrom. The bride having reached her destination, she and the bridegroom, with the "law" bound on his forehead, ascend a daïs, and the marriage ceremony at once proceeds. The proper service and legal settlements are read aloud; the ring is placed by the bridegroom on the bride's finger, or else a piece of gold or silver is given to her by him. A glass of wine is then blessed by the priest, and presented in turn to the couple, who drink the wine. The glass is dashed to pieces against the ground by the bridegroom, with a covert meaning that he wishes they may never be parted until the glass again becomes perfect. After offering congratulations the visitors disperse.

Next day the bride sits in state to receive presents of jewellery, gold lace, silk handkerchiefs, or money, which are placed in her lap, and for some days afterwards entertainments, according to the position and circumstances of the people concerned, continue to be given. Some weddings cost a great deal of money, and as many as 150 persons sup or dine at one time.

At the conclusion of the wedding at which I

was present, sweetmeats were handed round, as also sweet drinks; but their flavour was not appreciated by my unaccustomed palate.

The dresses of the bride and other ladies were truly gorgeous. Silk, in many-coloured hues, was bravely set off by lavish adornment of gold embroidery in rich and peculiar patterns; and gaily-coloured silk handkerchiefs tied about the head contrasted admirably with dark and flowing tresses, brunette complexion, and languid, kohl-stained eyes. A finer set of women it would have been difficult to find.

When the ceremony was concluded the two principal guests—in this case Consuls—walking on either side of the bride and holding her hand, led her through every room of her new house. She was then placed sitting in bed with her back against the wall, to open her eyes at leisure, with one of her friends beside her. My visit then ended.

The Jewish maiden wears her hair uncovered; but at the close of the proceedings I have just described the bride's head is formally enveloped in a handkerchief after the manner of matrons. This covering is worn ever afterwards.

Such is the routine which custom imposes on the Jewish man and woman of the wealthier class in Marocco, who wish to enter the matrimonial state. If a man be at all lukewarm on the subject, the prospect of such an ordeal must often turn the scale against marriage. The disparity in age is often great; sometimes a girl of ten is married to a man of forty or fifty.

The Mountain, which is situated about three miles north of Tangier, is an elevation rising to about three or four hundred feet above the sea. I made several excursions to it. The way lay through the market-place, thence by a bridle-track over an open, sandy country. This presently merged into narrow lanes, by which access was gained to the villas and gardens of the townspeople. The vegetation here was very luxuriant, the hedges being formed by the impenetrable cactus, and shade obtained by lines of reeds, many of which grow to a height of fifteen feet. Aloes were also abundant, their spikes varying from fifteen to twenty feet. The chief road, which was so roughly paved as to resemble in many places the dried-up bed of a winter torrent, was skirted by wild myrtle, olive trees, vines, and our own familiar blackberry.

Apart from these beautiful environs, the Mountain itself is a charming spot, well worthy of a visit. Chiefly facing the north-west and the sea, it is of considerable extent, and, as may be supposed, splendid and varied views of the broken, rugged coast-line and the blue strait are obtained from its acclivities and summit. It is mainly composed of sandstone, and has an abundance of pure water, though some of the springs are impregnated with iron and others with sulphur.

The Mountain would make an admirable site for a winter sanatorium, for the influences of a fine climate would be operative at a height sufficient to secure fresh air without the disadvantages attending a greater elevation. To advantages of this kind would be added the exhilarating effects of fine scenery and a luxuriant vegetation. Several of the foreign residents at Tangier, the British Minister among others, have country houses on this hill. Mr. White, the English Consul, has a villa at its foot close to the sea. In the terraced garden were a great variety of exotic plants and trees, in the cultivation of which Mr. White delights. Mr. Martin showed me another finely situated villa, which he was getting into order for the occupation of visitors to this genial clime. The grounds were well planted, and one tree which flourished there struck me particularly on account of its beauty and the fine shade it afforded. It was a species of chestnut, having leaves very much larger than our chestnut tree—*Castanea vulgaris*.

CHAPTER II.

AN EXCURSION FROM TANGIER.

Taking a soldier for protection and Kaddúr as guide and interpreter, I made an excursion to the south of Tangier on the road to Larache. The weather was still (Sept. 12) very hot, and when beyond the shelter of the town the heat was increased by a strong, oppressive east wind. Kaddúr and I rode wiry little horses of good mettle, and the soldier was mounted on a mule. For a long time our way was over a succession of small elevations like sand-hills on the sea-shore. The chief vegetation of this tract was the palmetto, which grew in tufts, having sandy, arid places between them.

We passed a great number of Moors returning from market with camels, horses, and mules. These were the only signs of industry seen on the road. At two hours from Tangier my aneroid showed that we had reached a height of 400 feet above the sea. At this spot there was a well, but the water, from being constantly disturbed by the feet of animals, was very dirty. Yet water in such a sultry atmosphere is indispensable, and I learned from Kaddúr how to extemporize a filter. Unloosening a fold of his turban he stretched it across the vessel, thus straining the water as he drank. In this way we imbibed the tepid liquid. Beyond this well we traversed an extensive plain, partially cultivated with maize and durrha or millet. In the fields we passed we observed Moors lying about, prostrated, apparently, by the heat; whilst here and there one would be observed praying in a squatting position, the hood of his jelabeer so stuck up as to give to his, thus cone-shaped, figure the look of a white extinguisher. No Moor, of all we saw, was doing any kind of work. We passed the tomb of a Moorish saint. It was a small, white-washed, but ruinous, square enclosure, surmounted by a white flag. These places, although as in this case close to the road, may not be approached by Christians or Jews without risk of giving deadly offence.

Leaving the plain, we reached the summit of a range of hills running in a north-easterly direction, their height at the point we crossed being barely 400 feet. On the southern slope the stunted oak-trees and wild olives formed a forest that afforded shelter to wild boars and more dangerous occupants. Until recently these hills were the resort of numerous outlaws. Here we passed two guard huts made of branches of trees, each hut sheltering four guards in a crouching attitude. Further on the trees and scrub had been recently burned, so that over a large tract nothing could lie concealed. Kaddúr said this had been done to save the expense of watching. Upon hearing this I naturally asked, "Why had not the whole forest been burned?" To this Kaddúr replied with a knowing laugh, "Sultan want part to make money." The fact is, that a toll equivalent to a penny for every camel, horse, and mule, and of a halfpenny for each donkey, is exacted at these huts on pretence of guarding the pass. It took us three-quarters of an hour to cross this mountain, the ill-omened name of which was Malhamra. Thence we descended into a ravine, and a few minutes afterwards reached our stopping-place, a village situated on the slope of a hill. Reckoning the pace of the mule at four miles an hour—and it never stopped or slackened when once set going—the distance of this village from Tangier was nineteen miles. Its ruler was one Busellam Boisha. Until a few months previously he had been the Sheikh and tax farmer over a large district, but having been out-bought by a rival he was now only headman of his own village. He was a thick-set, very dark, pleasant-looking personage of about forty years of age. I had intended to commence roughing it by sleeping in the open air, but the Sheikh insisted on my using a bell-tent of his, which was soon erected under the shade of some old trees close to the village mosque. My dinner was cooked in his house close at hand. I liked the contrast of rough life for a time, and in some respects matters were more than rough enough to meet my views. For instance, salt being wanted, some filthy-looking, coarse stuff like gravel was brought in by Hamet, the Sheikh's son, who transferred it from his own dirty hand to that of his father, which formed my salt-cellar; but the milk was excellent, and the water-melons fine and acceptable.

During dinner the Sheikh sat with his eyes fixed persistently upon me. He was not only inquisitive but very candid. He inquired the price of meat in England, and when informed, wished with a sigh that he could send his bullocks there. When told that London contained nearly four millions of people, he simply observed that he did not believe the statement. The front part of his head presented the marks of two frightful sword gashes received in a terrible fight. With regard to the outlaws of the neighbouring hills, it was alleged that it was a very long time since any murder had been committed, and to make the assertion more forcible it was added that it must be about two years. The Sheikh had two wives, the one brown and free, the other black and a slave. Kaddúr spoke of him as being very rich in flocks and herds, and I was told afterwards in Tangier that from £1,000 to £1,500 would fully represent the value of his property.

My bed, which was merely a mat laid on the

ground, was not only hard but hot, for the night was almost as sultry as the day. About midnight I was suddenly awakened, and, being alone, for a moment I was panic-stricken by the presence in the tent of what seemed to be some wild beast from the adjoining forest. It proved to be, however, only a large hungry dog from the neighbouring village, which, in search of food, had jumped the pack-saddle that partially closed the tent door. Unfortunately for me, this first attempt having proved successful, it was repeated again and again, and thus, in spite of maledictions, as soon as I dropped off to sleep so surely was I roused by that persistent dog.

One of the objects of my journey was to reach a river called Wad Mather, which flows near the village. It abounds in shebbel, sometimes called the salmon of Barbary, and although not known to take the fly, I was ambitious of trying my skill, and, if possible, adding it to the list of fish in which the angler delights. I was up early on the following day, and a walk of about half a mile brought me to the river. It was about forty yards wide, with banks which were flat and uninteresting. I had soon the satisfaction of seeing the shebbel rise repeatedly, sometimes with merely an eddy in the water like a large trout, but more frequently jumping high above the surface. It was a slender, clean-looking fish, apparently from two to three pounds in weight.

Kaddúr said the fish jumped out of the water because they were fighting with each other; so little do the Arabs know or care about things of the kind. Twice a shebbel rose to my fly, but although for fully an hour various sea-trout flies were tried, I was unsuccessful in landing a fish. This could hardly be wondered at, considering the state of the weather, the sun being excessively hot and bright, and a strong east wind blowing. It is to be regretted that I had but this one opportunity of fishing at this place, but it was at least made certain that this fine fish will, under favourable circumstances, afford good sport to the angler. On getting back to the tent the thermometer was found standing at 90° Fahr. It was thus too hot to do anything, so we all went to sleep.

I tried to tempt the Sheikh by the present of a revolver to get me a shot at a wild boar. But although these animals are numerous in the neighbourhood they are not easily seen. The Sheikh excused himself by saying that he was building and could not leave his workmen. A wall was being made in connection with the mosque, but the work seemed more like that of children at play than of men in earnest. The most exacting trades-unionist could not find fault with the manner in which the Moors contrive to show a minimum of result for the pay they receive, whatever that may be.

In the evening I went out shooting through a beautiful glade. It was flanked by picturesque over-hanging rocks, and finely wooded with clumps of trees like an English park. A great flock of black goats was passed, who followed the call of a man to their night quarters like so many dogs. Three or four hares were seen, and a few partridges, a brace of which was bagged. Close to the tent a huge scorpion was found, which, having been first disabled with a stick, I managed to get into my cigar-case. The prize was exhibited to Kaddúr, who, believing I was ignorant of the malignant nature of the creature, exclaimed with a sense of feeling and an earnestness for which one would hardly have given him credit, "Throw it down—it a bad thing. O God, it kill you!"

The Sheikh's house, which was a little distance from the tent, was a long, narrow building covered with thatch, and resembled an Irish cabin without a chimney. A considerable space around it was enclosed with a strong hedge of cut, thorny shrubs. Into this his cattle and flocks were driven at night. The few dwellings which formed the village were constructed on the same principle, but on a smaller scale.

The mosque was literally founded on a rock, which cropped above the surface. Its walls were of rough boulders rudely put together, and its roof was of thatch in want of repair. The interior, though small, was not unlike a country smithy, but the floor was scrupulously clean.

It being Friday, and the Mohammedan Sabbath, I had the fullest opportunity of observing what went on in the mosque. There seemed to be a perpetual Sunday-school; it commenced at 5 a.m., and was continued until 8 p.m., and whenever I returned to the tent the same service or form was being carried on. Half a dozen boys sat in front of the teacher, who, stick in hand, was prepared to punish any show of inattention on the part of his scholars. The portion of the Koran they were engaged in committing to memory was written on a board, which was passed from hand to hand. One boy after the other took up the recitation in a loud, sing-song, monotonous voice. It must be granted that only a strong religious feeling could suggest this troublesome discipline. The fanaticism of the Mohammedan is respectable, because in matters of faith he is painstaking and generally consistent.

As there was little or no twilight, it was dark at seven o'clock, and this confined me to the tent and such amusement as the society of Kaddúr afforded. A specimen of our conversation, taken from my notes, may not be uninteresting. Kaddúr's great object, he said, was to make the Mecca pilgrimage; and, if possible, to die in the holy city for the sake of a glorious immortality. Should he return, no money would thenceforth tempt him to travel with a Christian. Then, in the fervour of enthusiasm, Kaddúr exclaimed, "Come with me to Mecca! I'll swore you'll go the heaven." To which, having replied that my ignorance of the Koran would be a serious obstacle, he began to give me the first lesson: "*La illah a ill allah;*" but he was interrupted and sternly rebuked by the soldier, who was a more serious Mussulman. The truth was, Kaddúr was lax in his conduct, notwithstanding his professions. Although he would not eat with me, he drank my brandy only too freely—a very unorthodox proceeding.

Kaddúr was proud of his knowledge. He informed me that "thousands of Moors ignorant, know nothing, like wild boars; never sick, never dead, never anything." By this he intended to convey that they never think of sickness, or death, or anything. He also told me that tigers are common in England, and that Lord St. Maur had been killed by one there while engaged in hunting. The foundation for this legend was the fact that this nobleman had been some time previously at Tangier for his health, and died soon after leaving.

On the following morning I obtained the aid of a local sportsman, who took me through some millet fields, where fair sport at partridges was obtained. He brought us also to a garden belonging to his father. The old man gave us delicious water-melons, the most refreshing of all things under a burning sun. His garden was provided with an irrigating wheel, which is not seen often in Marocco.

My breakfast on returning to the tent consisted of partridges and fresh figs. The cookery was not bad, except that the butter used by the Moors spoils everything with which it is used on account of its rancid taste.

The mosque proved to be used for various purposes besides those of religion; as a town-hall for the villagers to discuss their affairs in, and as a dressing-room for the Sheikh. I saw him having his head shaved, and other personal matters attended to in the holy edifice. The Sheikh took a very inconvenient fancy to my rifle. Wanting, he said, to conciliate a certain governor in the interior, he wished to present him with the weapon. But, even under this pressure, its ownership was not changed; and he was obliged to be content with other compensation for his services.

We left the village on our return to Tangier shortly after mid-day, and soon overtook a man coming with merchandize from Arzilla. He informed us that on the previous day before he left that place there had occurred a sad event. A Jew boy was seen drinking by some fanatical Moors at a sacred fountain. They instantly killed him by cutting his throat. So much for freedom of action in a country where coroners and juries are alike unknown.

Though women are jealously guarded in Marocco, their condition among the lower classes is far from enviable. We met one groaning under the weight of a huge load of household goods, while her husband stalked on a few yards in front with no encumbrance whatever except his gun. It was late in the afternoon when we reached Tangier.

CHAPTER III.

CASA BLANCA.

I LEFT Tangier for Mogador in the French packet "Verité," on the afternoon of September 23rd. We steamed along the rock-bound lofty coast to Cape Spartel, seven miles from Tangier. This is the western extremity of the northern shore of Africa. It is the point often made for by vessels going to the southern ports; and also before turning eastward by those bound for the Mediterranean. For this reason a lighthouse has been established here by the maritime European nations. It is the only one in the empire, and was erected by a Belgian engineer on a spot granted by the Sultan and declared to be neutral ground. It is a substantial structure in the Moorish style of architecture, and its commanding position on a high plateau adds to its effectiveness. The administration of this lighthouse is undertaken in turn by the various consuls at Tangier. The extreme point of land is formed by a large rock that projects high from the water. Above the sides are worn by the action of the waves into the most fantastic shapes. The beautiful paper Nautilus is found about this Cape. Not far from the lighthouse, and close to the sea, there is a remarkable cavern of large extent, within which millstones are quarried on a somewhat extensive scale. The stones intended for the small hand corn-mills used throughout the country are, when conveyed to Tangier, sold at about six shillings each.

After turning the right-angle of land of which Spartel forms the apex, our way lay well clear of the coast in a south-westerly direction to Casa Blanca, our first stopping-place. The run of one hundred and sixty nautical miles from Tangier to Casa Blanca occupied nineteen hours. The morning of our arrival was dull and rainy, with a strong south-west wind blowing. The roadstead is quite unprotected, and a heavy sea was rolling in from the Atlantic. This made the vessel a very uncomfortable resting-place as she lay at anchor about half-a-mile off the town. Steam was kept up in constant readiness, so as to enable us to get away at a short notice. Seven or eight schooners at anchor close to us were dancing madly to the wild music of the wind. The one thought uppermost among the passengers in the steamer was to get out of the discomfort. But it often happens that vessels with passengers and cargoes for the different coast towns are compelled to pass one or more of them without stopping, even after having delayed a day or two, and are obliged to leave without communicating with the shore.

It was long before any boats put off to us, and when they did arrive there was another long delay; for we had to summon resolution to get into them, and to parley as to the exorbitant demands of the Moorish boatmen. No wonder that these fellows ask to be well paid for their perilous work. It is no uncommon thing on this coast for boats to be upset and lives lost in the tremendous surf. What makes the idea of being upset particularly unpleasant is the presence of great numbers of hammer-headed sharks, as these voracious creatures abound all along the coast. Only a few months previously, four masters of vessels that lay in the roads, three sailors and a Moor, were drowned by the upsetting of a ship's boat, while attempting to navigate it through this dangerous piece of water. The Moorish boats are large, high in the bows, and strongly built. They are rowed by four men with short, clumsy oars, which an English boatman would disdain to handle.

At last we left for the shore, and my first impressions of an African surf are not to be forgotten. Once within its clutches, it was a neck-or-nothing game, and if ever delay was dangerous it was here.

Watching the opportunity while outside the seething water, the men impelled the boat with their utmost strength on the crest of the ingoing wave. The tremendous velocity gained by this impetus caused, for an instant, the boat to rise high in the air on the swelling surface, and then as suddenly dip down the sheer descent of the subsiding water. This was the critical moment; for were not the crest of the next wave as rapidly gained, that which followed inshore would swamp the boat. The wild excitement of the scene beggars description. With wild shouts and frantic gestures, the reis, or captain, at the helm, urged the crew to renewed exertions; and they, straining every nerve, yelled like madmen in response. Some Jews in the boat cowered down and looked like lifeless bundles; but though the foam dashed over passengers and crew alike, we were all, thanks to Moorish strong arms, soon safely landed, and with no greater inconvenience than a thorough wetting.

Dar el Beida, or Casa Blanca, "White House," is built on the ruins of Anfa, a town said to have been founded by the Romans. Anfa was destroyed in 1468 by the Portuguese, but they abandoned the place in 1515, soon after they had rebuilt and renamed the town. The plain on which it is placed is of great extent and very fertile.

If we must acknowledge disappointment on landing at Tangier, it was greater still in the case of Casa Blanca. Viewed from the sea, its compact-looking walls, batteries, and couple of minarets, give it a respectable appearance; but, inside the walls, it is the dirtiest, most tumble-down place ever seen. Some of the Consulates are substantial buildings, but most of the other houses are in bad repair. There are also many waste spaces. Of these not a few are covered with reed huts, in bad repair, in which, when we saw them, many Arabs, wretchedly poor, were encamped. The streets and open spaces were covered with fetid pools of stagnant water, and in these, as elsewhere, was every species of abominable filth. The wonder, altogether, was how people could exist in such a place; and, as might be expected, the public health was at a low ebb. The population is about 4,000, of which a large portion are native Jews, and about a hundred are Europeans. Remittent fever had greatly prevailed, and the mortality among the Jews, in connexion with whom the number had been alone ascertained, had for some time been at the rate of ten and twelve daily. Some Europeans had also died, and one of our passengers from Tangier was a priest belonging to the Spanish Mission, sent by that religious body to fill up a vacancy. The worst climate on the African coast could hardly show a higher rate of mortality. When I returned here (November 6th) this had not materially lessened. The cholera epidemic of 1868 lasted nearly seven weeks, during which 563 persons fell victims to the disease. Notwithstanding all this sickness, the place does not contain one European medical man.[1]

I walked round the walls, which were twenty feet high, and made of *tabia*. They were supported at short intervals by square buttresses, and at longer intervals were small, square, castle-like towers, like those left to us in the town walls of medieval England. The country all round was flat and marshy, but there were good fig-orchards, and some fine palm-trees. The castor-oil shrub grew luxuriantly, as did also the aloe-plant; and it may be worth remarking that I did not observe the latter in any of the places I visited south of Casa Blanca. Just outside the gate, on the land side, was the slaughtering ground, where the offal of animals festering in the hot sun added to the pollution of the town. Fortunately it was well supplied with water, though this was also sadly polluted. The town was skirted on its southern side by a stream made serviceable in turning the wheel of a little flour-mill. This wheel was horizontal, and, though of the rudest construction, was on the principle of a turbine-wheel lately introduced from America into England as a great novelty. Close at hand was a well-kept saint-house of large dimensions. Within the surrounding enclosure grew a graceful palm-tree, the rich foliage of which relieved the glare of the whitewashed walls.

[1] "Le Choléra au Maroc en 1868." Par A. Beaumier. Paris, 1872.

At Casa Blanca we could obtain no reliable news of the Sultan; but a vague rumour was afloat that fighting had been going on in the interior. How difficult it would be in England to realize the existence of an army in the field constantly engaged with the enemy, say in the Midland Counties, and yet that no particulars as to its movements should be current in London! Yet the distance would not be probably greater than that between the Sultan and his Casa Blanca lieges. The condition of things in Marocco was somewhat similar to that of England when the Norman William invaded our shores, and the high-roads of the kingdom were mere trackways.

The export of Casa Blanca chiefly consists of maize and beans. This and Mazagan are the chief ports for these articles of produce; and, in addition, Casa Blanca exports more wool than any other place on the coast. The bar at the mouth of the river on which Rabat is situated, nearly sixty miles to the north-east, causes much of its produce—consisting of wool, carpets, and wax—to be shipped at Casa Blanca. Carpets and slippers are sent in large quantities to Gibraltar, from which place they are transhipped to Alexandria. Our steamer lost the first day of her stay here, on account of bad weather. The next day was employed in getting out our cargo and shipping maize for the Canary Islands, and during the night following we bent our course again for the south.

The coast for a long distance here is flat and uninteresting. Azamoor, seated on a low hill, was sighted in the morning, and at the opposite side of a wide bay lay Mazagan, our next stopping-place, and here we anchored.

CHAPTER IV.

MAZAGAN.

MAZAGAN, or El Bridjah, in the province of Dojualla, is 210 sea-miles south-west of Tangier, and 50 sea-miles from Casa Blanca. It is situated on a peninsula, and owes its origin to the shipwreck of a Portuguese vessel bound to the coast of Guinea. This was in 1502, and it is stated that the mariners took refuge in a tower found on the spot. By whom this structure, called the Tower of Albureja, was built is not clear; though it was probably due to some previous enterprise of the Portuguese. No mention is made of Mazagan by Leo Africanus, so that it could not have been a place of importance in his day.[1] The shipwrecked mariners were so pleased with the climate and fertility of the soil that, leaving twelve of their number well armed and fortified in the tower, the

[1] Leo Africanus was a Moor, born in Granada, who spent a great part of his life in Africa. Much contained in the remarkable accounts of his travels in Marocco, to which he appended the date A.D. 1526, is applicable to the present day. The translation of his work, from which I shall have frequent occasion to quote, was by John Pory, London, 1600.

remainder returned to Lisbon to ask permission of the King Don Manuel to erect a fortress. This having been conceded they returned with men and materials to carry out their purpose. But they were almost immediately attacked with such fury by the people of Azamoor, as also by the neighbouring tribes, that they were glad to take refuge in the tower. They were soon compelled to abandon their position and return to Lisbon. Again they made their representations to the king, who, in 1509, resolved to construct a square fortress, flanked at each angle by a tower. The existing tower of Alburcja was incorporated into the east angle, and as this was of great height it became the watch-tower of the fortress.

The three newly-built towers were called respectively the towers of Segouha, of Cadea, and of Rebate. This last afterwards became the prison for the nobles. Twenty-five cavaliers and 100 foot soldiers constituted the garrison of the fortress.

At the suggestion of the Duke of Braganza, who visited Mazagan on his way to the conquest of Azamoor, the King of Portugal again turned his attention to the new settlement. In 1513 he sent one of the best architects in his dominions to add to the strength of the fortress, and to build a town. This was square in shape, and enclosed within walls in which were three gates. The principal gate, that on the land side, was entered by means of two drawbridges. Another gate, facing the sea, served for communication with the shipping; and there was a third gate in the north-east wall, but this was soon permanently closed. The wall which enclosed the town measured about 4,500 feet (French) in circumference. It contained four churches, eight religious houses, and twenty-five streets, and the population soon numbered 4,000 souls. The fortress, which occupied the centre of the town, was provided with great stores of grain, of ammunition, and everything necessary for a siege. It also contained a prison and a hospital. More than a hundred bronze cannon with two mortars served for the defence of the place.[2]

During the whole time of their occupation, a period of 268 years between 1502 and 1770, the Portuguese never ceased to be exposed to attacks from the Moors. In the year last-mentioned the Sultan Muley Mohammed Ben Muley Abdallah sent an army—it is said, of more than 100,000 men—against the place. After the siege had continued some time the King of Portugal, Don José I., taking into account the frightful sufferings of the garrison and the impossibility of holding the town, except by constant bloodshed and at great loss, resolved upon giving it up. The defenders hearing this determination, in respect to a spot which they

---

[2] These details have been left by Don Luiz Maria de Couto de Albuquerque de Cunha, who was one of the garrison at the time the order was received to abandon Mazagan.

had so long and so dearly held, laid numerous mines, which were fired as soon as the enemy entered. In this way 5,000 Moors are stated to have perished. Mazagan was the last stronghold of the Portuguese in Marocco.

On their return to Portugal these valiant warriors were coldly received, and were soon afterwards sent to Brazil, where they founded a colony, to which they gave the name of Vilha Nuova de Mazagan, in memory of their former dwelling-place.

At the present time Mazagan has many fine specimens of Portuguese architecture. The massive fortifications towards the sea are quite perfect, and in former times were formidable works. A large ruin, which is the most prominent object in the place, is, doubtless on account of the dungeons which it contains, called by Europeans the Palace of the Inquisition; but there is no proof that the building was ever devoted to the purpose of this oppressive tribunal. One fine room I entered was fifty feet in length by twenty in breadth. The remains of the four towers which formed the angles of the fortress were still visible, and also the ruins of a cathedral. But the work which struck me as most worthy of note was a magnificent cistern for storing surface water. Its roof, which is below the soil, was constructed of a series of flat, groined arches, supported by forty-two pillars of stone. It was unquestionably a Moorish work, dating from a period prior to Portuguese occu-

VILLAGE OF CONICAL-SHAPED HUTS.
From a Photograph by the Author.

To face page 67.

pation. It was still used for its original purpose. Light was admitted by a circular aperture in the centre of the roof, while an entrance, provided with steps, led to the water. When stones were thrown from this entrance, a great crowd of bats, which made the cistern their home, rushed out.

The walls of the town were surrounded by a broad but then empty moat. They were thirty feet wide in some places, and twenty high, forming on the top a fine promenade, from which was obtained a good view of the surrounding flat, uninteresting, but fertile country. From this place, towards the north-west, was seen an Arab village made up of conical huts, which resembled the barley-stacks of an English homestead. There was also a new saint-house within view; this showed that canonization is still practised in Marocco.

Mazagan has now but one gate, and its population is reduced to 2,500 inhabitants. Of these about 800 are Jews. It owes its commercial importance to the great fertility of the surrounding country, the soil of which is admirably adapted for the growth of cereals and beans. There is also a large and increasing trade in wool. Most European nations are represented here by consuls or consular agents.

There was a small port or dock in connexion with the fortifications on the north side of the town, but it was only sufficient to admit very small vessels. Those of larger size are obliged to anchor about a mile and a half off the shore. The wrecks of two steam-vessels that appeared above water proved the treacherous nature of the roadstead.

There were seven Spanish and Portuguese sailing vessels at anchor, loading grain for the Canary Islands, of which the agricultural industry lies in the production of wine and cochineal, the inhabitants being mainly fed by imports from Marocco. Mazagan has also a good deal of traffic with Rabat, and beans and maize are exported to England in considerable quantities. The Sultan's victories had been celebrated here with more than ordinary zeal. Salutes were fired, powder play practised, and the shops decorated with little flags the size of pocket-handkerchiefs; there had been, in fact, quite a gala-day.

Notwithstanding its filth, its rough-paved streets, which retain all manner of abominations, the cesspools formed here and there by breaches in the pavement, and the entire absence of sewers, the town is not generally unhealthy. There is little remittent fever, and typhoid fever is unfrequent. During the cholera epidemic of 1868, the mortality reached twenty-five deaths in a day. Ophthalmia is very prevalent, and is attributed, with good reason, to contagion through the medium of flies.

The summer is not so hot as in some other

places on the coast. The warmest part of the day is about 6 a.m.; later on, the sea-breeze commences to blow, and continues throughout the day, accompanied by a grateful fall in the thermometer.

The neighbourhood of Mazagan would afford good shooting. There are plenty of partridges (the desert partridge is not uncommon), quails of two kinds, woodcock, snipe, plovers, and curlews. The numbers of small hawks, owls, ravens, pigeons, storks, and starlings that were flushed in the ruins of the old town astonished me greatly.

Fish abound, and one method of catching them is by enclosing large spaces on the flat shore with rude walls of stone; these being covered when the tide flows in, and left dry when it flows out, the fish which then happen to be within the enclosure are taken by the fishermen.

When I returned to Mazagan (November 5th) I found that rain had fallen there on almost every day since the first of October. The streets were so full of green puddles that it was difficult to get about. It is not easy to explain why Casa Blanca was so deadly, while this town, placed apparently under the same conditions, was not unhealthy in any marked degree.

CHAPTER V.

MOGADOR.

Our next port of call was Saffi, but Saffi refused to receive us. Although the weather was fair, the surf on this part of the coast made it impossible to communicate with the shore. So, as it not unfrequently happens, the captain was obliged to pass on, trusting to the chance of being able to deliver the Saffi portion of his cargo on the return voyage. On the morning of the fifth day from leaving Tangier, the town of Mogador was discerned rising out of the sand-hills by which it is partly surrounded. Mogador is 138 nautical miles from Mazagan, and about 350 south-west of Tangier. It is the model town of the Moors, and from a distance has some claim to the name by which it is commonly known to them—*Suira* (the Beautiful). There is an island to the southward of the town, and the entrance to the port lies between the northern end of this island and a dangerous reef of rocks.

The vessel anchored at about half a mile from

the landing-place, and was immediately surrounded by native boats. A man dressed in European clothes, and in whose face the Arab and the European were plainly blended, accosted me in tolerable English, and I accepted his services for conveyance to shore. This man's name was Ali, and he was at first a great puzzle to me, but subsequently this was explained. His father had been a member of a troupe of Arab jugglers, who thirty years previously had visited London. While there the man married an English woman, and of this marriage Ali was the offspring. Poor Ali was sadly crippled by rheumatism, but he gained a livelihood by means of his boat and the patronage of the English residents.

I was hospitably received by Mr. Yule, the representative of D. Perry, Esq., of Liverpool and Mogador, the principal merchant of the place. Mr. Perry's house was built in the Moorish style, with a spacious patio in its centre. The lower apartments were used for stores and offices. Strings of camels from the interior, laden with olive oil and other merchandise, were received into the patio. There was something primitive and refreshing in the directness and simplicity of the whole proceeding. The upper apartments opened on to a wide gallery, supported on pillars that ran round the patio. The ceilings of some of the rooms were finely decorated in Arabesque patterns and bright colours.

My stay here, including the longer visit on my return from the city of Marocco, extended over some weeks.

Mogador is in latitude 31° 30′ N., but notwithstanding this approach to the tropics, it has an equable climate. As a health resort I regard it as superior even to Tangier. But its distance from Europe and present want of accommodation are drawbacks from which Tangier is free. M. Beaumier, Consul of the French, has resided a great number of years at Mogador, and has made its climate a special study. I am mainly indebted to him for the following remarks. He also placed at my disposal some valuable meteorological tables.

Notwithstanding the imperfections of its sanitary provisions, the town is remarkably healthy. This in a great measure is to be attributed to the ventilating and cooling action of the trade winds. Copious rains of short duration prevail from the end of November to the commencement of April, but chiefly in February and March. The south wind sometimes blows with great violence, and occasionally there are thunderstorms. At times rain continues for three or four days together, but the winter cannot be regarded as wet. As a rule, the sky is clear and the climate most enjoyable.

Rain rarely falls during summer and autumn. A strong north wind then prevails along the coast

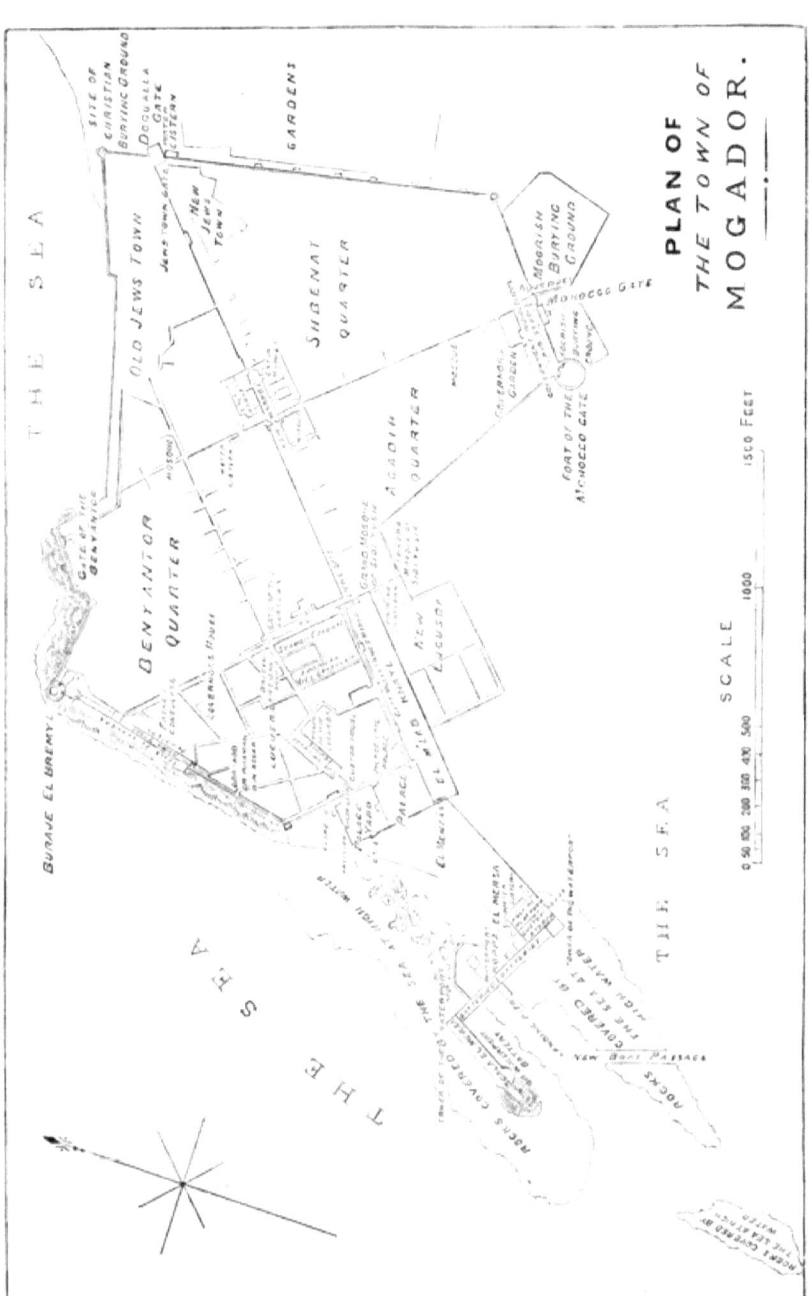

from Cape Cantin as far as Mogador. The town is built partly on sandstone rocks and partly on the sandy shore of the Atlantic, in such a way that in certain states of wind and tide the place is surrounded by the sea without being ever flooded. There are reefs of rock at the north of the town upon which the waves break with great violence. The spray is carried by the wind into the town in the form of invisible particles of sea-water, and at times people's clothes and hair become saturated. This is regarded as very healthful, but it has great disadvantages: iron rusts, and leather and other articles become mouldy in spite of care. The north-east wind is the great benefactor of the place. Whenever the temperature rises this increases in force, after which the thermometer falls. It begins to blow at about 9 A.M., and increases till midnight, and from that time the night is calm.

It is remarkable that the sirocco (S.E. wind), the terrible scourge which is experienced with fatal effects a little inland, very seldom, even in a modified degree, reaches Mogador. The towns on the coast to the north of Cape Cantin, as well as those of the interior, are more or less subject to this wind. The position of Mogador explains the immunity. Although in the latitude of the Great Sahara, the town is situated far enough to the west to be outside the range of the desert wind. Places a little further north and more to the east are within its burning track. On rare occasions a perfect calm exists for a day or two, and this is the worst weather experienced at Mogador. The temperature then reaches, though it rarely exceeds, 80° Fahr., and the sky, usually very bright, is overcast; the atmosphere seems thick, and a sense of lassitude and sleepiness is experienced.

Mogador contains about 15,000 inhabitants, of which number about 6000 are Jews and 150 Europeans. The town is comparatively new. It was built in 1760 by the Sultan Side Mahommed ben Abdullah ben Ismel, and derived its name from the adjacent sanctuary of Side Mogodol. But it is, as already said, best known to the Moors as Suira, on account of its beauty. It is the only town in Marocco which has been laid out with a view to regularity of plan. Like most Moorish towns, it is divided into two parts, the citadel and the outer town. The citadel contains the public buildings and the houses of the foreign merchants. The Jews' quarter is in the outer town. It is isolated and inclosed by walls; but many of the better-class Jews live in the same localities as the foreign merchants. The town is supplied with water by an aqueduct which brings it from a river about a mile and a half distant. In the part of the town occupied by Europeans the streets are of good width for a place in which wheeled vehicles are un-

MOGADOR FROM THE SEA.
From a Photograph.

To face page 70.

known, and are kept fairly clean. Moreover, the drainage is here effected by sewers.

The view of Mogador from a house-top conveys the idea of dreamy solitude. The bright sun shines out of the clear blue vault upon the white and dazzling walls of the silent town. The atmosphere seems to make itself visible by that strange transparent waviness which lulls the senses and invites repose. Looking westward, nothing is in view but one boundless expanse of blue sea; while on every other side, except at a long distance, nothing is to be seen but sand. Close to the water the sand is level and firm, but towards the east it is thrown by the violent winds which prevail in summer into irregular hills of considerable height, the size and even the position of which are entirely altered from time to time.

Mogador is the capital of the fertile provinces of Haha, but, in consequence of its position, it has no immediate rural connections. Its inhabitants live by commerce, and its food supplies are brought from a considerable distance. Unlike Saffi and other towns, grain is seldom exported from Mogador. The fine olive plantations of the country to the south yield abundance of oil, which forms a large article of commerce. Various gums, almonds, beeswax, ostrich feathers, gold, some ivory, goatskins, wool, and sundry other articles, are also exported. Many of these articles are brought to Mogador by caravans from Timbuctoo and the Soudan.

There are several horse-mills for grinding corn; and when I was at Mogador, a small steam-mill was for the first time set going. It excited the jealousy, rather than the wonder, of the Moors; for, as it has often happened in similar cases nearer home, they were afraid that the new machinery would throw those working in the horse-mills out of employment.

A good deal of Marocco leather, chiefly of that fine yellow colour of which slippers are so universally made, is produced at Mogador. There are also some soap factories, but the manufactures are not important. The shops are like those at Tangier, except that at Mogador there are none of those hybrid establishments in which we see the influence of European ideas and customs in combination with those more primitive of the Moor.

A dispensary has been for some time established in the Jews' town, which has been the means of effecting much good. The late Sir Moses Montefiore, the universal benefactor of his race, was a liberal donor to its funds. It is open three times a week, and the attendance of patients ranges from about thirty to forty. There was a hospital containing a few beds, but it was closed for want of support. Dr. Thevenin, a French medical man, and an enthusiast in his craft, has charge of the dispensary, and to his courtesy I am indebted for many opportunities of professional observation.

The poorer class of Jews at Mogador, as in all the

other towns of the empire, presents, generally speaking, an unhealthy appearance. They suffer from the effects of bad food, want of outdoor exercise and ventilation. Yet the Jewish population does not succumb, as might be expected, to severe disease. Ordinary fevers are of rare occurrence among them, and fevers of the remittent type are so uncommon that some years pass without a case being treated. I saw no case of pulmonary consumption, and Dr. Thevenin believes that it is not indigenous. The cholera epidemic of 1866 passed lightly over Mogador: two per cent. only of the estimated population fell victims to it, while the mortality at Tangier was four per cent.; at Mazagan, nine; and at Casa Blanca, fourteen per cent. Indigestion, as might be expected, is very common, as are also rheumatism and diseases of the skin.

Generally speaking, the Moors are averse to receiving medical aid from the infidel, but prefer trusting to the prayers and charms of their priests. My own practice among the better class of Jews, and a few of the Moors of good position, was at times more extensive than I desired. I would gladly have been excused acting the part of amateur physician, when I had only recently and temporarily left behind the fag and responsibility of professional life.

As I was on intimate terms with several Jewish families, I had many opportunities of being present at their ceremonies and entertainments. I was particularly indebted to the High Priest, Signor Joseph Elmaleh, for many acts of kindness. A Jewish wedding which took place at Tangier has been already described. Here, at Mazagan, I witnessed a circumcision, which was celebrated with much rejoicing. It took place, according to the law, on the seventh day after the child had been brought into the world, and in the presence of the mother while still confined to bed. The room was crowded with guests, and there was a small band of hired musicians and singers. One of the songs, among other points, declared that the mother had done well to have given birth to a son, who, worthy of praise, should be held in honour. Had she brought forth a daughter, she would have been highly to blame; those about her would have beaten her with a stick; and so on, in the same strain.

Many of the Jews of Mogador wear the costume of Europe, and are educated gentlemen. They have been to England or some other place abroad, and thus profited by their intercourse with the world. Others of their race, who have not had these advantages, are much on an intellectual level with their Moorish neighbours, and live and dress in the same manner. Some of the Jew merchants are rich, although hardly so in the English sense. But in Marocco there are few luxuries, and money bears a high value; a given income may therefore be regarded as worth double what it would be in

England. There are no costly equipages to be maintained, and there are not even public promenades. The result is, that although the ladies possess expensive dresses and jewellery, there is not the same temptation as with us to constant expenditure on these matters.

The Jewish houses of the better class are large and substantial, and built in the Moorish style. They are, generally speaking, comfortably furnished in the European manner, though often with indifferent taste, there being too much glitter and too little regard to proportion and relative effects.

The Roman or, as now called, Turkish bath has sadly degenerated in Marocco. There are many baths in Mogador, and by great interest I managed to gain access to one while it was unoccupied. It was a fair specimen of its class. The anteroom and cooling-room combined was a small apartment opening to the street, and crowded with various articles; there was also a sort of den to receive the bather's clothes, and beyond this were two small arched rooms parallel with each other. The first or outer room, which was very dark, had a moderately high temperature, and was furnished with a tap and cold-water supply. Separated by a door, the room beyond was absolutely without light at all. There was no ventilation, and the smell such as to lead me to beat an instant retreat. Yet in such wretched chambers the less fastidious Moors pass much of their time. The use of the bath is unknown among the Jews.

I visited the Governor of Mogador, a fine-looking Arab, about forty-five years of age. He was an important personage, yet his pay was said to be only a dollar a day; but his perquisites were various and valuable. For instance, there was a large number of soldiers at Mogador, and from the sum allowed by Government for each man the Governor took the lion's share. He is obliged, however, to send periodical presents to the Sultan, like every one in a similar office. The Governor wore a jelabur of fine white cloth, and was seated on a mat in the anteroom of his house. A crossbill, in a revolving cage like a squirrel's, which was turned by the bird, was his companion. The Moors are fond of pets of all kinds. The Governor was friendly and pleasant in manner. He told me, with much satisfaction, that he had done the Mecca pilgrimage. We had a long conversation, among other things about corporal punishment, which he constantly ordered to be inflicted. He maintained that beating is the best preservative against crime; but that it ought to be inflicted, as was the case formerly, by the force of the arm from the elbow only. He also said that it was a punishment in respect to which much judgment should be used, as the mere idea of being flogged would almost kill some sensitive men. I spoke of the great advantage that would result from a railroad between the city of Marocco and the coast, but his only reply was a waive of the hand. The dislike entertained by the Moors to any European innovations is very remarkable.

The Moors who work at loading and unloading the steamers at Mogador communicate with the captains and crew in a peculiar jargon, which they suppose to be English, but which bears hardly more resemblance to that tongue than Anglo-Saxon does to modern English. It is true this Anglo-Moorish dialect is not copious, and can therefore be soon acquired; but no unaccustomed person could possibly understand a conversation held in it. I was as a listener often amused, and, with the assistance of Captain Hogg, here present a scrap of the lingo *verbatim*. It must be premised that the Moor who acts as stevedore or headman of the men employed in loading and unloading the steamers has frequently great trouble with his gang. The men are by no means fond of work, and it is difficult to keep them in the hold. They stow themselves away in odd corners to smoke kief. Under these circumstances the stevedore goes to the first mate, and the following odd sort of conversation ensues:—

Stevedore.—" Mr. First Mate. This man nithing sot down. Me speak, em sot down. Him speak, catch em smoke. By em by sot down, me speak, em catch em mate. Him speak, never mind for mate. What for this? This no good ewar! Where is what for?"

Mate.—"What man nithing sot down?"

Stevedore.—"This man," pointing to delinquent.

Mate.—"Go down for below. Nithing sot down quick! catch en stripes, no good sot down for smoke, plenty work, quick down for below. Nithing quick; go for ballast; wark quark." Thus urged, the rebellious workman descends to the hold and to his work."

The phrase "go for ballast" is used in various senses. As used above, it means that under certain contingencies the mate will throw the man overboard. If any one dies, it is also said, "He go for ballast."

The captain is styled "Reis"; the second mate, "Mr. Sticky-mate," an epithet doubtless derived from his frequent use of the stick; the steward, "Stoure"; the sailors, "silors"; etc.

This style of conversation, or, more correctly speaking, jumble of words, is extremely ludicrous; carried on as it is with great volubility, violent gestures and flashing eyes. Whether the words "wark quark," which so often occur, be Moorish or "pigeon-English," I could not ascertain, though they seem to imply some such meaning as belongs to our phrase, "It's like your impudence."

There was a Moorish beggar at Mogador, Moses by name, who devoted much attention to me when

we happened to meet in my strolls about the town. He knew a little English, and it was amusing to hear the way in which he applied this knowledge in aid of his calling. The Moor believes in flattery, and Moses applied it without stint. Here is a specimen of the running fire of compliments he would pour into my ear as we walked along :—
" Fine fellow! Clean man! Buy all Mogador! Englishman one man all over world," etc., etc. Who could resist such blandishments, or not indulge their repetition at the small cost of a few reals?

CHAPTER VI.

EXCURSIONS FROM MOGADOR.

The Island at Mogador is rather more than a mile from the southern extremity of the town. It is nearly half a mile in length, extending along the shore, with a breadth at the widest part of about five hundred yards. Thus situated, the island might be supposed to form a natural breakwater against the impetuous roll of the Atlantic. But in this respect it is of little use. The water intervening between the mainland and the island is shallow and exposed to the headlong rush of the waves, which sweep round its northern extremity. Here is the entrance to the port. From its narrowness it presents during violent gales from the west a scene of awful and, perhaps of its kind, unequalled grandeur; for the waves, breaking as they do on the rocks at both sides of the channel with a perpetual upcast of white foam, seem animated by a savage fury. At short intervals a mountain of water, backed by the tremendous force of the ocean, rolls swiftly but smoothly inwards until checked by the rocks within the port. A ground swell is thus raised in which no craft can remain at anchor. For these reasons, Mogador as a port is a mistake, and it is questionable whether these natural defects would be rectified by the outlay of any amount of capital; even if they could, and the port were made really serviceable, there is much reason to suppose that the trade which might follow, though calculated at a high figure, would not be sufficiently remunerative to repay the expenditure incurred.

On a few occasions of the kind described, steam vessels have been surprised within the port, and compelled at all hazards to face the imminent peril of running out. The townspeople relate how, with bated breath and beating hearts, they have witnessed from the beach or from the housetops these courageous efforts. It is told how captains, watching their opportunity, have urged at the instant of a lull, and at the highest speed, their vessels over this treacherous path. How that the gallant captains were met by the incoming waves; how their vessels were dashed backwards and forwards, then to one side, now to another, like a cork on the surface of a waterfall, and were momentarily expected to be split into fragments against the rocks. But the next instant the inward rush of water placed them in a position from which the attempt could be renewed till it culminated in success. Then a spontaneous cheer would arise from all who witnessed these feats of gallantry and nautical skill, and each beating heart would be relieved from an intense anxiety. Bravery of this sort, no less than any other, deserves to be held in honour; for a cool head, strong nerves, and all the qualities necessary to make up the heroic nature are absolutely required.

Only vessels provided with steam-power can attempt, with any certainty of success, entrance to the port. Very few sailing vessels now resort to it, and these are chiefly Spanish from the Canary Islands. When they are overtaken by a gale such as that I have described, they are almost invariably driven from their anchors and hopelessly wrecked. It is the custom of the crews to consult their own safety by abandoning their ships in good time. Some years ago an English captain, as renowned for his cool courage as for his experience of the port, persuaded his crew to follow his example and stand by their vessel. They did so; and, though deserving a better fate, perished to a man.

As an agreeable change, the island is a favourite resort of the European residents of Mogador. But the Moors and the Jews seem unable to understand why people should take the trouble to move for a purpose so indefinite or useless. Many well-to-do Jews told me that, although natives of the place, they had never set foot on the island. I had the pleasure of spending a couple of days there with some of the English residents at Mogador.

This island is the quarantine station of Marocco, and is occasionally used for the purpose. Steamboats destined for Tangier, and containing Mecca pilgrims from Alexandria, have been compelled, on occasions of an outbreak of cholera, to proceed to this place, nearly four hundred miles further. This most justly has been considered a great grievance, though it is one which at present admits of no remedy.

There were a couple of good houses on the island, in one of which we took up our quarters. It consisted of a patio, or courtyard, the four sides being surrounded by apartments. These afforded ample room for the ladies and gentlemen of the party; and our mattresses served for seats as well as beds. But if, thus far, the Moorish habits were adopted, we lived otherwise in the true style of English profusion, and during our sojourn in this retreat all experienced as near an approach to a state of mental and physical inaction as those who are neither Orientals nor true believers can attain, for the days were charming and the calm nights simply delicious. The air, tempered by the fresh sea breezes blowing unchecked over the island, rendered endurable the direct rays of the sun. Looking over the island, the sandy soil was seen to be overgrown with scrubby bushes and green succulent plants, which contrasted favourably with the arid mainland. The sky was of the deepest blue; while at night the stars, reflected in the ocean, appeared as though magnified. Of these, some were new to the northern stranger, and, as might be fancied, returned his gaze with a staring lustre. On the land side of the island the gurgling waves were heard in dreamy monotony, while on its seaward side the restless billows plunged into the caves and crannies of the cliffs with a power and rush of sound, the sublime effect of which cannot be described.

The northern end of the island is very precipitous. In this direction a large piece of sandstone cliff had been detached, probably by an earthquake, in such a manner that the water could flow between it and the mainland. Rising like a straight wall some hundreds of feet out of the sea, that portion of it facing the island was pierced by a great natural archway, through which, in calm weather, boats could pass to the opposite side. The ledges of rocks, as also the top of this detached cliff, were the resort of great numbers of cormorants and other sea-birds. Still more populated was the interior of the archway. It was the home of innumerable wild pigeons. Many of these were constantly flying about the island, and, from specimens we shot, they appeared not to differ in plumage from the ordinary blue-rock variety, which they also resembled in rapidity of flight. At sunset and during the short twilight these birds would arrive at the island in huge detachments. If, after they had settled, a gun was fired, the air was instantly filled with a dense and fluttering mass of animal life. The birds, however, soon returned to their resting-places, and at daybreak were again on the wing, flying far inland in search of food. This habit probably accounted for the regularity of their departure and return. Aware of this, sportsmen from Mogador take up their position at certain points on the mainland, and shoot them down in great numbers. The thing for wonder was how the birds, scattered as they were during the day over a wide extent of country, collected together at the approach of night, and flew away direct in compact bodies to their accustomed resting-places in the inaccessible rocks.

Immense flocks of starlings also roosted under the shelter of the same rocks. It was an interesting sight to witness the eccentric movements of these birds as they approached the island. At a distance their compact phalanx resembled nothing so much as a black cloud constantly changing its shape. At one moment it was elongated, the next it rapidly whirled round its axis, then became a more compact body, was now triangular, and now of no regular outline. A moment later it ascended towards the sky, then, descending swiftly, swooped along the ground. This method of going to rest was certainly extraordinary, considering that during each day these birds had of necessity traversed great distances in rapid flight.

One night we tried fishing, though with little success, from the high rocks beneath which there was deep water. As everywhere else, fish in these latitudes are capricious, and will not always take the bait. The best time for fishing here is on a dark night. Our rods were strong, finely-tapering reeds five-and-twenty feet in length, and the lines were of wire, to prevent them from being bitten across, for the fish are most voracious. The bait consisted of pieces of octopus. These our attendant Moor prepared for the hook by seizing a portion of the phosphorescent and semi-putrid mass with his teeth, and there thus holding it, then he separated it into pieces with his hands. It was a proceeding as savage as it was sickening.

The island is too small to harbour game, but it abounds in wild cats. These are said to live entirely on fish which have been thrown on the rocks, but small birds form, more probably, their chief food.

The edible hawk—so much esteemed as a delicacy—is procured from this island. The flesh of the hawk tribe is regarded by us as totally unfit for food; yet one species is so much in request in South Marocco, that the birds are sent from Mogador as presents to the Sultan. I was not so fortunate as to meet with this delicacy, neither was I able to ascertain the species, but it is a small bird somewhat resembling our sparrow-hawk.

Adjoining our house was a little mosque, which the pious care of a Government, intimately blending in itself all the authority of Church and State, had provided for the residents. Early and late the solemn cry of the muezzin was sent forth, to die away upon the waters; but we soon found that this good man was not so punctual in his movements as to render them a regulator for our watches; in fact, he seemed to ascend the tower just when it suited his convenience. Neither, so far as I could judge, was his cure of souls extensive, for, generally speaking, priest and congregation were united in his own person. Even with this liberty as to time, his life must have been wearisome and monotonous in the extreme, for we were told that during the period of twenty years he had never once left the island. Its permanent residents consisted of fifteen men, chiefly ragged soldiers, who were the custodians of five batteries placed around the coast. The guns were iron thirty-two pounders, placed *en barbette* from three to five in each battery. All were deplorably rusty and honeycombed, and not a few had been dismounted and spiked by the French. Many others had been thrown into the sea by the same hands.

When the French, under the orders of the Prince de Joinville, landed here, they met with a most resolute resistance from the garrison of some hundred Moors, who fought with the desperation of men that expected no quarter. On both sides great slaughter ensued, numbers of the Moors perishing in their attempt to swim to the mainland.

About a mile and a half south of Mogador is a Shluh village, called D'Jerbet. It is situated on the sea-shore, a small river running close beside it. From this cause, probably, almost all the inhabitants were more or less affected with remittent fevers, and the condition of some was very deplorable. This was the more remarkable, as at this date no cases of fever were known at Mogador. Mr. Yule enlisted my services for these villagers, and we visited the place together on several occasions. This gave me the opportunity of inspecting the interior of the houses, and of making myself familiar with the general economy of a Shluh village. The one in question was enclosed by high walls of tabia, and the interior in some respects resembled a maze, for a series of narrow passages or lanes run between the enclosure, each house having a walled-in yard, in which the cows, mules, and poultry of the proprietor were housed at night.

In making our visits to this village we were sure to be assailed by a number of the most savage dogs I ever saw. Without doubt these brutes would have torn us to pieces if they had not been driven off by the men before we dismounted from our mules, for they seemed to be imbued with the true spirit of Mussulman exclusiveness, and resented most fiercely all intrusions of infidel strangers into the precincts of the faithful. The villagers appeared to be industrious. They lived partly by farming and partly by acting as carriers to Mogador. They are also sportsmen in a way. Seeing some pigeons in confinement, I ascertained that these were used for decoying falcons into a net. The latter birds are reared on the island already described, which is opposite the village, and being rare, their captors are considered fortunate if they take a dozen in the year. The falcons are thus highly prized, wealthy governors and others sometimes giving as much as £20 for a specimen. Many find their way to the Sultan himself.

The houses consisted of narrow rooms opening on to the courtyard; usually a single room formed the entire house. It had no windows, and depended for light on the open door. At one end was the bed of the husband and wife, the children sleeping on a raised sofa-like bench placed along the walls. The other end of the room was filled by a large chest, a simple cooking stove fed with charcoal, millstones for grinding corn, some cooking vessels, and gourds for holding water, milk, and other things. The walls were limewashed, and sometimes bordered with a decoration resembling the repeated form of half an egg in a bright colour. Bowls of the handsome pottery in common use were hung against the walls by means of strings passed through holes in the bottom rims. Bird-traps, ingeniously made from the rib of a sheep or goat, showed the juvenile taste for sport. The floors were scrupulously clean, and the whole appearance of the house reflected credit on the inmates. The locks and keys were of wood, such as are used in many Eastern countries.

How is it that in dwellings such as these, buried from the world and unconnected with, at least, its modern phases of civilization, a greater taste and a truer feeling for colour and ornament are found than in the homes of corresponding classes among ourselves? The cottage of the English labourer, the cabin of the Irishman, the bothy of the Highlander, are alike undecorated by any art belonging to the occupants. Celt and Anglo-Saxon alike seem to have little innate æsthetic feeling, or at least it requires peculiar circumstances and aids for its development. But the Esquimaux who carves his pipe, the South Sea Islander who decorates his paddle or his weapons, the negro of Central Africa who scratches figures on his gourds, or the Moors in the seclusion of their villages, exhibit a conception of, and inherent taste for, art rarely discoverable in the nature of our uneducated classes.

Most of my patients were women—a circumstance to be explained by the absence of the men from the locality during the day, while the women were exposed both day and night to the noxious emanations from the river. Some of the women were fine specimens of their race, their features being regular, their figures good, and their hands and feet small. The younger women had their eyelids blackened with kohl and their hands stained with henna after the approved  method. Many were tattooed on the chin with the figure represented in this woodcut. It is a cabalistic sign intended to ward off the influence of the evil eye.

It must not be supposed that the domestic virtues did not flourish in this benighted village— virtues which we are apt to suppose belong almost exclusively to a different religious dispensation than that of the prophet of Mecca. It is true that poverty alone prevented the villagers from being polygamists. But that is a question of morals which would be decided differently by the Christian citizens of Utah and New York. I can only say that if paternal and filial affection, patience in adversity, gratitude for help, and resignation to the will of God are Christian virtues, these Mohammedans possessed them in a degree higher, it is certain, than many so-called Christians. One middle-aged widow who was seriously ill had brought up a large family by the proceeds of her labour at Mogador, to which place, when in health, she daily repaired. An old weather-beaten man, who had a certain shyness about him, proved to be a Spanish renegade. One little incident of medical practice must be told; it may convey a valuable hint to some anxious mothers. A miserably nourished infant was brought to me for advice; it had not been weaned, but, as it did not thrive, the mother had given what she considered to be the most strengthening aliment within her reach—walnuts chewed to a pulp in her own mouth, and then transferred to that of the child.

I made several shooting and other excursions into the country in company with my friends. In some places partridges were very numerous, but, owing to the high cover, were difficult to shoot. In sandy places, overgrown with tall broom, we could often hear them rising on the wing close at hand and in great numbers, and this without seeing a bird. The country was in many places very picturesque, the ground being broken by well-wooded hills. The date-palm was hardly to be seen; but the argan-tree gave the landscape a character of its own.

The argan, like many other trees in Marocco, has a local distribution. It is only found south of the river of Tensift, and at no great distance further south it again disappears. The province of Haha contains many large forests consisting entirely of these trees, and the oil pressed from the kernels of their fruit forms an important article of diet. They are not lofty trees, but, by their tendency to spread, afford most grateful shade. The leaves are small, of a dull green colour, and surrounded by thorns. The bark is furrowed longitudinally and cross-ways, so as closely to resemble the armour-like skin of certain antediluvian creatures.[1]

The largest known argan-tree was about four miles from Mogador. It was of great age, and I found that, while it was not more than twenty feet in height, it covered a space of ground seventy-two yards in circumference. The trunk, which was very rugged and unequal, measured near to the ground twenty-six feet, and from this point soon branched out. The branches extended more or less horizontally, and drooped so as to rest on the ground. From these other branches were sent upwards, this giving the appearance of several trees in a group. This tree was a favourite resort of picnic parties from Mogador; and the Moors, mistaking the object of these visits, have concluded that the Christians have adopted it as their saint-tree.

Another more distant excursion, but somewhat in the same direction, was to the Sultan's garden. It was beautifully situated and

---

[1] Referring to this province of Haha, Leo Africanus wrote:—
"Likewise there are found in this region certain thornie trees, bearing a gross kind of fruit, not unlike unto those olives which are brought unto us from Spain; the said fruit they call in their language arga. Of this fruit they make a kind of oile, being of a fulsome and strong savour, which they use, notwithstanding, for sauce and for lampes."

well supplied with water, which in this country implies luxuriant vegetation, but it was utterly ruined and neglected. The house was in a tumble-down condition, and the ground overrun with weeds; but there were some fine trees, the relics of former care and cultivation. In this neighbourhood we saw great numbers of partridges, and the spoor of wild bear was frequent.

Another tree abounding in these forests was the ararthuja-tree, *Callitris quadrivalvis*, a plant allied to the cypress, yielding a durable wood much employed for building purposes. But its trunk grows to no great height, while the branches are not large; and these circumstances have made an unmistakable impression upon the architecture of the country. The tree is of slow growth and not conspicuous for beauty, but it is valuable to the world at large on account of its yielding gum sandarach, a substance useful for making varnish. This gum forms one of the exports peculiar to Mogador.

The long-standing fame of the thuja-tree has given it a place in ancient history. It was the citrus-tree of the Romans, and yielded the citron wood which, in the palmy days of Rome, attained a price unknown for such articles even in our own age. Pliny thus refers to this tree and its uses: "In the vicinity of this mountain" (one of the Atlas range) "is Mauretania, a country which abounds in the citrus, a tree which gave rise to the mania for fine tables; an extravagance with which the women reproached the men when they complained of their vast outlay upon pearls. There is preserved to the present day a table which belonged to M. Cicero, for which, notwithstanding his comparatively moderate means, and what is even more surprising still, at that day too, he gave no less than one million sesterces (about £9,000). We find mention made also of one belonging to Gallus Asinius, which cost one million one hundred thousand sesterces. Two tables were also sold by auction which had belonged to King Juba; the price fetched by one was one million two hundred thousand sesterces, and that by the other something less. There has lately been destroyed by fire a table which came down from the family of the Cethegi, which had been sold for the sum of one million four hundred thousand sesterces, the price of a considerable domain. . . . The largest table that is made from a single piece of wood is the one which takes its name from Nomius, a freedman of Tiberius Cæsar. The diameter of it is four feet, short by three-quarters of an inch, and it is half a foot in thickness, less the same fraction. While speaking on this subject I ought not to omit to mention that the Emperor Tiberius had a table that exceeded four feet in diameter by two inches and a quarter, and was an inch and a half in thickness; this, however, was only covered with a veneer of citrus wood, while that which belonged to his freedman Nomius was so costly, the whole material of which it was composed being knotted wood."[2]

Sir Joseph Hooker, President of the Royal Society, has kindly supplied me with specimens of the veneer, procured at Algiers, where the wood is used for cabinet work, which is sold in Paris at a very high price. The varied markings of this material allowed the Roman connoisseurs the opportunity of fixing standards of excellence according to the rarity and other qualities of each specimen.

Ordinary arar wood has no beauty whatever, and that which was so much esteemed appears to have been knots in the wood, the product, like the pearl, of disease. On this point Pliny again affords us some interesting information. "These knots are properly a disease or excrescence of the root; and those used for this purpose are more particularly esteemed which have lain entirely concealed under ground; they are much more rare than those that grow above ground, and that are to be found on the branches also. Thus, to speak correctly, that which we buy at so vast a price is, in reality, a defect in the tree."

[2] Pliny: "Nat. Hist.," book xiii., chap. 29: Bostock's translation.

CHAPTER VII.

JOURNEY TO THE CITY OF MAROCCO.

THE European residents at Mogador seldom go to the capital; years sometimes pass without any one making the journey, as it involves much discomfort and some risk. It happened fortunately that Mr. Broom, an English merchant of the place, wanted to petition the Sultan in reference to a long unpaid debt owed by an influential Moor who lived in Marocco, and, hearing of my intention, resolved to accompany me. His knowledge of the country and the natives was of great service, and we set out with a much smaller party than I intended to have taken. In ordinary times the number would have been sufficient, but we afterwards found that more numerous guards were greatly needed.

Our party, besides ourselves, consisted of Leo, a Mogador Jew, interpreter, valet, and handy man in general; Ben Ahia, a Moor, with a strong dash of negro blood; and Mohammed, our soldier and official protector, a slightly-made, good-looking Shluh. Two other wild-looking Moors made up our party, one of whom, nicknamed Timbarkate, was an athletic and amusing fellow, a keen sportsman, and, as he subsequently admitted, a rascal of the first water. We were seven in all, mounted on mules—strong animals trained to go at a steady pace of four miles an hour for the greater part of each day. All except Leo were well armed; the soldiers and the muleteers with long Moorish guns and daggers, while Mr. Broom and I carried shot-guns for sport and revolvers for protection.

The Moors excel in packing for a journey. Four mules carried all our equipments. Panniers made of strong grass interwoven, were first filled with various requisites; of these, each mule carried a pair, across one of which the mattresses were packed, serving as a seat for Leo. The tent and other bulky things were stowed away in like manner on three other mules, all of which had riders. The soldier, like Mr. Broom and myself, was unencumbered by baggage.

We left Mogador early in the afternoon, and, striking eastward, traversed the sandy plain on which it is situated. Just outside the town we passed a Moorish funeral. A great crowd of turbaned men accompanied the corpse, which, borne by sorrowing relatives, was about to be placed coffinless in the earth, the crowd singing, as it went, a solemn dirge.

Here an instance of the custom in Arabia and the wisdom of the precepts of Mohammed is worth remarking. It was, no doubt, copied from the Jews, like circumcision, etc. Mohammedans have always buried their dead outside the towns, while we have only recently arrived at the conclusion that this is a sanitary necessity.

We passed, a little way beyond the town, a powder magazine, as also a small building which could only be regarded as a monument of Moorish incapacity for progress. It had been, till recently, used for the manufacture of percussion caps, under the superintendence of Europeans; but, difficulties arising, no efforts appear to have been made to overcome them except by readily throwing up the manufacture.

Our way now lay through miles of deep sand, covered with nothing but the waving branches of the artim, or white-blossomed broom, which grows to a considerable height. Then commenced a tract in which the sand disappeared and the argan tree flourished. In some places these trees were so large and numerous as to form a forest of considerable extent. It was a beautiful tract, as seen when the slanting rays of the sun lighted up the rugged and gnarled trunks of the old trees, and, as a landscape, was worthy of Ruskin's descriptive power. As we passed along we flushed covey after covey of partridges, and longed to go in pursuit. At last Timbarkate, seeing one of the birds on the ground, succeeded, by a peculiar circumventing method used by the Moors, in approaching close enough to shoot it with a ball from his clumsy weapon. The gesticulations and self-applause of this wild fellow, as he triumphantly brought in the bird, were highly amusing. I killed a beautiful hawk, the skin of which, when shown at Mogador, was said to be that of a bird unknown there.[1]

Soon after, a cavalry soldier, mounted on a fine horse, overtook us, saying he would accompany us, as our destination was the same. We found him a pleasant fellow; but neither then nor afterwards could we get any satisfactory account of where he came from, or under what orders. We conjectured that he was sent as a spy on our movements. Our ride to-day was, on the whole, very pleasant. The air was balmy, the heat not excessive, while there was a sense of exhilarating freedom in thus exchanging the shut-in Moorish town for an open, yet finely-wooded country. Not only was the argan tree abundant, but also the arar and wild olive. As no rain had fallen, the ground was parched, and but for the trees the country would have been a desert. On the left, fine views were obtained of the picturesque Iron Mountains. Had there been grass, the scenery would have been similar to that of an English park; and as it was, some of the tree-covered hills at a distance resembled the wooded heights of Surrey. The road, although in some

[1] It proved to be *Melierax polyzonus*.

places a mere bridle-path, in others expanded into
one fairly wide and worn smooth by the feet of
mules and camels.

As we left Mogador late, this was a short day's
journey of not more than twelve miles to the inzella
of Mangat. It is undesirable to travel at night,
and therefore it is always best to stop at an inzella,
or place appointed by the Government for the reception of travellers. These inzellas are situated
at convenient distances on the line of road between
different places. They consist of enclosures, more
or less spacious, surrounded by high walls, or
sometimes by almost equally secure fences made
with closely-packed branches of the thorny zyphu-
shrub. A custodian is appointed to take charge
of each station, and, as there is generally a village
in connection with the inzella, the head-man acts in
this capacity. It is his duty to set a guard at
night, so that travellers under his protection may
not be surprised by the robbers and freebooters
with which the country abounds. Camels, horses,
mules, and asses are also received into the
enclosure. Fires are lighted by the travellers for
the preparation of meals, and they sleep stretched
on the ground in the open air, or, more rarely,
in tents.

The people of the inzella receive a mozonna
or two (even the latter sum does not amount to
a penny) for each animal taken into the enclosure;
yet such is the poverty of the Arabs that they

sometimes prefer to cross mountains in order to avoid these small charges. When Europeans arrive they are surrounded by a crowd full of curiosity, who, inspired by the hope of high pay, are generally civil and obliging. Live fowls, eggs, milk, and bread are brought for sale from the adjoining huts. Butter is also to be had, but no untrained stomach can endure it. As for both bread and milk, it will be better for the traveller, if he values his peace of mind, not to trouble himself about the sanitary condition of the dwellings from which they have been brought, nor the state of the woman's hands through which they have passed.

It is desirable not to stop, if possible, at an inzella near the bounds of a province. The reason is, the ruffians of the adjoining province pass from its jurisdiction, and congregate at the enclosure. In order to do away with the great evils arising therefrom, it sometimes happens, as in the case of the inzella near the sanctuary of Sidi Moktar, where formerly four provinces met, that the boundaries have to be altered, since a sanctuary cannot be disturbed.

On September 30th we were astir early, but a vexatious delay occurred. The bridle of one of the mules had been stolen, and we had nothing to replace it with. By the offer of a small reward it was at last brought back. The Moors are much given to thefts, and the ingenuity with which they excuse or rebut a charge brought home to them is sometimes as amusing as it is provoking.

During the delay my companion and I employed ourselves in shooting doves, which abound about the villages in wooded districts. The species was the same as I had met with in the north. It was nearly seven o'clock A.M. when we left the inzella, and, after a ride of about an hour and a half, we passed piles of stones which form the boundary between the provinces of Haha and Shedma. Two hours later the station Kil'atu l' Hassan was reached, where, under the shade of some olive trees, and close to a well, we stopped to breakfast. Near at hand, perched on a hill in the full glare of the scorching sun, was a large saint-house. It had a defiant aspect, and could not be approached. Moreover, the manners of the inhabitants of the place differed from those of the Mogador people, and indicated that as we advanced inland sullen glances would change to looks of hatred.

After leaving this inzella we passed by the wayside a heap of stones, the purpose of which it was difficult for a stranger to guess. It was a murder cairn, and they are not infrequent in the country. A poor wretch had at some time or other been waylaid on the spot and sent to his last account. Forthwith it became the duty or privilege of devout passers-by to place a stone on the place, and this had been done, till now a considerable heap stood there. This custom may have arisen more from a superstitious than a religious feeling, but, with all its faults, there is something in the creed of Mecca which tends to soften and humanize the hearts of rough untutored men.

Our way lay through many miles of palmetto tufts, with hardly, so far as we could see, any sign of cultivation. Afterwards the soil became sandy, and for some distance the broom again prevailed. Beyond this there was an abrupt rise of ground, on the crest of which my aneroid indicated a height of 1,400 feet. A mile farther on, at a height of 1,250 feet, and distant from Mogador about forty-eight miles, the vast plain of Marocco opened out. The whole country was here covered with an ugly, low-sized thorny bush.

It was dark when we reached Ain O'must, our stopping-place. We had had a hot ride of forty miles, and both men and animals were tired and thirsty. As soon as we had dismounted at the inzella, some of the mules which were set free, guided by unerring instinct, rushed downhill through the darkness to a spring at a considerable distance. Mr. Broom and I followed, only to find that the water, stirred up by the feet of the animals, was thick with mud. Yet so great was our thirst, even in this state it was acceptable. On returning to the inzella our men protested that they were too tired to pitch the tent, and that it was unnecessary as the night was fine. A little firmness soon got over this difficulty. Next the villagers declared they had neither eggs nor fowls, and it was only by threatening to report them to the Sultan that necessary supplies were obtained. Altogether we had a chapter of troubles, but there was also something to amuse.

Just outside the gates of the inzella a number of Moors seated in a circle were gravely discussing the topics of the day, among which our persons and personalities were on the *tapis*. The proper method of treating us was also a point discussed. We could see their white turbans moving to and fro in the darkness, and we felt that our suppers might depend on their decision. These *réunions* among the Moors show that they are a clubable race. Indeed, every village would seem to have its open-air evening club.

We were not sorry to get away from this inzella, for, as seen in the early dawn, our fellow-travellers and companions of the night were an unsightly set, whose company we did not covet. Soon after leaving, I shot an owl about the size of a thrush; a matter not worth mentioning, except for the temporary mutiny it raised among our men. The row was quelled by my promising not to kill another. Here, as in some other countries, superstition protects the birds of Minerva. The country traversed was undulating, stony, and barren, with hardly any vegetation but the small sidra shrub. The ground was thickly pierced with rat-holes, although it was difficult to conjecture what the wretched vermin found to eat in such a parched desert. Squirrels were also seen, and it afforded our Moors something of the excitement of the chase to hunt them from bush to bush. This uninviting country is scantily inhabited by a tribe of indifferent reputation, who long ago were removed here from the Sahara. Some of these wild fellows, who were working at a deep well at which we stopped, were unencumbered by any covering except what the last demands of decency required.

At about a dozen miles from Ain O'must, on the right-hand side of the road, we passed the famous sanctuary of Sidi Moktar, already mentioned. From Sidi Moktar to Seshoua was a dreary ride of nearly twenty miles, under a burning sun, and over a stony parched soil which threw back upon us the sun's heat. At one place, close to a curiously-shaped hill, there is a large dilapidated cistern without water, and in this state it has long remained. Yet every summer men and animals die of heat and thirst in this part of the route between the metropolis and the coast. Thus it is that a despotic government cares for its subjects!

Close to Seshoua, and at about a quarter of a mile to the left of the road, is another curious hill. As we approached it was deceptive, appearing nearer than it really was. It was flat-topped, and resembled a loaf of sugar with its upper half removed, and rose abruptly out of the vast plain. Between this hill and the river traces of a ruin, covering a considerable space, were observed. They appeared to be foundations of stone buildings, but we could obtain no information with respect to them.

At last, after anxiously scanning the horizon many times in vain, a welcome fringe of oleanders was discovered. Wherever in its own arid climate this beautiful shrub grows, water is certain to be at hand. The sight infused fresh vigour into all, for we had ridden about thirty miles and were nearly exhausted. For a great part of the way we had suffered much from thirst, as the Arabs, who seem to have no forethought, had neglected or wasted our supply of water; and we resolved in this important matter not to trust to them again.

As water in this climate means life, Seshoua presented an agreeable contrast to anything we had seen since leaving Mogador. Irrigated fields, in which maize was springing up, presented that shade of delicate green which is so grateful to the eye. Various trees and shrubs abounded in rich profusion. How gladly we threw ourselves from the saddles under the perfect shade of luxuriant olive trees from which the fruit was constantly dropping! What value the river had in our eyes as we drank draught after draught of its tepid water! Our paradise, it must be owned, was a trifle too warm. My thermometer, hung under the trees, indicated 94° Fahr. A strong north-east wind was blowing at the time, yet the air was as hot to breathe as the water was warm to drink. Although ascending rather rapidly after leaving the level of the seaboard, the temperature quickly increased. At Mogador the heat rarely exceeded 80° Fahr.; at Seshoua, eighty miles inland, where the elevation is 1,200 feet, the heat was exceptional, even for the tropics.

The object of our early arrival and delay here was to fish. I was desirous once more to try this sport in a Marocco river. After refreshing ourselves, we went down to the stream, though in the fierce heat it required an effort to do so. The sight and noise of the flowing water, with its verdant banks, excited that kind of vivid pleasure which a sudden and agreeable contrast always imparts. The river, which flows into the Tensift, was very low. The volume of water did not exceed that of a good-sized mill-stream, but its worn banks and rather extensive bed, broken here and there by little islands, showed that in the rainy season its dimensions are considerable. We used for bait bread moulded on the hook, and also bits of meat, selecting the deepest pools to cast in. We were rewarded by the capture of a number of small fish, which took the bait freely. The sport would have been good under more favourable circumstances. But shade was wanted, and we felt uncomfortable as to venturing amid the overhanging shrubs, lest we should be regarded as intruders by a puff-adder, or some other deadly reptile, attracted, like ourselves, by water and protection from the sun.

Our fishing was also greatly interfered with by the voracity of creatures we never bargained for. Again and again the bait was taken from the hooks without the usual indication of a fish seizing it; but, on drawing one of the lines quietly up, it was observed that the bait was followed to the surface by a large tortoise. Having discovered the secret, we were able to bring the enemy into view repeatedly. Afterwards, as if getting bolder by success, this and others of its kind began to swallow our hooks, and our lines were broken in the attempt we made to pull them out of the water. At last, by great management, I contrived to land a floundering fellow weighing several pounds. He behaved in so reserved a manner that nothing was to be seen of his head, for the line passed deeply beneath his uncouth armour. By pulling the line strongly, both head and neck were slowly protruded, and the hook was found firmly embedded in its jaws. To regain this, we decided on a surgical operation; so, keeping its neck steadily extended by means of the line, I proceeded to operate with my penknife. But no sooner did cold steel enter its flesh than back flew the head, as if governed by a powerful spring, into its tortoiseshell case, and snap went the line with a whiz, leaving the operation, unless with the aid of chloroform, hopelessly unfinished, and myself as hopelessly deprived of a hook.

This water-tortoise (*Leprosa Clemmys*) is common in the rivers of Marocco. They may be observed poking their heads just above the water, to breathe; but their power of remaining long under the surface must also be great. They often crawl out of the water on to the banks, off which, when disturbed, they plunge with a loud splash which is startling. I wanted Timbarkate to carry off my sport-destroyer as a trophy, but with the most ridiculous grimaces of disgust he absolutely refused to touch it, pointing out that it emitted a most disagreeable smell. It shook my faith, for the time, in the purity of the element I had recently so largely imbibed. There was, however, no need for apprehension that a thirst such as we had experienced would not get over this and far greater scruples. This water-tortoise is very voracious, and, as we proved, devours with equal readiness vegetable and animal substances.

A practical inconvenience arising out of Leo's religion had to be met. Our delay here would cause us to arrive in the city on the second, instead of the day following our leaving this, and that day would be the holy *Rosh-ha-Shanah*, or New Year's

Day of the Hebrews; on which, being a strict holiday, no orthodox and pious Jew, such as one finds in Barbary, would travel. Nothing else could be done but to send him on with the cavalry soldier, who agreed to escort him. Our own arrangements were also so disturbed as to make it necessary for us to send on our tents under their care.

The inzella here was surrounded by high walls, and as the night, like the day, was extremely hot, we resolved to brave all risks rather than pass the night in that stifling enclosure. We hoped to find cooler quarters in the open, under some fine trees, and proposed that we should watch by turns for protection; but no persuasion could induce our soldier to agree to this plan.

There was nothing to be done but to put our mattresses side by side in the inzella, and try to sleep as best we could. I had been consulted professionally by several of the villagers, and they were obliging and attentive; but nothing could compensate for the drawbacks of that terrible night. The floors of all the inzellas are covered to the depth of some inches with straw broken short, leaves of trees, together with the dried dung of camels and other animals. This compound harbours innumerable insects, from which we had already suffered more or less; but on this sultry night all the insect world seemed to have combined against us. We tried to eat a frugal meal of bread and milk and boiled eggs, but no sooner was a candle lighted than it was extinguished by a host of assailants in the shape of gigantic moths, bizarre grasshoppers, and, worst of all, great foul-smelling flying bugs. This was the least part of our troubles, as we managed to dine in the dark; but when, wrapped in our jelaburs, and otherwise partially undressed—for it was impossible to retain all our clothes—we lay down to sleep, we found ourselves at the mercy of far more malignant enemies. Fleas, bugs, ants, midges, mosquitoes, and other insects for which we could find no name—all things, in short, which could crawl or fly—seemed on that night to make common cause against us. They attacked with suckers, with pincers, and with burning awls, till we were almost frantic. I was constantly expecting that a few scorpions would give a finishing touch to our misery, for there must have been many in the old walls close to where we lay. What would have been the end of it is hard to say, had it not been for a sovereign remedy which was fortunately at hand. I had with me a box of Persian powder, and wherever the intruders were thickest we rubbed this into our skins. The effect was almost magical. At these spots the invasion was subdued, and by constant applications of the powder we gained comparative ease, till at length, worn out with worry and fatigue, we rested and slept.

One of the drawbacks to travelling in this country is vermin, and the apprehension of losing blood from the parasites of the Moors was much more before my mind than its loss from their daggers. Even the constant use of the bath, the shorn heads and scrupulously clean clothes of the upper classes, do not in all cases fit them in this respect to be trusted. The theory of equality leads to a constant intermixture of classes. The saint whose clothes are never washed or changed, and are consequently a mass of filthy rags, elbows the governor, or sits beside him. The servants constantly squat close to you, and every divan or seat that is sat upon involves a risk.

Oct. 2.—We gladly left the uncomfortable quarters long before daybreak. The whole plain was mainly covered with sidra bushes. In the dawning light we saw some gazelles gracefully scampering away through the bushes. At about ten miles from Seshoua we reached the village Al Buydá, where there was a small but swift stream of good water. The huts of this village were conical, appearing like an assemblage of large beehives. They closely resemble those found in the interior of Africa, but are not met with in the north of Marocco. Some young girls came out and offered us water to drink. They wore necklaces of large beads, with amulets of various kinds, and rudely-engraved rings of unsoldered brass. Water, as usual, had produced its effect here in the shape of green fields and fine trees.

We crossed here the bed of a dry winter torrent, which forms the boundary between the province of

I

Woled-Aboussebáh and Bled-Ahmar mentioned in the narrative of R. Adams.[2] This tribe came from the Sahara. Here some rough-looking tax-collectors sat, crouching under the shelter of a few cut branches of trees rudely put together. Every animal passing from one province into another must pay toll, but no demand was made upon us.

About ten a.m the inzella of Mzoudia was reached. This place, which is about thirty miles from Marocco, boasts to be something more than an inzella. It is a stronghold of the Government. There is a square space enclosed by walls about twelve feet high, with an adobe tower rising to thirty-five feet. The people here were extortionate, asking us about three-halfpence each for eggs, or twelve times the proper price. They were a rough set, and were surrounded by a pack of ferocious dogs. The heat was again excessive, and men and animals were almost unable to proceed. Our unwarlike soldier especially complained, so we rested about three hours.

From this place the plain was thickly covered by a shrub about three feet high, which continued all the way to the palm groves of the city. It gave the country a monotonous and dreary aspect. But in this district there is a good deal of cultivated land, and also many fields of wheat stubble were passed.

[2] London, 1816, page 135.

On the left-hand side of the road, near Mzoudia, were three small isolated hills called Kudiyat-hill Ardhous. According to local tradition, Ardhous or Arthous was the name of a celebrated Christian of a remote period, who buried an immense treasure in this locality. The passage which leads to the treasure is thrown open on one particular day every year, but always in a different spot. As nobody knows either the time or the place, no one has been fortunate enough to obtain the treasure but the Cherif who defended the neighbouring sanctuary of Cherrady against the arms of Muley Abd-er-Rahman. A portion of the buried hoard was employed in making war against the Sultan, who nevertheless succeeded in destroying the sanctuary and dispersing the inhabitants.

My friend M. Beaumier believes that this treasure story, which is implicitly credited, is founded on the fact of a gold-mine having been worked here in ancient times. The abundance of quartz found on and about the hills makes this probable.

Our journey to-day was about thirty miles, and we passed the night at the inzella of Mshra-ben Kara, another walled enclosure with a rickety wooden gate. There was another acceptable little river here. I was awakened during the night by some big drops of rain falling on my face. This was the first indication of the wet season, but nothing more resulted, and the barometer remained steady.

Oct. 3.—We left early, and soon passed two small streams, and at about three miles from Mshra crossed a larger one. Not more than a dozen yards from this we reached the river Nifys, which, from bank to bank, is at this part about eighty yards wide, but the water, except where pools were formed, was at this season a mere stream easily forded by horses. The river takes its rise in the Atlas chain, and, flowing through the plain of Marocco in a north-westerly direction, discharges itself into the Tensift. Its source accounts for the variable volume of water it contains, and its impetuous torrent during the rainy season. It then becomes dangerous to cross, and, as it happens every year, is even impassable for many consecutive days. Curiously enough, another satellite stream was passed about the same distance from the other bank to that already mentioned.

A little beyond the spot where we crossed the river, we passed the inzella El Youdy, or inzella of the Jews, so named because it was established in consequence of the murder of some Jews at or near the site. From this point as we passed onwards we found the colour of the earth to be a reddish brown, and much of the land was under cultivation. Gradually the magnificent palm-trees of Marocco, at first indistinctly seen on the horizon, came more and more into view, and with them the grand ridge of snow-peaked mountains. The city itself was distinguished by its towering fringe of green. At length, after a ride from Mshra of about sixteen miles, we reached a bridge over a stream. This formed, at about two miles from the city walls, the boundary of the palm groves. Here we halted, and were met by a courier, who then galloped back to herald our approach.

The small number of people met with on the road was remarkable—a great many miles were traversed without our seeing a soul. Now and then we passed a sombre caravan of half-a-dozen camels, headed by the leader on a donkey. But the trade between Mogador and Marocco is not considerable. Men travelling on foot were not common; but at the wells were generally groups of men or women employed in drawing water. When the women were by themselves they were by no means reserved; they did not seek to cover their faces, but rather displayed them with the fullest coquetry of their sex.

The intense heat of the weather, considering that October had been entered on, was quite unlooked for; nor could we have conjectured it from the temperature at Mogador. But in the interior the heat of summer is continuous until the autumnal rains have cooled the soil.

In this journey one thing struck me forcibly— the peculiar distribution of the vegetable products; this, without doubt, arises from great diversity of climate and soil within comparatively short limits. It almost seemed as if the trees and herbs of the soil, like the people who inhabited it, were influenced by those exclusive tendencies which prevent people of one race or one religion from mixing with another. Thus, as I have shown, first a tract covered with broom was passed through; this was succeeded by the argan forests; then came an expanse overgrown with palmettoes; then broom again; then a small thorny shrub, the name of which I did not learn. To these followed the sidra shrub; then one called sheeah; till finally came the palm groves about the city of Marocco. Much of the soil throughout this great extent of country was evidently of the finest quality, and it was lamentable to see how little it was turned to account. Here and there, at long intervals, were a few fields of maize stubble, still fewer of wheat or barley; while in the neighbourhood of rivers would occur patches of green maize; but throughout the whole journey neither a man nor an animal was to be seen at work.

The plain of Marocco lies between a range of low hills on the north and the Atlas range on the south. It is from twenty-five to thirty miles across, and in the direction of east and west seems interminable. The soil is for the most part fertile, but in some places sandy. Rounded stones of quartz, flint, porphyry, and cornelian are variously found.

CHAPTER VIII.

RESIDENCE IN THE CITY OF MAROCCO.

On nearing the city we were met by a cavalcade of mules and riders. At the head, as leader, was Sid Bu Bekr Bin Hadj l'Beshire, to whom I had already forwarded several letters of introduction, or rather of strong recommendation. The cavalcade, as it advanced, had a most picturesque effect, consisting, as it did, of four or five Moors of the higher class, who were clad in snowy robes, and had their mules set off by handsome trappings. They were attended by servants, also mounted.

After riding together for some distance we alighted in a garden, or, more correctly speaking, orchard, which was surmounted by high walls of *tabia*. There was no sign of cultivation in the way of flowers or vegetables, but an abundance of flourishing trees, which, being principally olives, afforded grateful and necessary shade. Under these, Moorish carpets were spread, on which we seated ourselves in a circle. A tea equipage had been sent previously from the city, and by means of a portable fireplace, fed with charcoal, the grateful beverage was soon supplied. The teapot and tray were plated, and, as is customary in Marocco, drinking-glasses were substituted for china cups. A kind of well-seasoned forcemeat called keffsa was also served with bread. This had been moulded around slender sticks, and was now cooked by placing the sticks across the fire, in the same manner as the morsels of meat called in the East kebab. Plates and dishes were not wanted, as the sticks were handed to us in relays, and the hot meat was picked off as from a bone. Smoking followed; then more tea-drinking; and in this way two hours soon passed away.

During conversation, we learnt, to our dismay, but then not so fully as was actually the case, that the city of Marocco was in a very disturbed state. The Sultan was not looked for at any particular time, although it was known that he was temporarily stationed about eight days' journey to the north. From the hostility of the intervening tribes communication with him was uncertain, and the reports sent to the coast of his victories were, for political reasons, intended to mislead. After all the cannon-firing, powder-play and wild revelries we had witnessed, this seemed strange news; but it was true, or nearly so, although just then we were unable to see its bearings on our own safety.

A ride of twenty minutes brought us from our resting-place to the Doukkela gate of the city. The road leading thereto was through lanes and spaces bounded by walls built of *tabia*. These enclosed gardens filled with trees of various kinds, such as the orange, lemon, citron, olive, date-palm, walnut, mulberry, almond, pomegranate, apple, pear, peach, and other fruits. Evergreens grew also in great luxuriance, and included the cypress, cedar, and myrtle. Roses and jasmines were also present.

We were requested not to display fire-arms in our passage through the city, observance of which was at once insured by having all the guns packed on one of the baggage mules. We noticed, although at the time we did not attach proper significance to the fact, that Bu Bekr and his friends went quickly away just as we approached the gate. Before leaving, he cautioned me on no account to stir from the house allotted to us, unless accompanied, in addition to our own guard, by some soldiers supplied by the Governor of the city, to whom I had letters of recommendation from the Governor of Tangier.

Thus entering the city, our way lay through waste places, and narrow winding streets, in parts much crowded. With the exception of some spitting and hissing noises from the mob, and their generally sullen looks and muttered curses, there was little to record of my first impressions of Marocco except its likeness to the Oriental cities I had visited. Most things, however, wore a more African tinge. The black race was more numerous here, and there were many indications that the western Arab is several degrees lower in the scale of civilization than his eastern co-religionists.

Sid Bu Bekr had quite an exceptional position in the city. Without being a governor or a courtier, he was wealthy, and, what was more important, he enjoyed exemption from being squeezed to disgorge his wealth, being under English protection, and is one of the largest slave-dealers in Marocco. Some years ago a leading commercial firm in Mogador conceived the idea of extending their trade to this city by consignment of goods on commission. As there were no European residents, the firm were obliged to obtain the services of a Moorish citizen, and also, for obvious reasons, to take care that he was protected by the *ægis* of British power. Thus it was our new friend Bu Bekr became rich, and that his property and person were comparatively secure. As a natural sequence of circumstances he became a man of power; more so, it was stated, than that of many governors. But this solitary pre-eminence had its drawbacks. He was envied and hated by his countrymen, and an attempt was soon made to poison him.

As no Mohammedan ever dreams of placing

men, and above all strangers, on familiar terms with his family, it becomes necessary, in the exercise of hospitality, and where no hotels exist, to provide guests with house-room.

In Marocco it is the practice to give strangers an empty house, situated either in one of the numerous gardens within the walls, or else in a street, with the use of a garden elsewhere; for during the hot weather it is usual to pass much of the day in the open air on carpets spread underneath shady trees. We expected a garden, but only a small house in the Moorish quarter was assigned to us. On dismounting at the door we were by no means favourably impressed with the appearance of our residence. It was situated in a narrow, but fortunately not filthy street, and its windowless walls of uncoloured clay and little dingy door gave it an aspect altogether sepulchral. Had the words, "Abandon hope, all ye who enter here," appeared above the door, they would have seemed not out of place. There was but a single story, and narrow stone stairs conducted to our quarters, which were two small rooms on either side of a central square room. Two other rooms were also on this floor.

A man accustomed to be boxed up within glazed windows feels instinctively out of place when housed without windows at all. I had often tried to realize the domestic life of antiquity, but never successfully, till thus necessitated to inhabit apartments which derived light and air from the door alone. Our rooms were, in all essential points, identical with those in ancient Roman houses, and thus one at least gained a new experience.

The interior of the house proved superior to its outside promise, for it was bright and clean. The central room was fourteen feet square and of good height. In the middle of the roof was a square opening or *impluvium*, crossed by iron bars, through which the sky was visible; but there was no corresponding tank or *compluvium* to collect rain-water in the floor, only a grated aperture through which the water could run off. The ceiling was decorated in an arabesque style, of which the prevailing colour was green. As already stated, two narrow rooms opened from this central one. To these, handsomely arched doorways gave admittance, the sills being paved with coloured glazed tiles. One we used as bed and sitting-room, the other was assigned to our servants and guards. The doors were of unpainted wood, and, for greater convenience, each was pierced with a smaller one. Both walls and floors were covered with a smooth compound or stucco, in the use of which the Moors excel; the walls were white, with a dado of a rich reddish-brown colour, which was quite Pompeian. The mattresses and carpets belonging to our tent were the only furniture. A young Moor, to act as cook, was added to our establishment by Sid Bu Bekr, and we at once settled down to keep house in Marocco with a sense of grateful rest after a long and hot journey. Yet it must be added that there were many indications which foreboded us no good.

Our troubles soon commenced. We had, in fact, fallen on evil days. The inhabitants, always hostile to the Kaffir, as the unbeliever is called, were just then in a state of almost open revolt. Accordingly, next morning (October 4th) I received a message from Sid Ibrahim Geroui, Governor of the city, in reply to my letters of introduction, that it was impossible for him to send us any guards or even to receive me. He was himself in a critical position. Were he to supply us with soldiers, the fact would become known to the townspeople, and draw down upon us the hostility of the faction opposed to him. He advised us to use great caution in going about, and to appear always in the Moorish dress.

Owing to the reverse the Sultan had experienced, a revolution had taken place in the city a month previous to our visit. El Geroui, a powerful ruler of the adjoining country, had deposed Ben Daoud, then governor, and, imprisoning him in his house, still kept him there. On this account the townspeople were divided into hostile factions, and only two days before our arrival there had been much serious fighting in the streets. Great precautions were being taken to prevent an outbreak.

In all Moorish towns the gates leading into the country are closed after sunset, and in this the capital, the Jewish quarter is also isolated and unprotected. In addition to this, every street is at each end provided with a gate of its own, and this not merely one easy to climb, but a solid piece of woodwork set in a massive archway. As some of the streets are very short, these defences are in consequence very numerous.

At night they were all closed and strongly guarded. As for ourselves, we found that we were little better than prisoners, with a certain liberty of action. When we went out, those who remained within immediately secured the door, and the same precaution was taken upon our return. We saw that Sid Bu Bekr was uneasy about our safety, and it was quite evident to my companion that the object of his own mission would be fruitless. He gave up all thought of making any claim against the Moor indebted to him, as to do so in the then threatening state of public affairs would be an act of sheer madness.

As for myself, it was equally plain that my plans would be greatly interfered with. It has been already stated that the Cherif of Wazaan had given me a letter of recommendation to Muley Hassan, the Sultan's eldest son, from which I expected much consideration. It was supposed the Sultan could not refuse the Cherif a request, although such a letter was an exceptional favour, and one not previously given to a European.

It had been generally believed that the Sultan would enter the capital about the time of our arrival, and I had hoped for a presentation to that potentate, and by such means to gain access to information and to secure an influence not otherwise obtainable. But the Sultan had not arrived, and no one could form an idea when he would. It might be in a week, a month, or longer. We therefore resolved to wait the course of events, and see as much of the city and neighbourhood as circumstances would permit.

Our great difficulty was about guards, as the men clamoured for an addition to their number. We only managed to pick up one, but whether in case of need he was to be depended on was uncertain.

Attended by our whole retinue, all well armed, we sallied out on foot to the Jewish quarter, in search of the house of Signor Abraham Korkos. This gentleman, to whom I had forwarded a letter of introduction, is the principal Jewish merchant in the city, and also acts as agent for the Sultan. We had some distance to go, but beyond sundry dark scowls and maledictions from those we met, and for which we were prepared, nothing occurred worth noticing. We found on our arrival that Signor Korkos, who had invited us to breakfast, was unfortunately very ill; bu his son worthily performed the duties of host. The spacious house inhabited by these gentlemen was built, as customary, round a central court, and furnished in the Moorish fashion. Our breakfast consisted of the staple dish, kuskusoo, omelets, pigeons cooked in argan oil, forcemeat, mutton, and sweet potatoes, together with wine from Deminet, which, mixed with water, forms an agreeable beverage. During conversation we learned much as to the true state of public affairs. A courier had just arrived from the Sultan, who was at Tedla, four days' journey to the north. It was quite true that the imperial arms had met with a check, but this sultan was the first who had attempted to enter the refractory province. He was now fighting his way therefrom, and might be shortly expected in his southern capital, which he had not visited for five years, where he was anxiously looked for.

I had afterwards the opportunity of visiting several Jewish families, and of observing their habits. The women here did not seem so remarkable for beauty as in other places in the empire. The application of kohl to the eyelids, and of henna to the hands, appeared universal among them when young.

A little circumstance occurred during one of my visits, the narration of which will illustrate the Oriental apathy prevailing here. Though so simple, I could scarcely contain my gravity. While conversing with a lady, I observed that her eyes, which were inflamed, attracted to them a number of troublesome flies. One in particular so posted itself that it could stoop over and thrust its proboscis between the lids at the inside corner of one eye. Each time this was done the lady merely shut her eye with a jerk, instead of using her hand to sweep off the pest. The fly, as impassive as its victim, merely backed a little, withdrew its sucking tube for an instant, and then began again. In small things, as in more important matters, passiveness was the rule.

Oct. 5.—We were awakened twice during the night by a strange rustling noise in the room. I thought it was caused by a rat, but my friend's more practised ear attributed it, and rightly, to a snake which had issued from a hole in the floor of the anteroom. These household snakes are not venomous, and are never molested, as they perform the office of cats in killing rats and mice.

We visited Sid Bu Bekr in his newly-built house in the street called K'art Ben Alud. He received us in a room with small glass windows, which were decorated with finely-wrought iron of Moorish workmanship. In place of chairs were low divans covered with carpets and luxurious cushions. We saw also a European clock, which was undergoing a cleaning. Tea was served in really beautiful china coffee-cups by a black female slave of fine figure, and everything about was perfectly clean and neat. Afterwards our friend showed us his bedroom, which was partially covered by an English carpet. His bed was arranged on the floor, and over it hung a talisman in the form of a small picture representing the soles of Mohammed's shoes, which were covered with well-executed inscriptions from the Koran. At the top of the picture were some antique characters, which the Moors themselves could not read.

It was, as may be supposed, a step beyond the strict rules of Moorish decorum for Sid Bu Bekr to admit Christians even to his house; beyond this he could not go, and his harem was, of course, closed to us. But its inmates were not altogether invisible, for on passing from room to room we observed, through lattices and half-opened doors, numerous dark and gleaming eyes peering above the white cloth which concealed the lower part of the features. The curiosity excited by our presence was apparently intense.

Sid Bu Bekr endeavoured to excuse the conduct of his friend, El Geroui. "Had the latter," he said, "had timely notice, he would have sent to Mogador and prevented our undertaking a journey to Marocco at a season so unpropitious." "Such," El Geroui had declared, " was the state of public affairs, that it was God only who was keeping the people quiet. He neither could nor would undertake to protect us or answer for our safety, and could only depend on Bu Bekr to aid us privately. He had sent a despatch to that effect to the British consul at Mogador." For himself Bu Bekr added, "that it was quite true that a guard of the governor's soldiers would be injurious rather than serviceable, as the people would attack us in order to get him into trouble with the Sultan, who would not probably reach the city yet for some time." This information was far from satisfactory.

Having obtained our mules we rode through the city to the Bab Aghmat, or south-eastern gate, and then turning to the south crossed the little river Ixia. On the right was a large Moorish cemetery, towards which a funeral procession was wending its way. Carefully avoiding it, we pushed on over an extensive piece of level ground used as a government wheat farm. The extremity of the city walls being reached, there commenced the long, high earthen wall which surrounds the garden of the Sultan. This, called the garden of Aguidel, is of great extent, and contains some buildings. A gate which we passed had architectural pretensions, and was fortified with a few small guns. To the interior we were unable to gain admission, but, judging from the glimpses obtained, there was nothing lost. Like other gardens we had seen, it was merely a vast orchard, and though containing many fine trees, was wholly neglected, the ground, for the most part, being a mere garden of weeds.

Re-entering the city by the same gate, we rode through much waste and neglected ground. Here were women washing clothes at the aqueducts, and men lounging about or praying devoutly. In one place gunpowder was in the process of manufacture in a manner the most primitive, as were also other articles in ways as simple.

At length we reached the object of our search: the far-famed mosque known as Katoubia. It stands in an open part of the city, adorned with gardens, and will be presently described.

During our long rambles on this day we avoided, as much as possible, all crowds and thoroughfares; nevertheless we were, as usual, the object of curses and invectives. Many of these would not bear translation, one of the mildest being, "May God burn your father, Christian dog!" The Moors consider it the greatest insult to curse the parents of those they hate.

My first experiment with the Moorish costume in full was not satisfactory, for hitherto I had only worn the jelabur. The weather was sultry, and my efforts to keep on the ill-fitting yellow slippers while walking were most fatiguing. It was also very irritating, whether walking or riding, to have

the haik continually falling down. This garment is a long white sheet worn folded in a peculiar way round the body, while one end is thrown over the left shoulder. These mischances were not solely due to inexperience, for the Moors themselves were constantly adjusting the end of these flowing garments as they walked along, often to the danger of the eyes of passers-by.

It was obvious enough that our disguise was only a rough one. In spite of turban and beard, sun-burning, and flowing robes, we were easily recognized as Europeans by any Moor who met us. At a little distance, however, the disguise was sufficiently effective to keep us from being mobbed, more particularly as when under observation we always kept moving.

Oct. 6.—On this day we went early to the grain-market, which is held in an open space in the centre of the city. Wheat and Indian corn were being sold to customers, while the camels and mules which had conveyed these articles to the city stood about in great numbers. As there were said to be many rough fellows here, we avoided their proximity in passing through. We had also been cautioned on no account to tread upon the corn exposed for sale. The Moors have a superstition in respect to this, and would have made it a pretext for attacking us.

As I had a desire to see the interior of the principal jail, a request was made to Bu Bekr that he would obtain from the authorities an order to admit us; but he failed in this, and therefore we resolved to endeavour to get in through our own address.

This prison, though not very extensive, was at this date much crowded, containing, it was said, a thousand inmates. As the food supplied to those who have no friends was limited in quantity and bad in quality, and the sanitary condition of the place was bad in the extreme, the mortality among the prisoners was great.

The prison was, as we found, situated in a much-frequented thoroughfare; and opposite the entrance we saw the vice-governor of the city seated on the bare ground, with his back against a wall. He was engaged in trying causes, and a little group of litigants and witnesses were crouched around, the eyes of all being fixed with eagerness on the judge. There was in the whole proceedings much of the pathetic and comic intermingled. It was just one of those scenes which, having been transmitted from the eye to the brain, becomes, so to speak, photographed thereon, and can at will be recalled.

The kadi himself was a fine old man—spare, erect, and his looks kind in an exceptional degree; I ventured, therefore, to address him, and asked permission to see the prison, which was courteously granted. Believing that the permission was sufficient, we entered the gate, our men conveying a quantity of bread as a present to the prisoners. Reaching a courtyard covered

with trellised vines, we found a number of
guards, through whom we passed, and had
already reached a passage leading into the
interior of the prison, when, in spite of
remonstrances, we were pushed back to where,
on one side of the court and on a kind of
daïs, three magnates were seated in state.
Before these worthies we were placed, and
one of them, a certain Muley El Gralli,
with a look and tone of voice the reverse of
complimentary, told us he did not care whose
permission we had, we should not see the prisoners, and that we must go away with all speed.
I replied that we were Englishmen, who had no
other object in view than to see as much as
possible of the country; that I had a letter from
the Cherif of Wazaan to the son of the Sultan; that
therefore his conduct was not only uncivil but
unjustifiable. His tone was now altered. He
civilly explained the difficulties of the case, the
disturbed state of the city, and added the number
of prisoners was very great, and that the keys of
the prison were sent every afternoon, for greater
security, to the Sultan's palace. He also said he
could not grant our request, but promised that our
offering of bread should be distributed among the
most needy prisoners. With this we had to be content, as our friend the kadi could not or would
not interfere; and, to say the truth, we had seen
enough of this gloomy, ill-omened place.

The three men referred to seemed to form a sort of court-martial, the city being in a state of siege. For convenience, apparently, they thus sat within the walls of the prison to order the putting quickly under lock and key any one they thought proper, whether delinquent or not. Each one in power was afraid of the other, and the state of general distrust was indeed lamentable.

After this we managed to see a good deal of the markets and shops of the city; but to these subjects I shall refer farther on. Before the day was over our government soldier absconded—a circumstance which did not look favourable. It was the result, we feared, of an intrigue, in order that it might appear, should any calamity befall us, that we had been going about unprotected by a soldier, as required by the authorities in the case of all Christians.

Our manner of life in the house was the same every day. Nothing favoured that feeling of security which we associate with the idea of being at home. But the men enjoyed their rest greatly, as also the food provided for them, and made themselves merry after their own fashion with feasting and music. The boisterous merriment and flute-playing were at times rather oppressive; and the street noises had a painful interest not easily forgotten. Sometimes the shouting and uproar of a crowd met our ear, and then we felt that, should an outbreak occur between the rival factions, the presence of infidels accredited to one side would not be forgotten by the other. Under these circumstances, the possession of an American rifle capable of discharging eighteen bullets without reloading was an unspeakable comfort. We felt that the narrow stairs could long be defended by our superior weapons, and that even if destruction at last overtook us, it would be only after a resistance most disastrous to our assailants.

The gossip of the town picked up by our servants amused us greatly. In imagination we were transported, as it were, to the remote days of Greece and Rome, when, although art and literature had both reached a point of surpassing excellence, there were no printing-presses to give ready expression to the opinions and desires of the populace. Yet news must have been as eagerly sought after in those stirring days as in our own, and its acquisition was probably cultivated with an assiduity we can now scarcely realize. And such was the bent of the citizens of Marocco. All our movements appeared to be as well known as though daily chronicled in a penny newspaper. The Moors are naturally communicative, and, as happens in India, the bazaars take the place of clubs for the interchange of news. Therein, therefore, our affairs were discussed, and we heard, among other things, that the city authorities were, for politic reasons, very uneasy about our safety. Rumour also confirmed what we had been previously told, that, though we anxiously awaited that event, no time could be depended on for the Sultan's arrival. This was likewise the opinion of Signor Korkos, who undertook to forward my letter to Muley Hassan. Signor Korkos would not listen to my proposition that we should try to make our way to the Sultan, as it was impossible, he said, to tell the exact state of the intervening country, and, considering the excitement of the tribes inhabiting it, the risk of such a journey would be very great.

It is surprising how soon, through habit, one becomes reconciled to what at first was disagreeable. After an experience of some days, we grew accustomed to sitting on the floor, though at first it was very irksome, the soft Moorish carpet being all the furniture thought necessary for ordinary domestic life; and thus we gradually learned that a number of articles seemingly necessary to Europeans may easily be dispensed with.

Our food was not bad. It consisted of fowls, pigeons, and partridges; but the cooking spoiled it. The birds were invariably served soaked in argan oil, to like which requires long habit. Fowls formed an invariable dish, and they were always brought alive to the house. The first indications of dinner were the cries of the unhappy birds while in the act of being killed. This is a somewhat savage way of whetting one's appetite; but it is the invariable custom to cook animal food immediately after death. A bird commonly called tabib (the doctor) was our constant companion at meals.

A message was sent us through Bu Bekr from the prison magnates to the effect that we might inspect that place. They probably thought it would be wise to conciliate us; but we had by this time learned to estimate at their true value promises and engagements made by such people; for it appeared to be a general habit to make offers and promises, and then evade fulfilment by paltry tricks. We were tired of this sort of thing.

Our runaway soldier turned up, but as to where he had been or what he had been doing we could gain no satisfactory information. On this day we paid a second visit to Signor Korkos. On our way, while passing the prison, an emaciated corpse, scantily covered with dirty rags, was being brought through the gate. Lying stretched on a board, beyond which the uncovered head and feet projected, it was a sad spectacle of dishonoured humanity, though in keeping with the dismal place from which it issued.

As on a former occasion, our breakfast, or rather

luncheon, was excellent, and consisted of many articles, among others of a roast turkey; and it is a curious circumstance that this bird is peculiar to the city. Not one can be had anywhere on the coast, except such as are occasionally brought from Marocco as rarities. A sheep had also been killed for us; but it could not be used, as it had on inspection been found unlawful.

When the meal was over, we ascended to the flat roof of the house, from which a good view of the city and neighbourhood was obtained. It was only, indeed, when in this the Jews' quarter that we felt secure enough to look about, as it were, freely. I availed myself of the opportunity to take a view of the place by means of the dry photographic process, and this (which is here reproduced in a wood engraving) gives a good idea of the general appearance of the city with its narrow streets, terraced roofs, and windowless houses, its mosques and gardens. In the distance, on the right, the majestic Atlas chain appears. Such is the purity of the atmosphere that it is difficult to realize the true distance of the mountains from the city; sixteen miles is about the true measurement, but it seems to be not more than eight. The lofty tower of the Katoubia is seen to the left of the mountains. The woodcut gives a good idea of the large space covered closely with houses, viewed in a north-west direction from the quarter of the Jews. Even supposing that

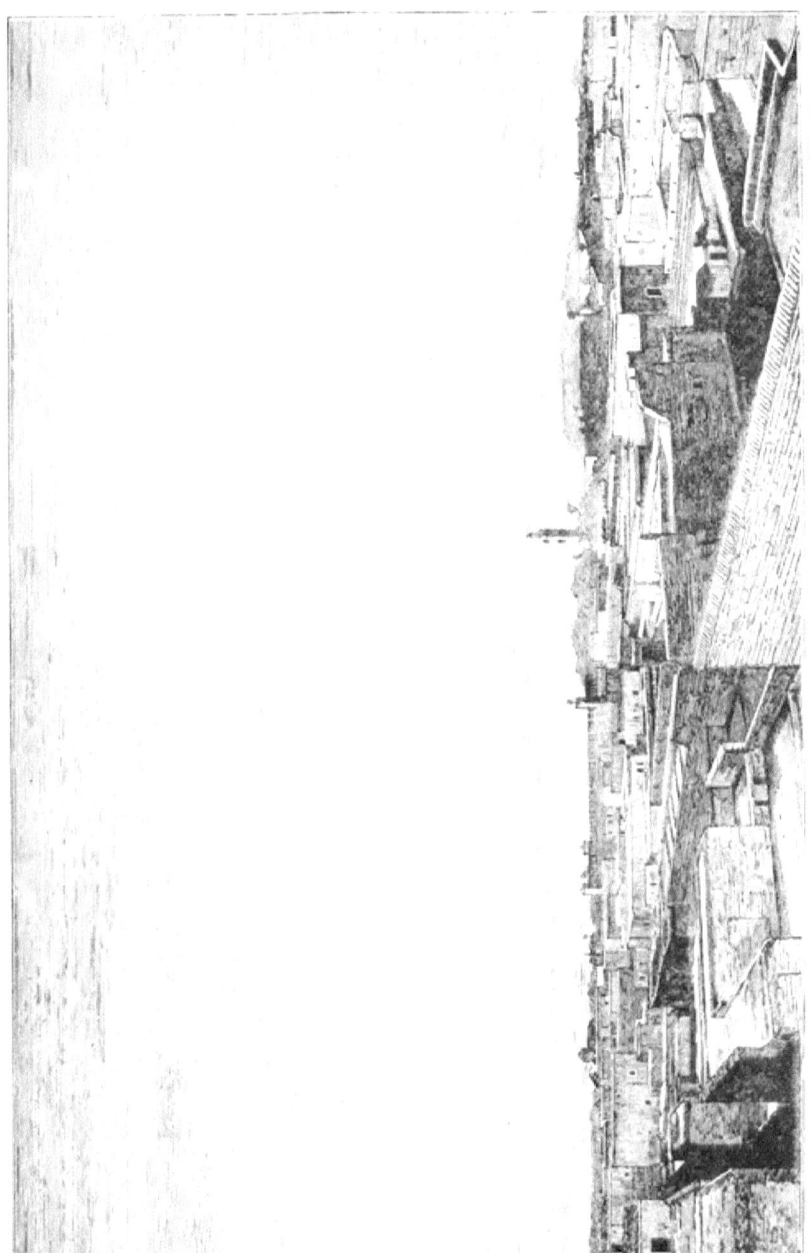

CITY OF MAROCCO.

[To face page 140]

one had the choice, perhaps no better point of view could have been selected.

We rode afterwards to the large open space called Djemaa El Fna, where festivities, as also markets, are held. It is commonly full of people. The first thing was to look for the heads of the Sultan's enemies nailed to the wall set apart for such exhibitions. We were informed before reaching the city that these heads were to be seen in hundreds. But we looked in vain, as might have been concluded from the state of affairs so lately revealed to us.

Proceeding farther into the square, we observed a snake-charmer and a man with monkeys, the place being noted for these exhibitions. I requested the former to begin his performance, and the man at once pulled out two hideous reptiles from a basket and began to flourish them about his head. A crowd of roughs, men and boys, rapidly collected. We kept aloof as much as possible, nevertheless the mob showed signs of hostility and began to jeer. Some man in authority, who was near, ran immediately to the snake-charmer and stopped the performance. We saw at once that our position was not safe, and that this interference was for the purpose of checking an imminent disturbance. But the worst part was that our guards began to avoid us, so that it seemed likely we should, in case of a row, be deserted. Our interpreter, Leo, on this occasion gained golden opinions. We could not, by the most generous interpretation of his ordinary conduct, attribute to him personal courage; but now, seated on his mule, he harangued the populace, and seemed for the instant to keep them in check. "The Christian gentlemen," he said, "had not come there to eat Moors, but to see what was to be seen, to learn what they could, and do good if possible." His speech was short, for we all thought it prudent to beat a retreat as fast as spurs could induce our animals to move.

As soon as we had distanced the hooting crowd an amusing incident occurred. Ben Ahia rushed up to me with flashing eyes, and the veins of his dark forehead swollen with rage. He, that never could be induced to speak two consecutive words of English, now gave vent to his thoughts with the utmost energy and volubility. "Missur Doctor! Leo one rascal! Kill all! Too much brandy! Too much d——m Scotch!" By this he clearly implied that Leo, by his delay with the crowd, had endangered our lives, and that the reason he had acted so was because he was under the influence of brandy. The words "d——m Scotch" puzzled us, but were subsequently explained. Among the Mogador men the term "Scotch" has a meaning of its own, and one not complimentary. Some years previously a dissipated Scotch sea captain, of herculean build, was detained with his vessel

SNAKE CHARMER.

[*To face page 142.*

in that port. Whenever he came on shore he was in the habit of thrashing the Moors in the most merciless manner and without provocation. He became, therefore, so much dreaded and hated that the name of his nation has, in the Mogador jargon, come to mean a bully of the worst class. As for Leo's conduct, there could be no doubt that an over-liberal allowance of mahaya at breakfast had been the exciting cause of his unwonted fire.

We rode from this market or open space through the city to its north-western extremity, and out by the Doqualla gate; our object was to visit El Hara, the village of lepers, a little way outside it.[1] The village is of considerable size, and surrounded by walls. There is only one entrance, close to which is the sanctuary of the patron saint, Sidi Ben Nor. On this account an objection was made to my entering the village; but a number of lepers soon made their appearance and were very friendly. Many of them showed no outward sign of disease. They form a community apart, and have a mosque, a prison, and a market of their own; they buy and sell, and also cultivate the land. The number of lepers was stated to be about 200. Many of them came from long distances—from Haha, Sus, and even the Sahara. Some had resided thirty years in the village, and there were a few very aged people among them. The village had also a Jewish

[1] See Jackson's account of visit to it in 1788. In "Account of Timbuctoo, etc." (London, 1820), page 90.

quarter, but though a few years previously it had held five residents, not one was there at this period of our visit.

Notwithstanding the rigid separation of the leper population, the Moors show little or no fear of contagion; they pass to and fro into the leper villages freely, though the lepers are not allowed to enter the city. Some of them were miserable objects. We saw them about the city gate, either slowly dragging themselves along or else seated on the ground, loudly appealing to the charity of passers-by.

In the group which congregated about us in the village, the alteration of the voice was a very marked symptom. Many spoke with a huskiness which denoted that the terrible malady had attacked the windpipe; in some cases a tubercle on the forehead, or at the side of the nose, was all that made it imperative on the lepers to separate themselves from the healthy. Some had lost, more or less, the fingers of both hands; others, the toes of both feet. No application is made to the corroding sores, nor is any internal remedy used. Washing at the sacred well of the saint-house, which is supposed to possess virtues, is all that is required or attempted in the way of cure.

There were more women than men in the village, so the lepers informed us; but this might be due, in this case, to polygamy. The children of leprous parents are, as we also learnt here, sometimes, but not usually, diseased. The causes assigned for leprosy were overwork, and drinking cold water while perspiring; and the lepers added that God sends the disease to punish people for their sins. Some of those we saw made pretence of medical knowledge. The Governor of Mogador told me that he had, when in Marocco, been treated by one of them, and he showed me the marks on his arm caused by the actual cautery then applied.

We reached our house about eight o'clock, and dined on fowls stewed, as usual, in argan oil. While at dinner Mr. Broom remarked that the oil had an unusual taste, and no sooner did we lie down after the meal than we both became exceedingly unwell. Fortunately Leo did not eat, as was his custom, any of this food after we had dined, as he was observing a rigid fast.

Strange to say, the cause of our illness did not occur to me; and if it had, no antidotes were at hand. Our symptoms were great pain and prostration, together with those referable to a strong cathartic. We passed a wretched night, and lay the next day prostrate, and without the power of taking food. I do not wish to dwell on this disagreeable episode, though there can be no doubt our food had been poisoned. The use and effects of arsenic are well known to the Moors, and poisoning is a common crime among them. In this dastardly attempt to destroy us, this potent drug had been probably used.

During this wretched day the effect which our condition had upon the people surrounding us was remarkable. Both the soldier and Moorish servants would come and look at us in silence, then go away, but soon return. We afterwards found that all were of the same opinion as to the cause of our illness, and fully expected we should die. As for Leo, his attention deserves a passing tribute. Indeed, it was a most fortunate thing for us, as well as himself, that he did not eat the poisoned food. This he afterwards attributed, with much fervour, to the interposition of God, because the attempt was made on a day when his religious observances preserved him from danger. We thought it prudent to observe great reticence on the subject.

Oct. 9.—We felt very unwell this morning, and our position was anything but reassuring. The attempt to poison us might be repeated, or our lives be attempted by open violence. We no longer wished to remain for the Sultan's arrival, but to get away as speedily as possible from this inhospitable place. This desire became paramount with us. Although as yet not strong enough to travel, we resolved to go out, feeling sure that what had occurred to us was widely known; and that even before the attempt was made some few were in the secret. There would be satisfaction in an open display of ourselves to our enemies, and we resolved, should any attack be made, to retaliate to the utmost of our power.

The first thing we did was to visit Bu Bekr. He was unwilling to admit that while under his protection we had been subject to an attempt on our lives. He was very anxious to be acquitted of all blame in the matter, and referred to the letter he had caused me to write for despatch to the Consul at Tangier on the very morning the attempt was made, stating that he was taking every means for our protection. He suggested that our illness might have been caused by the food of which we had partaken in the Jews' quarter, and mentioned other improbabilities which tried our patience to hear. In conclusion, he offered to assist me in seeing everything in the city and neighbourhood; at the same time highly approving of our resolve to leave for the coast as soon as possible. The truth was, our presence was an embarrassment to him, which we, on our part, were anxious to remove.

At his suggestion, we rode out of the city to see the garden of Muley Ali, one of the Sultan's sons. It contained an abundance of fine trees, and a large alcove much out of repair. In front of it was a fountain without water, and around it were a number of little conduits, so arranged as to form antique Arabic characters, which together expressed a passage in the Koran. We also visited a bridge over the Tensift, situated, as Bu Bekr had assured us, at no great distance, but which we found was a full hour's ride from the city. His object, we saw at once, in suggesting this visit, had been to get us out of the way. The bridge, he had told us, was a marvel of construction. It proved to be a very ancient structure, eighteen feet in width, thrown across the river at a place where it has a breadth of two hundred yards. The water was still very low, and many of the arches were dry; but altogether it was the best evidence of public spirit we had yet seen in the country, and must have been built long before the present lamentable condition of political and social affairs.

Bu Bekr had proposed to meet us on our return and accompany us to the Sultan's palace and other places. We accordingly met him and some of his friends, but he began instantly to find fault with our delay, and pretended it was then too late to carry out his intention of showing us places of interest in the city. Far from well, and very tired, we passively acquiesced. for we had no inclination for further exertion that day. But we perceived at once that a Moorish dodge was being practised, there having been no intention, and probably no power, to make good the proposal and gratify our curiosity. I had already had many occasions for observing the specious and ready falsity of these people and their roundabout methods to deceive.

We rode on amicably together, but when approaching a market held just without the city walls, our pretended friends sneaked off in advance, and finally left us altogether. Nothing could be more evident than that they were afraid to be seen in our company. On reaching our house we had immediately fresh evidence of the incorrigible propensity of the Moors for lying and deceit. Our cook, not knowing that we had just left Bu Bekr, greeted us by saying that that gentleman had sent his respects, and hoped we had enjoyed our ride. We were disheartened and weary, and at once resolved to leave Marocco for Saffi next morning, and accordingly the evening was occupied in making preparations for our departure.

In reference to the motives which led to the dastardly attempt to deprive us of life, we give the opinion current among the Moors. As already stated, the city was divided into two factions, the majority espousing the cause of El Geroui, the ruler in power; the minority that of Ben Daoud, a man of notoriously bad character, who had been recently deposed. Thus Ben Daoud, being an unscrupulous man, and giving full scope to the maxim, "The end justifies the means," had, there is little doubt, commissioned one or more persons to attempt our lives. The chief motive was, that as soon as the Sultan should enter his capital, an international difficulty would be ready to embarrass him, and that then, being given to understand that this murder of two Englishmen had followed El Geroui, the usurper's, accession to power, the deed would be placed to his account, and his cause be damaged in the eyes of the Sultan, while that of his rival, Ben Daoud, would be proportionately benefited.

The hatred commonly entertained by the Moors for Christians renders it impossible, as already stated, to travel in the interior of Marocco, unless specially provided with at least one government soldier, who, obtained through a consulate on the coast, is responsible for the safety of his charge. In a fanatical place like the city of Marocco, or the city of Mequinez, the Christian is exposed in two ways to risk of open violence. He may be stabbed by a fanatic when off his guard, or, what is more probable, may get surrounded by a crowd, and a disturbance begun by boys may end in his being spat upon, then buffeted, and trampled on by men, encouraged by each other in their savage work. We had, by using great precaution, escaped these dangers. But such insidious destruction as had been prepared for us could not be easily guarded against, and must have been deliberately planned by the two men provided for us by Bu Bekr. One was a young fellow of obliging manners, who lived in the house and acted as cook. The other was a man who did not live with us, but came when his services were required to make purchases and execute commissions. On these men suspicion naturally fell, and on our reporting the matter at the consulate, after our arrival in Saffi, Mr. Hunot, the British vice-consul, promptly undertook to investigate it. The poison administered must have either been put into the dish off which we dined, or mixed in the argan oil at the time of purchase.[2]

My companion had met with singularly bad luck during his residence in Barbary. In the February previous, while making a country excursion in the neighbourhood of Mogador, he

[2] This investigation led to no results, although the evidence given by the Moorish soldier and servants, before the government adools corroborated our statement. The affair was referred to the Sultan, and it was demanded that the suspected persons should be sent to Saffi for examination, but without effect. One of the suspected persons was said by the authorities at Marocco to have absconded, and the other to be too unwell to be moved. In the correspondence which ensued between our minister plenipotentiary and the vice-consul, the latter was enjoined to be careful "that no arbitrary act of cruelty be committed by the authorities on vague suspicion upon any Moorish subject, Jew or Mohammedan." This so far was right, but it was very unsatisfactory to those who barely escaped the worst consequences of a foul crime that it was not promptly and vigorously sifted. The matter was some time afterwards inquired into on the spot by Sir J. D. Hay, but with no success. Different absurd explanations of our illness were offered, such as that it was caused by the corrosion of the copper cooking-vessels, but these vessels had been in constant use previously. Arsenic does not always destroy life, even when freely taken into the system. An account of the poisoning of sixteen persons was published lately in the *British Medical Journal*. All suffered severely: in every case the poison acted as a strong cathartic; but in the end all recovered.

It may be well to caution future travellers against allowing their food to be prepared by Moors about whom they know nothing. I found, when too late, that European residents who know the country well make it a rule not to partake of any dish cooked by a strange Moor unless he is seen to eat part of it himself.

was set upon by three ruffians, who first fired at him without effect, and then stabbed him so seriously that he escaped death almost by a miracle. He had alighted from his mule for the purpose of gathering flowers, and his soldier was some distance in the rear. The motive in this case was apparently the same as that which led to our being nearly poisoned. An unpopular governor had been recently appointed in the province in which the attack was made, and the intended assassination had been apparently undertaken for the purpose of obtaining the Sultan's sanction to this man's dismissal.

Thus it was that I was compelled to turn my back on the unexplored glorious Atlas range, then in full view. The year before (1871), Dr. Hooker, now the distinguished President of the Royal Society, accompanied by his friends, Messrs. Ball and Maw, made a successful ascent of one of the summits of this range, and the valuable results of their explorations in botany and geology have been contributed to science. But Dr. Hooker travelled when the people of the country were comparatively tranquil. He was provided with a special guard, and an autograph letter of the Sultan's, procured by our Foreign Minister, in which all governors and kaids were enjoined at their peril not only not to molest, but to afford him every possible aid. These privileges I hoped to have obtained from the Sultan, with whom, as already stated, I looked forward to a personal interview in his southern capital. As the case stood with my companions and myself, we had the very doubtful advantage of seeing the Moors in all their savage turbulence, and, being almost entirely at their mercy, we regarded ourselves as very lucky in escaping with our lives.

CHAPTER IX.

THE CITY AND ITS NEIGHBOURHOOD.

The investigation of the city of Marocco and its neighbourhood was in the strictest sense "the pursuit of knowledge under difficulties." Yet ceaseless perseverance effected much, and I saw a great deal of this semi-civilized place.

Marocco is called by the Moors Marakech; the derivation of this is unsettled, but it is supposed to have been taken from certain wells that in early ages existed on its site. In the vicinity are still traces of the ruins of a Roman town—Bocanum Hermerum. The modern city of Marocco has claims to antiquity. It was founded in the year 454 of the Hegira, or 1072 of the Christian era. One Sid Youssef Ben Tachenfin built a mosque, as also a citadel, wherein to store his wealth; then his followers and many people of the surrounding country, seeking the protection of this citadel, raised houses around it. After the death of Youssef, his son Ali fortified the growing city, and adorned it with other mosques and public buildings. Its progress at that period seems in-

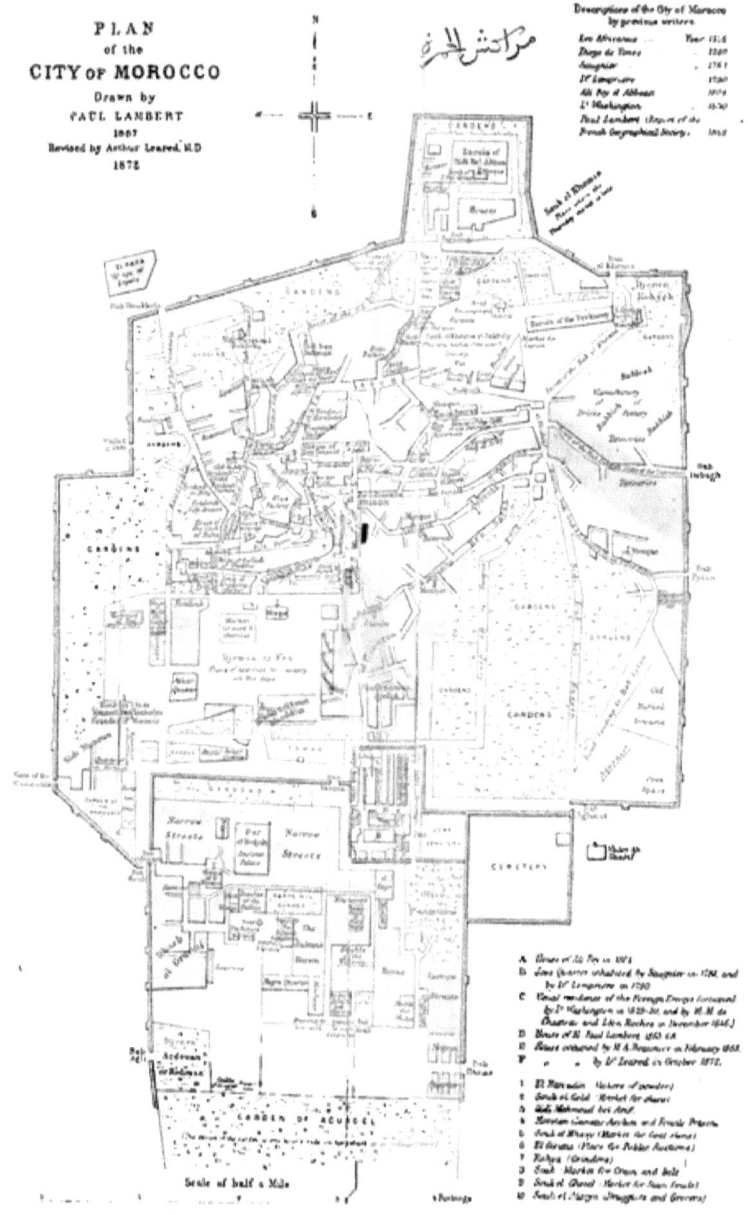

credible. Before the death of Ali it is said to
have contained 100,000 families. It was surrounded by a strong stone wall, and thus protected,
the inhabitants flourished and soon excelled in the
arts and sciences; and so greatly as to lead the
Moors of Spain, Algiers, and Tunis to send their
children thither for instruction. The spoils of
Andalusia flowed into the favoured city, and the
addition of an active commerce with the interior
of Africa soon raised it to a position of great
wealth and corresponding luxury. The fall of
the Moors in Spain was the first cause of its
decline; civil wars interrupted its commerce; vast
numbers of citizens emigrated therefrom; till in
the end it was brought into that state of decay
and partial ruin in which it has since remained.
"This noble city," wrote Leo Africanus, "is
accounted to be one of the greatest cities in
the whole world." Having regard to the space
enclosed within its walls, it is still entitled to be
called "great," but its grandeur and nobility have
utterly vanished.[1]

[1] In writing the following account of the city of Marocco,
I am indebted to Mr. Lambert, of Tangier, for much information. He lived as a merchant in the city for five years, and
adopting the Moorish dress and customs, speaking the language
fluently, and mingling with all classes of the people, he acquired
a more accurate knowledge of the whole subject than was
possessed by any European. He sketched out a map, which is
here reproduced, and, considering the difficulties of such an
undertaking, it is wonderfully accurate. Mr. Lambert also wrote
an account of the city, which was published in the *Bulletin de
la Société de Géographie*. Of this I have freely availed myself

Nothing can be finer than the scenery which surrounds Marocco. Situated in an immense plain, it is flanked on the north, and for some distance towards the east and west, by a splendid wood of date palms, to which the citizens constantly resort for the sake of enjoying the pleasant shade. It is bordered on the east by gardens, and beyond these the country is open to the foot of the Atlas mountains, portions of which grand chain reach a height of 10,000 feet. The lustre of the snow on their summits has a singularly fine effect against the deep blue background of a cloudless sky. Viewed from a house-top it is a scene on which to dwell with pleasure, and one which for the time leads the spectator to forget the drawbacks to existence in such a place.

The tract of country in the midst of which the city stands rises gently from the mountainous district in the west to the Atlas chain; and from

It may here be stated that another of the very few Europeans who have lived for any length of time in the interior of the country is Mr. Archibald Fairlie, C.E., now of Cannon Street, London. He was for some years in the service of the late Sultan. Large mills for the manufacture of cane and beet-root sugar, machinery for cleaning and pressing cotton, and other works, were erected in Marocco under Mr. Fairlie's superintendence, and, what is remarkable, entirely by native labour.

Mr. Fairlie was regarded favourably by the late Sultan, and with respect by all classes of people. This was largely due to the fact that he always upheld the dignity and good faith of an English gentleman in his dealings with the natives. All the improvements which Mr. Fairlie laboured so hard to introduce have long since vanished under the combined influence of ignorance and despotism.

measurement made by myself with an accurate aneroid barometer, it lies about 1,500 feet above the level of the sea. The city walls are thick, and average in height twenty-three feet; and the area within is very extensive. Square turrets flank a portion of the walls, though many of them are in a ruinous state, and in parts there are none at all.

That portion of the town lying north, forming a sort of peninsula, is surrounded by walls of a later date than the rest, and contains the sanctuary of Sidi Bel Abbes. These walls were raised at the end of the last century, by order of Sidi Mohammed Ben Abd Allah. All of them are made of *tabia*; and in the entire circumvallation are seven gates, in addition to two others which lead direct into the Kasba. As seen from without, the city has a compact and strong appearance; but it is needless, perhaps, to add that, in relation to advanced warfare, it may be regarded as quite unfortified. About two-thirds of the space enclosed is taken up with gardens or covered with rubbish. The gates are placed in massive archways, within which are guard-houses. The streets leading direct from these gates are usually of good breadth, but in other parts of the town they are narrow and, particularly in the wet season, very filthy. The makers of gunpowder procure saltpetre from these street-sweepings, and the men employed in this work are the scavengers of the city.

The houses of the superior classes are almost all built upon the same plan—that of a central courtyard surrounded by long, narrow rooms. One of these serves for a kitchen, in which cooking is carried on by means of charcoal fires. The other rooms are used for reception and sleeping, and accommodate the ladies and children of the family. Near the entrance-door, a narrow staircase leads to the first floor. This is called the *Joueria*, and here it is that the master of the house receives his friends. Each house has a well which supplies water for the laundry and for ordinary use, but drinking-water is obtained from the public fountains. In some instances the horses of the owner divide with the ladies the occupation of the ground floor; in other words, one room is a stable.

The narrowness of the apartments in the best houses of this country cannot fail to attract the attention of strangers. They are, generally speaking, of good height, but are very long in proportion to their breadth. This arises from the difficulty experienced in obtaining native wood of sufficient length for the floors. The width of the rooms, in consequence, seldom exceeds ten or twelve feet. The importation of foreign wood has of late years caused these limits to be in some cases a good deal exceeded. The interiors are usually plastered, and adorned in various colours with arabesque designs and verses taken from the Koran. The lower stories of almost all the houses are made of *tabia*, which means mud. The nature of this mud varies in different districts. At Terodant, in the south, *tabia* walls are formed by earth and straw intermixed. But those of better quality consist of a mixture of one-third each of lime, clay, and small pebbles, mixed together with water, and beaten down in a movable mould, which is raised as the wall progresses. The upper story of many houses is constructed with bricks of good quality. The tower of the Katoubia is the only building of stone in the city, there being a great scarcity of this material in its vicinity. The best houses are situated in the quarters named respectively Zaouïa-el-Hadhar, Sidi Abd-el-Azyz, Kat Ben Aïd, and Ruad Zeetoon. These quarters are more secure than others from attacks of thieves. A street which communicated between one quarter (*Darb*) and another, is bordered only by little shops or merely by blank walls. As previously said, the exterior walls of houses are blank; all windows being made to open on the interior courts. The Djemaa El Fna, of which we had such a disagreeable experience, is the great assembly place of the people. Here the jugglers, gymnasts, snake-charmers, and comedians perform in the evenings before the crowds seated around in a circle; and here it is also that the scum of the population constantly prowl—men ready for tumult and plunder on any pretext, and, should it further their ends, as ready to take life.

The mosques are numerous, and some of them are spacious buildings. The pride of the city is the one called El Koutubiga, or the mosque of the booksellers. The angles of its square minaret, or tower, correspond with the four cardinal points of the compass. It is 220 feet in height, and, being of the same dimensions at top as at bottom, it has an imposing effect. On the top there is a small turret, or lantern, from which the name Smà el Fannar is derived. The tower consists of seven stories, and the ascent from one to the other is effected by inclined planes instead of stairs. It was built in A.D. 1197, during the palmy days of the Moors, by Guever, a Sevillian architect, who about the same period constructed the Tower of Hassan at Rabat, and the Giralda at Seville, from the same designs, by order of the Emirs Almohade, Yacoub, and Mansour.

The mosque is a large building of brick, much out of repair. The interior, which is never seen by Christian eyes, contains many marble pillars, said to have been brought from Spain. Beneath the floor there is a cistern as large as the building itself, which is used by the Moors for ablutions.

Leo Africanus, in his description of this mosque, remarks, " The roof is most cunningly and artificially vaulted, and I have not seen many fairer temples ; "

and he adds, in relation to both mosque and city, "Albeit you shall hardly find any temple in the whole world greater than this, yet it is very meanly frequented; for the people do never assemble there, only on Fridays. Under the porch of this temple, it is reported that in old time there were almost an hundred shops of sale books, and as many on the other side over against them; but at this time I think there is not one bookseller in all the whole city to be found." This account was written more than three hundred years ago. Even then this once populous and enlightened city had fallen into great decay, and now little more than barbarism and misery prevail.

Notwithstanding the present neglect of literature, the science of astronomy is not altogether lost among the Moors. In February, 1868, when Mr. Beaumier visited Marocco, a partial eclipse of the sun was visible, and the *savants*, desiring to make some observations, were obliged on this occasion to use the tower of the mosque of Ben Youssef, instead of that of the Kotoubia, the usual observatory. The reason for change was simply this. The harem of the Sultan's brother, Muley Ali, was at that time in the neighbourhood, and it was feared the philosophers might be induced to direct their eyes and their thoughts downwards, in place of fixing them on their sublime task.

The mosque of Ben Youssef is, as regards height, next to Kotoubia. El Moussen and El Mansoury are also large buildings. One of the gates of El Moussen is said to have been brought from Granada by Mansour, the fourth sovereign of Marocco. An archway of stone, curiously wrought with arabesque sculptures, called Bab Aquenaou, is also said to have been brought piecemeal from Algisiras.

There are twenty-one public baths distributed over the town and citadel. The method of bathing is identical with that of the Turkish bath; but the buildings in which the processes are carried on are mean structures compared with those of the East. Men are admitted from sunrise to mid-day at a charge of a mouzouna (less than a halfpenny) each, and women from mid-day to nightfall at two mouzounas each.

There are three prisons. The largest, to which we have already referred, is formed by excavating the earth to the depth of about seven feet, and then raising an arched roof supported by pillars. Daylight is scantily admitted through openings guarded by iron bars. The prison contains a reservoir of water and a mosque. All criminal prisoners have irons riveted upon their legs, and some have an iron collar and chain attached to the neck. No food is provided by government; the prisoners, generally speaking, are supported by relatives or friends. In default of these, they support themselves by making mats, baskets, and cushions, or else they live on alms. Those who are unable to work frequently die of hunger.

Justice in Marocco, as often elsewhere, has a keen eye to business. Whenever an unhappy wretch is suffered to leave prison, he has to pay ten ounces—about tenpence English money—for the use of his irons. Another two ounces has to be paid to the talib, or scribe, who makes out the order for release; and a present has also to be given to the Mekhazni, or jailer, who conducted him to prison, and who, at his deliverance, is at hand.

But prior to the payment of these fees, a preliminary and often most difficult arrangement must be made. A sum, arbitrarily fixed by the kaid, must be paid to him for the prisoner's release. The amount is always an extortionate one, being usually regulated by the means of the relatives or friends. After much negotiation, and many appeals, an abatement is at last effected. It also sometimes happens that the kaid, after receiving the sum agreed upon, demands still more before the prisoner is released, or else, after release, he recommits him to prison until a further sum is extorted.

The prison in the citadel is devoted to prisoners of state, such as rebellious or refractory governors of provinces. Its walls enclose an uncovered court around which are little cells, and in the centre is a subterranean chamber. Food is provided by the authorities, but the prisoners are almost always supported by their friends.

There is a jail in the quarter assigned to the Jews, and in which they are imprisoned when charged with ordinary misdemeanours. But when guilty of grave crimes they are relegated to the foulest and most unwholesome portion of the great city prison. Opposite to this stands the *Márly-tun*, or madhouse. Lunatics reputed dangerous are fastened to the walls by means of a collar round the neck, and a very heavy chain. This chain is lengthened at night just sufficiently to allow the unhappy wretch to lie down on the bare ground, and the whole of the inmates are fed upon bread supplied out of the revenues of the mosques. The first floor of this institution is used as a jail for women. They do not wear fetters, but they are compelled, like the rest of the prisoners, to pay a sum of money before they are released. The women detained here are chiefly those of reputed bad lives, and all such are arrested in the streets during the night.

There are a great many markets for the sale of merchandise. One of these, Sok-el-Djedid, is devoted to important woven fabrics, and the English visitor is half-surprised by the sight of familiar marks and names. But the goods of Manchester find their way everywhere, and to few places in reality more out of the world than to this semi-savage city of Marocco.

In the Sok-el-Atàrin, sugar, tea, and drugs are sold. The Sok Smata is for the sale of shoes. The blacksmiths, carpenters, and butchers have each a street communicating one with the other. These streets correspond to the bazaars of the East, and are not inhabited at night, except by guards. The communicating gates are then closed.

The wholesale merchants have their warehouses and offices in what is called a fondouk, or caravansary. The principal fondouks are Ranjia, Djêdid, El Melah, Selem, Hadj-el-Arbi, and Sid Amara.

Besides these fondouks there are a great number of others which are used as inns by strangers coming into the city with their donkeys and camels. These are filthy places in which accommodation is afforded at the charge of one mouzouna a day for each person, and two mouzounas for each beast. The master of the establishment is responsible for the safety of the animals, but he does not supply them with food.

A fondouk, if belonging to a merchant, is generally on a large scale, the courtyard being surrounded by a number of rooms which are used for the storage of bulky articles. The rooms on the floor above, around which is a gallery, are devoted to more portable wares. In the case of fondouks used as inns, the courtyards serve to contain the animals, and the small rooms surrounding them shelter the owners and other visitors.

There are two weekly markets, one held on Thursday, the other on Friday; the former, known as Sok-el-Khemis, is the principal one. It is held partly within the town in the open space, Khemis Dakhalani, and partly outside the gate, Bab-el-Khemis. Camels, horses, mules, and asses are sold in it. On the sale of each animal a guarantee that it has not been stolen, verified by a notary, is required. The Friday market, held in the Djamaa El Fna, is for the sale of horned cattle.

In the centre of the city, close to the market for spun materials, Sok-el-Ghezel, is that for slaves. This, which is the principal market in the whole country for the sale of negroes, is held during the hour before sunset on Wednesdays, Thursdays, and Fridays. The slaves are brought direct here from Soudan and Sus.

Near at hand is the grain and salt market, Rhabba del Gimh. A toll of three ounces is taken here on each load which enters the markets, and this produces a considerable revenue. A toll is also charged at the gates on all country products, with the exception of corn, as they enter or leave the city. There is another direct tax, *enkess*, of about two-and-a-half per cent., which is levied on all articles sold, even when such are of local manufacture, and it is laid also upon all goods sold by auction. These various taxes are annually farmed out to the highest bidder. The monopoly for the sale, in the city, of tobacco and kief, yields a return to the Government of about £6,000 annually.

Marocco is not a manufacturing city like Fez or Rabat, and such textile fabrics as it produces are of inferior quality. The only manufacture in which it excels is that of leather: the colours produced in this material are chiefly red and yellow.

There are within the city a great number of horse-mills for the grinding of corn; and without, near the Bab Rob, about a dozen small water-mills; but the poor grind their corn at home in small hand-mills. The millstones are obtained in the neighbourhood. Meal is sifted in small sieves by women, the sieves being made by Jews. Bread is sold in flat cakes in the open streets. It is of good quality, but much impregnated with grit, owing to the soft material of which the millstones are composed.

The palace enclosure of the Sultan faces the south and the Atlas mountains. It is outside the city, but is surrounded by equally high walls. It covers a space of about 1,500 yards long by 600 wide; and this is divided into gardens, in which are pavilions. There are two large courts, *mchouar*, or places of audience, around which are arranged apartments for the ministers, secretaries, and guards. The Treasury, containing, it is said, a large amount of specie, adjoins the house inhabited by the Sultan whenever he visits his capital city. The floors of the rooms in the palace are paved with various coloured tiles; but, with the exception of mats, carpets, and cushions, they contain no furniture.

There is only one charitable institution in the city; it stands at the northern extremity, and is known as the Zaouia, or sanctuary of Sidi Bel Abbes. Here destitute persons receive alms and find an asylum for the night. It is also a place of inviolable refuge for criminals, and those who seek its protection take care not to leave till pardon has been secured. There are, however, occasions when little faith is placed in the promised clemency; and then it is the custom for those seeking it to go forth wrapped in some drapery from the tomb of the saint, and accompanied by the head of the sanctuary. The presence of the Sultan or governor is then sought, and pardon is often obtained.

In Marocco there is no law of *mortmain*; on the contrary, everything is done to encourage the growth of ecclesiastical property, and thus the mosques and holy places are very richly endowed. Bequests are frequently made by piously disposed Mussulmans; and these, which are called *habous*, can never be alienated. One-third only of the net rental, or sum accruing, is devoted to use; the other two-thirds being employed in enlarging the capital by the purchase of houses and lands. In this way, and by additions from other sources, ecclesiastical property is constantly and greatly increasing. The value of the *habous* appertaining to the sanctuary of Sidi Bel Abbes is estimated at £200,000 in value.

The city of Marocco has an abundant supply of water. To this are due the verdure of the gardens, and the fine quality of fruits and vegetables. It is conveyed into the city by aqueducts leading from the hills Misfeewa and Muley Brahim.

The fountains are numerous, which, as well as the reservoir and aqueducts, being the work of former ages, are for the most part in bad repair if not in ruins. One reservoir, El Mouezin, has been recently well restored. Close to our house was a handsome fountain decorated with a Moorish arch, and finely carved in old arabesque ornament. The name of this fountain was *Shup-wa-Shrub*, which means, "Behold and drink." It bears the architect's name, Maamun. To this is added "Allah be praised that I was able to finish this work." This directness and simplicity of expression have always characterized the Semitic races, and the style and taste of the decoration are in this case quite in keeping.

The Jews' quarter is in the southern part of the city. Enclosed by high walls, it is about a mile and a half in circuit, and is bounded on the south and west by the Kasba. It is called El Mellah, the salt place, in allusion to the utility of the Jews, and often in derision *El Messous*, the place without salt, by which term their worthlessness is implied. The gates are guarded by Moors appointed by the kaid. It is built of tabia, like the rest of the city; and although this is a lasting material when treated with care, it soon, from neglect, becomes ruinous; many dilapidated houses and tumble-down walls exist in this as in the Moorish quarters.

Here and there, a large cubic mass of earth, as it seemed from the street, pierced by a single aperture for the door, denoted the house of an affluent owner. But these houses are exceptional,—I speak from experience, having entered a number of dwellings in various quarters, and especially in poor neighbourhoods. Just then the rainy season had commenced. Already fetid pools, formed by water in which decayed vegetables and still greater abominations were soaked, were to be seen before almost every door that opened to the streets, or else into the little courts, around which the houses are, in some cases, grouped. Under such conditions it is marvellous how people exist. The fact that the vital processes are maintained almost shook, at the time, one's faith in the necessity for enforcing sanitary laws. But the mortality must be prodigious, though there are no registrar-general's reports on death-rates to reveal the fact. What wonder that these poor people are pallid and worn, that numbers of them are constantly sick with intermittent fevers, that to meet any free from ophthalmia is the exception; and from this cause the proportion of blind people among the general population is very great. The houses are wretched tenements, consisting usually of a couple of small rooms with low ceilings. Few of these have windows, though, during the day, the open door affords light and air. But, as the occupants have no idea of the necessity of ventilation, the atmosphere of the rooms must be stifling when the doors are closed at night. In addition to this evil, all that is objectionable, as regards decency and order in our own overcrowded dwellings, must necessarily prevail. Yet, in justice to these poor Israelites, it must be added that the rooms were, in general, clean; the walls were limewashed, and the matted floors, unencumbered by furniture, had a neat appearance.

The inhabitants of the Jewish quarter are industrious and painstaking. Here, as in other places, they devote themselves more to sedentary occupations, such as that of the silversmith, engraver, shoemaker, or tailor, than to laborious outdoor trades. Jewish butchers are, however, numerous, and it speaks well for the practical value of a certain portion of ceremonial usages that the Moors deal with them in preference to butchers of their own persuasion, because of the care taken by Jews in the selection of animals for food.

As might be expected, this isolated community is superstitious and credulous in a high degree. They put full faith in charms and amulets, and, in order to control destiny, practise many things repugnant to our ideas. Some of the means resorted to for the cure of disease are especially of this kind.

The belief of these Jews in the "evil eye" is very steadfast. They assure you that far more deaths take place from this than from natural causes. The sign of one harmless piece of superstition may be observed in almost every house. The city of Marocco is greatly infested by scorpions. In order to keep such venomous intruders out of the house, a paper, on which is drawn a rude picture of one or two scorpions, is stuck on the door-post of every house. Above this, in Hebrew characters, is an array of mystical words, arranged on the principle of the ancient *abracadabra*. Below it, is written a solemn imprecation. The rabbi who prepares this precious document must, in order to make it effective, rightly observe certain circumstances. It must be written only on the first night of Sivan, near Pentecost, and previous to his labours he must immerse himself three times in a bath, and also cut his nails. When finished, it is as follows, except that the mystical part is given in English instead of Hebrew characters.

Epicoros	In	Apretata
Picoros	Nin	Pretata
Icoros	Ini	Retata
Coros	Gini	Etata
Oros	Igini	Tata
Ros	Ligini	Ata
Os	Bligini	Ta
S	Abligini	A

The translation of the inscription below these cabalistic letters reads thus:—

"O scorpion, daughter, daughter of a scorpion, be thou accursed by the strength of every power that exists. From the mouth of the Prophet Joshua, the son of Nun; from the mouth of the High Priest Judah Bar Eli; and also from the mouth of the High Priest Judah Bar Ezekiel; so that you may not pass the threshold of this door, nor hurt any Israelite now and for evermore. This is by command of the High Priest, Simon Bar Yuli. Amen." "They shall not hurt nor destroy in all My holy mountain; for the earth shall be full of the knowledge of the Lord, as the waters cover the sea."

A Jew told me that a short time previously he was an eye-witness to the efficacy of this imprecation. A large scorpion ran to the door of a room, and then stopped suddenly, as if stupefied; it was, in fact, a case of no admittance. Several members of his family were summoned, and all agreed in the truth of the prodigy.

The Jews are known to have much money and other valuables in their possession. On this account, in a country like Marocco, where banks and places of deposit for security are unknown, much uneasiness, in times of public disturbance, is inevitable.

This was the case at the period of our visit. For although it was stated that 500 men were nightly employed by the kaid in the protection of the Jewish quarter, depredations had already commenced, and the uppermost thought in every Jew's mind was this:—"What if our guards betray us?" "*Quis custodiet ipsos custodes?*" Nor was it pleasant to find, in this depressing state of public affairs, a strong feeling of distrust and jealousy among the Jews themselves. Their misfortunes, it might be thought, would have been a bond of union, yet, here as elsewhere, there were cliques and parties who talked of each other with bitterness. Thus, many of the Jews attributed the suspension of certain privileges, granted by the Sultan at the intercession of Sir Moses Montefiore, to the action of an influential member of their own community, who, they alleged, was, for substantial reasons, devoted to the interests of the Moorish government. They went even so far as to say that certain communications from England, intended for the Sultan, and sent through the quarter in question, had never been forwarded. But it seemed to me then, as it does still, that all this was unfounded suspicion, and, more likely than not, to be due to the erroneous impressions of a suffering and politically degraded people trying to fix blame *somewhere*. As for the late Sultan, although in the European sense a tyrant, and even cruel, he was not regarded as such by his own countrymen; but, on the contrary, they looked upon him as comparatively a mild ruler. He appears also to have been a just man, with every disposition to keep faith and observe engagements. But, as is too often the case with so-called absolute rulers, he was not master of his own actions; for public opinion, guided by a fanatical religion, cannot be disregarded. He was said to have been disposed to gradually increase the liberties of the Jews instead of curtailing them. For, according to an Arab proverb, as my informant added, "If you want to cook a camel you must first cut it in pieces."

The disqualifications and indignities to which the Jews are subjected in the city of Marocco, so far as they came under my own observation, were as follows:—1. They are never allowed to wear the turban. 2. In the presence of a governor, or when passing a mosque, they are obliged to remove the blue handkerchief with which the head is at other times bound. 3. They must wear black instead of the yellow shoes always worn by the Moors. 4. When they go from their own quarter into the Moorish town, both men and women are compelled to take off their shoes and walk barefooted; and this degradation appeared especially painful when one had occasion to walk with a Jewish friend through the filthy streets of the Moorish quarters. 5. A Jew, meeting a Moor, must always pass to the left. 6. Jews are not allowed to ride through the city. 7. They are not permitted to carry arms. 8. The use of the Moorish bath is forbidden to the Jews. 9. In the exercise of their religion they are restricted to private houses; hence there are no public buildings used as synagogues. This restriction applies equally to other parts of the empire, except Tangier.

No doubt there are other more or less annoying interferences with personal liberty which do not meet the eye. But the list given is enough to show that the grievances of the Jewish community are far from being merely sentimental. They live under the yoke of an iron despotism, and, as might be expected, betray this in their manner and appearance. The men are in general of medium height, but slender, long-visaged, and sallow. It is sad to see them walk with bowed heads and slow steps through the streets of their mother city; rather, indeed, a hard stepmother, who, while acknowledging their right to a harsh protection, subjects them to the taunts and ill-treatment of her more favoured progeny. Even the horse-play and practical jokes of the Moors are highly inconvenient to the Jew. Here is one instance:—In some seasons the gardens in and about the city are so productive that oranges are absolutely of no value except for pelting the Jews. It is, indeed, regarded as seasonable sport, like that of throwing snowballs in England, for which oranges are no bad substitutes. Woe to the unhappy Israelite who is seen in the streets, or on a housetop, during this saturnalia of the Moorish youth. Assailed by shouts and jeers, he is, unless saved by hasty flight, ridiculously besmeared; and, from the violence of the blows, he also runs the risk of receiving more serious injury. On this account the authorities have, of late, made efforts to suppress this curiously literal kind of "Orange riots."

Marocco, as regards Africa, is a cosmopolitan city. Its inhabitants include Moors, Algerians, Tunisians, Egyptians, natives of the Sahara, negroes from the Soudan, and occasionally negroes from Senegal are met with. Three languages are commonly spoken—Arabic, which is most general; Shluh, the language of the inhabitants of the Atlas and of the south; and Guennaoui, the speech of the negroes.

Without the aid of anything in the shape of a census it is extremely difficult to arrive at safe conclusions in relation to the number of inhabitants of a city spread unequally over a large space. The custom of shutting women up adds to the difficulty. Even the Moors themselves have very hazy notions on this subject. One of the citizens gravely assured me that the city contained some millions of people. But, so far as an estimate can be made, the following data, carefully put together by M. Lambert, are, without doubt, close to the truth. He has grouped, as follows, the people according to their occupations :—

Mussulmans—Landed proprietors and agriculturists	1,200
Ulemas and Adools	150
Talebs and students	800
Wholesale merchants	100
Traders (woven goods and groceries)	500
,, (haiks and carpets)	300
Shopkeepers (oil, wood, charcoal, pottery)	1,000
Manufacturers (haiks and carpets, &c.)	800
Carpenters, smiths, and sellers of old iron	350
Makers and sellers of ropes	250
Tanners, shoemakers, and cobblers	1,500
	6,950

Brought forward 6,950
Masons, labourers, and porters 2,500
Millers and bakers . . 600
Government employés . 400
Negroes belonging to the Government . . . 2,000
Soldiers, bokhary, and others 2,000
Mekhazny, soldiers in the service of the kaid, of the mohtasseb, of the kadies and others . . 500
Paupers, beggars, and vagabonds 1,500

16,450

By adding to this total of 16,450 males an equal number of females, as also an equal number of children of both sexes, together with 6,000 Jews of both sexes and all ages, the result gives the sum total of over 55,000 souls as constituting the population of the city of Marocco.

Although many of the Moors have a plurality of wives, beside female slaves as concubines, at least half of the males above specified have only one wife, or else are unmarried.

The town is governed by the kaid and a number of subordinates: namely, the khalifa, or vice-governor; Moulán 't 'dour, or chief of the night-guards; the mohtasib, or chief of the day-guards and administrator of the markets; two kadies, or judges and officers of public worship; and the nadhir, or manager of the property of the mosques and of the city. In addition, every branch of industry and trade has its amín or head man; and each quarter of the town has its mukaddim, and its special nadhir. This complicated system of government is well calculated to foster the systematic corruption which prevails in all places of trust. Yet it must be stated that in certain rare instances men in power gain for themselves a character for honour and honesty.

As might be expected in the case of such wild and undisciplined hordes as inhabit the city of Marocco, crime is rampant. Murders are of very frequent occurrence; and although the *lex talionis* is a leading doctrine of the Mohammedan religion, Moorish avarice almost always overrides revenge; and the friends of a murdered man are induced, for the sake of a sum of money, to settle the affair. One phase of European civilization has its counterpart in this city. Like their London brethren, the Marocco thieves devote themselves to special branches of their art. One class is addicted to stealing clothes from baths. Others take the slippers deposited in the porches of the mosque. Many follow the pursuit of stealing fruit from gardens. Others are pickpockets, who ingeniously cut holes in the hood of the jalabeer, which, when thrown back, is used as a pocket; or else they cut the string by which the scarrah or leather bag is suspended from the body. Many steal horses, mules, camels, &c.; not a few are professed burglars. All robbers are known more or less to his mukaddem, who turns his knowledge to account.

Whenever a robbery of importance takes place, the kaid sends for this functionary and informs him that a perquisition of the quarter will be at once made unless the offender be immediately named. It was stated that the golden age of thieves, which had lasted five years, had just terminated with the deposition of Kaid Ben Daoud.

CHAPTER X.

MAROCCO TO SAFFI.

We left Marocco on October 10th, being only too glad to shake the dust from our feet and turn our faces towards Saffi and the coast. Yet the palm-groves outside the city, having been refreshed by the late rains, looked more than usually alluring and beautiful.

We rode as far as the Tensift without a halt, and breakfasted under the fine shade of some noble date trees. Here, at this season, the river was contracted to a shallow stream, though its sands were a quarter of a mile in width. There was the usual fringe of verdure, and many kinds of beautiful little birds were disporting themselves among the shrubs. We observed some rooks perched on the palm-tops, but they looked singularly out of place, and, judging by their attitudes, it was with difficulty they kept their footing on the broad leaves.

Resuming our journey, we entered upon a

OUR HALTING-PLACE ON THE TENSIFT.
From a Photograph by the Author.

[*To face page 18.*

country made rough by rocks of quartz and slate, which in some places were arranged in perpendicular strata. About eighteen miles from the city we reached the base of a hill which rose from the level rather abruptly, and here the plain of Marocco ended. At the top of this hill, and at an elevation of 1,350 feet above the sea, we took our last view of the city, the tower of the Katoubia bearing south by ten degrees east.

Our way now lay over stony and arid hills, and it soon turned towards the north. Timbarkate signalized himself by dismounting and shooting a venomous snake which lay basking in the sun. A great uproar, as usual, followed, and numberless maledictions and expressions of disgust were wasted upon the dead reptile.

About four p.m. we reached the inzella of Emshras belonging to the Wuld Eliria Kabílah. As the place was well wooded we strolled a little way with our guns, attended by the old sheikh of the place. We saw several desert partridges, but did not get within range. A shot I made at a hare won the admiration of the patriarch. Indeed, his delight was unbounded, for he showed by pantomime, repeated over and over again, how the gun was raised and the hare turned head over heels while running at full speed. All the villagers were told of the exploit, and I was the hero of the evening. The extra civility of this sheikh was due, probably, to the fact that, when leaving Marocco, El Geroui had sent us a letter for delivery to him. We had not asked for such a favour, but the crafty ruler was only too happy to do anything which was likely to expedite our departure.

This inzella was only formed by a fence made of cut sidr shrubs, so piled one upon another as to form an impenetrable hedge. I was more than usually troubled here by applicants for medical advice; probably it was supposed that, being so good a shot, I must be a particularly good doctor.

Oct. 11.—We were early in the saddle, and soon after setting out saw in the breaking light a fox, a jackal, and some ravens. A great part of the journey was over a good but monotonous road, with but little surrounding vegetation, except the sidr tree. We passed the saint-house of Sidi Hamet Ben Brahim; and after that we had a long ride under a strong sun, made less endurable by want of water. Our mid-day halt was most uncomfortable from the same cause, and also from the want of shade, and it was long before water could be obtained from a distance. Except for some corn-fields seen towards the close of the day, the country passed through was barren. The distance travelled was about thirty-five miles.

It was three o'clock in the afternoon when we arrived at our halting-place, the residence of the governor of Bled Ahmer, to whom we had a letter from Bu Bekr. This residence was a huge building, which realized to the mind one of those fictitious castles so dear to the imagination of childhood, where giants once dwelt and innocent victims were confined, and which good and true knights, clad in the brightest mail, attacked and entered. Its grey tabia walls and crumbling castellated turrets gave it a dismal and forbidding aspect. Entering by the guarded gateway, we passed into a large courtyard, where were slaves and soldiers, cattle and horses. The quarters assigned to us consisted of an isolated open square, around which were apartments of the usual kind, long and narrow, and with no other furniture than matting on the floor. Yet even this approach to comfort was most welcome, for we were fatigued, and not as yet recovered from our illness.

The governor himself was reported to be unwell, and almost as soon as we arrived his brother came to inquire if I would undertake to cure him. I replied, "That, as far as I could judge from his brother's report, he was suffering from intermittent fever; I would willingly do my best for him, and should probably succeed." This message was conveyed to him, and was, without doubt, considered unsatisfactory, for I heard nothing further of him.

His brother showed great interest in my photographic apparatus. His surprise at seeing objects turned upside down when he looked through the camera was great. But explanation would have been fruitless. No doubt the whole process was attributed to the contrivance of the devil, with whom all Christians are supposed to be in close alliance; indeed, it being only through Satanic aid that the latter attain power to do so many things unknown to the true believer.

A great mess of kuskusu and mutton was sent us for dinner in the usual wooden vessel. It was so greasy and rancid that we did it little justice; but our Moors did not fail in this respect, and it disappeared with marvellous rapidity. Indeed, nothing we received from the governor's stores was at all good, except some tea; and this was excellent. A piece of candle was given to us for light, but more was refused. I contrived, however, to bribe one of the slaves with some gunpowder, with the result that he produced an ordinary composite candle. In short, my ideas of our reception by a governor received a rude shock. I had expected something approaching luxury, whereas our lodging and living were only shelter and the plainest food. Into the *penetralia* of the palace I had no excuse to enter, for I had not guaranteed to cure its owner. Some pretext of this sort was needed, as, without it, it was not permitted to show the Frank that inner sanctuary, where reigned supreme four legitimate wives and numerous frail beauties.

During and after dinner we were besieged by a staring crowd of Moors and slaves, who were anxious to witness and know all about our movements. One fine young black from Timbuctoo made private overtures to the effect that he would like to run away from his master and follow my fortunes. The worst part of this interview was the doctoring. Black and white alike had some complaint, a description of which I was expected patiently to listen to, and then cure, as the Americans say, "right away." At length, when wearied out and needing rest, we had the greatest difficulty in clearing our room. Medical reputation of this kind is highly inconvenient, and the practice it brings is not remunerative.

We were provided next morning with a dainty for breakfast, which we failed to appreciate. This was unsalted butter. We did not even taste it, for the smell was enough. The men, however, did not copy our abstinence, but ate voraciously and pronounced it to be of rare quality. Butter in Marocco is estimated according to age, as wine is by us; and this in question was, we were assured, a year old!

While making an examination of the castle as far as was possible, I came upon a sad spectacle. In the courtyard, near the entrance to our quarters, was an opening in the ground. It was the size of an ordinary skylight, strongly secured by bars, and was further protected by a low wall. The place was, in fact, an underground prison, and the barred opening the only entrance for light and air; for the door was like that of a burial vault.

Having an opportunity, I descended and examined this prison. It was simply an excavation without masonry, the size of a large room. In order to prevent escape therefrom, and to avoid the necessity of arching the top, the chamber had been sunk low in the earth, and the superincumbent mass above left proportionately thick. It would be impossible to imagine a more gloomy or depressing dungeon than this grave for living men. There was just light enough to show the horrors of the place, while the earthy smell made its resemblance to a tomb complete.

At the time the prison was almost empty. One fine-looking fellow, heavily manacled and secured by an iron neck-collar to which a strong chain was attached, lay on the floor. Three or four lesser culprits, heavily ironed, were in the courtyard. But this was an indulgence only allowed during the day, for at night they were sent below to share in the grave-like prison.

We tried, but failed, to learn the nature of the crimes these men had committed. But this much was certain, that trifling offences are made a ready pretext for arresting any one suspected of possessing money, and therefore capable of paying for release. But the Moor's endurance is as great as his avarice, and he suffers long before he parts with his hoarded wealth.

Among other qualifications which I got credit for was the repair of musical instruments. A musical box was brought to me to be mended, but I respectfully declined the job.

Game abounds in this neighbourhood. The governor had a brace of handsome greyhounds, and some of his retinue brought them out for us to course with. But the time at our disposal was too short to do more than start a hare, which was not killed. We also flushed a large covey of desert partridges, as well as many red-legged partridges, and several birds apparently of the plover kind, their wings being tipped with black.

We left the castle soon after mid-day, and, passing through a fertile plain, beheld a strange sight —what appeared to be a wide expanse of snow beneath a glaring and burning sun. This snow-like material was indeed a product of the sun, for it was a lake filled with salt. In winter it was a shallow lake of brine, which the rapid evaporative powers of summer converted into a solid mass. I rode some way out upon it, the mules' feet sinking as if in so much snow. Far out, men were employed in loading camels with the salt. This is a valuable article of commerce, for the product of these brine lakes—there being others in the country—is conveyed by caravans into Central Africa as far as Timbuctoo. I made the elevation of this lake 1,250 feet above the sea level.

From this place the road is level and good for some distance. About ten miles from the salt lake we crossed a range of hills, running north and south, and soon descended into a narrow defile about three miles and a half in length; its width and the elevation of the hill on either side being very uniform. The sun was setting, and the pass having a bad repute as the lurking-place of thieves, we hurried through, so as to be clear of it before darkness set in. After a journey of about twenty-one miles we stopped at an inzella, where, somewhat to our surprise, considering our previous experience, we were received with a spirit of genuine hospitality. The sheikh supplied us with fowls, eggs, and other things, and positively refused remuneration. It was a glorious moonlight night, and we dined in the open air. The cool breeze and subdued light, after the heat and glare of the day, were most refreshing.

We left early next morning, and soon passed on the left another governor's house. After this we crossed some barren hills, and then descended to a table-land possessing deep soil of a rich chocolate colour. Much of it was cultivated, and over a portion the caraway plant flourished. Then the signs of cultivation disappeared, and the palmetto-tree varied a landscape which soon became rugged and rocky. At last the town of Saffi was discovered nestling under deep hills, and washed by the blue sea. Our day's journey had been about thirty-three miles, and we entered Saffi early in the afternoon.

CHAPTER XI.

SAFFI.

WE were hospitably received by Mr. Hunot, the British Vice-Consul, and stayed some days at his house. Here we dismissed all our Moors, retaining only Leo. Subsequently, on my return north from Mogador, I again stayed a couple of days in the town, and, on this occasion, was indebted for the same kindness to Mr. Murdoch, the principal merchant of the port. In a place where there are no hotels, such attention from our countrymen is as valuable as it is well appreciated. It will thus be convenient to group together the events of both visits.

Saffi, or Assapi, as spelt by Leo Africanus, was founded by the Carthaginians, and is, therefore, a town of very great antiquity. It may be regarded as the capital of the province of Abda; it is surrounded by a high wall, and is placed between two hills. It was captured by the Portuguese in 1641. Extensive ruins of the castles and fortified places still remain. The population is about 8,000, of whom a considerable number are Jews. The sanitary condition of the place is very low. Placed under high hills, the summer heat is very great; and in this respect Saffi contrasts unfavourably with Mogador, situated two days' easy journey to the south. Another small town, called Rabat, lies close beside it, not more than 500 yards to the south. Rabat is in fact a famous sanctuary, presided over by its own governor, the privileges of the place extending on the one hand to the walls of Saffi, and on the other half a mile on the road towards Mogador. Here fraudulent debtors, highwaymen, and assassins live, for a time at least, without fear of arrest, under the eyes of the persons they have injured, and beyond the power of the law. To this subject of sanctuaries and their privileges we shall again refer.

Being one of the holy cities of Marocco, pilgrimages are made to the shrines at Saffi. It has many saint-houses, and the usual accompaniment of lazy priests, who live on the bounty of the devout. One saint-house situated on the side of a hill, just outside the town, is held in particular veneration. It is called the House of the Seven Brothers, or Woled Ben Jimero, that is, "the sons of Jimero." All seven died on the same day, and were canonized in a bunch.

But the remarkable thing is, that it is yet an unsettled question whether they were Moors or

Jews; for they are claimed as co-religionists by both sects, who alike venerate them. Thousands of persons flock annually from distant parts to receive the benefits which are supposed to emanate from the seven holy graves; among which, cures of affections of the eye are judged to stand pre-eminent.

The Sultan's palace, a large dilapidated pile, overlooks the town; it contains some fine rooms, with lofty and richly-ornamented ceilings. The part most important, and constructed of stone, is Portuguese work, and over the principal entrance heraldic devices are still visible.

On one of the terraces a few brass guns bearing the British arms were mounted, and on another were some of iron of moderate calibre, but honeycombed and rusted to the last degree. Some few artillerymen occupied the place, as my visit was on one of their *fête* days. The guns were of course fired, and the old walls shook with the sound; but neither walls fell nor guns burst, as might from the condition of both have been anticipated. The gunners afterwards entertained me at a midday tea party. In a ruinous part of the building I saw, to my surprise, and to my conviction that there is nothing new under the sun, a small cannon on the breech-loading principle, but it was utterly corroded and spoiled This piece had evidently centuries before been left here by the Portuguese, and proved that the germ of the Armstrong masterpiece was in existence at that early date.

In this palace I examined with interest a small but compact suite of rooms once belonging to a sultana of our own race. Though much out of repair, enough remained to show that they had been built and finished with care.

An Irish sergeant of sappers and miners was, by request, sent with some others from the garrison of Gibraltar to enter the service of the Sultan Sidé Mohammed. The man died soon after, and the widow, wishing to be sent home, sought an audience with the Sultan. It was granted, but with the result that his majesty, being smitten with the woman's charms, made her "an offer," which, notwithstanding all drawbacks of religion and country, was accepted. The renegade Irishwoman became the favourite of the harem, and in due time a son was born in this palace at Saffi. He was named Muley Yezid, though afterwards better known by the *sobriquet* of Lihyat Hamaá, or Red Beard, a characteristic derived from his mother's race. Ultimately he became Sultan, and in that capacity was the most sanguinary monarch known in the annals of Marocco. Our interpreter's great-uncle held a post of importance under the Government, but did not conduct its affairs according to Yezid's views, so the poor Jew was burned alive. This is but a single instance of his ferocity. He was in the habit of saying that the empire would never be governed well till blood flowed in a stream between the gate of his palace and that of the city. The savage acts of this Maroquin Nero were at times characterized by a jocoseness as singular as it was sanguinary. He would order the decapitation of a couple of his domestics, and then play at bowls with their heads. On occasions he would feast all the poor of a district at the expense of some rich bashaw. He was blessed and cursed by turns on account of his inconsistencies, which were characteristic of madman, fool, and despot. Yet in one thing Yezid was consistent; he was the steady friend of the English, to the exclusion of all other nationalities.

At length his unceasing barbarities excited a civil war, and Yezid was mortally wounded by a silver coin used as a bullet from a gun. In a previous attempt upon his life one formed of lead had failed to do its appointed work, and it was then concluded that magic made him invulnerable to projectiles formed of base metal. He was carried to his palace at Casa Blanca, where he survived but one day, yet it is said that in that single day, prompted by a diabolical spirit of empty vengeance, he caused more people to be put to death than during all his previous life. This occurred in 1792, when Yezid was in his forty-fourth year, and just as the second year of his savage reign was drawing to a close.

The surf at Saffi is so dangerous that the place is frequently inaccessible from the sea. It was amusing to observe the skill and daring with which the boats laden with grain were piloted to the vessels in the offing. Just beyond the landing-place is a large rock which at high tide is surrounded by water. This forms a look-out for a Moor, whose duty it is to signal to the boatmen when he thinks the surf is practicable for their boats. About every seventh wave is larger than the others, and the look-out man, counting this succession, guides his procedure partly thereby. But with every precaution accidents often occur, the bags of corn are overwhelmed by the surging waves, and lives are sometimes lost.[1]

Four or five miles inland from Saffi there is a giant olive-tree. To see it is a favourite ride, and the ladies of Mr. Murdoch's family were good enough to accompany me thither. The ground traversed was in a great part rocky, but in places the soil was highly fertile. The country then (November 1) was becoming clothed with the verdure of spring. Various bulbous plants were in bloom, and in some places we saw the beautiful and rare

---

[1] Captain Hogg, with whom I made the return voyage, told me that he had been nine years trading on the coast, and had occasion about six times each year to stop at Saffi, yet he had only ventured to go ashore three times. Such apprehensions for the safety of vessels prove the dangerous nature of the roadstead.

flower *Narcissus Broussonetii* in rich clusters, and were charmed with the sweetness of its perfume.[2] The pretty little *Narcissus serotina* was more diffused, and much less gregarious. In one place, where grew some vigorous plants of the white broom, we noticed that their slender branches were tied in numerous knots. The sanctuary of a favourite saint lies not far off, and at this particular turn of the road, where it first comes into view, pious Moors stay and make these knots. They are a sort of votive offering to the dead, as in olden days stone after stone was added by passers-by to the memorial cairn.[3]

This large olive-tree was held in great respect by the Moors, who called it Lallah Zobooja, or Lady Olive-tree. The glorious shade from the scorching sun which its mass of dark green foliage affords truly entitles her ladyship to high respect. The outside circumference of the tree was, as I ascertained, 120 yards, and the circumference of the main trunk, including irregularities, 28 feet. We judged the height to be about 43 feet. An olive-tree of these dimensions is, I believe, unknown elsewhere.

[2] Through the kindness of Mrs. Ford I have been put in possession of some bulbs of this plant. They have been grown successfully in the Royal Gardens, Kew.

[3] Unfortunate Moors murdered in travelling. The same as the custom of each passer-by dropping a stone on the grave. Numbers of these cairns are found wherever you go inland.

But this eccentric old lady seems to have discovered the secret of marvellously extending her limits and of renewing her youth.

The lower branches grew upwards till, bent by their own weight, they became horizontal, and rested upon the ground. Here, Antæus-like, they renewed their strength: taking root, and throwing out perpendicular branches, they blended their foliage with the parent tree. One curious effect of this process was apparent—the branches were much thicker a long distance from the trunk than they were close to it. In some cases

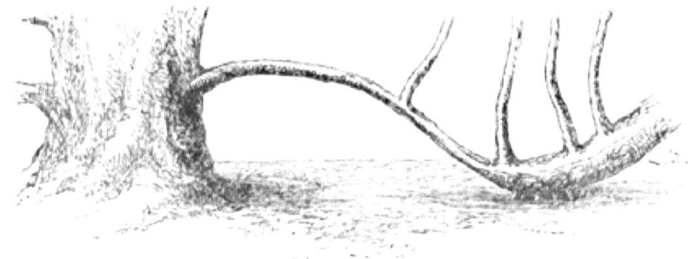

a branch, after it had left the ground, was three or four times as thick as the portion between the main trunk and the soil. A little consideration explains the anomaly. The first part of the branch was nourished by sap from the parent tree alone, while the second not only enjoyed this advantage, but derived still further sustenance from the independent life its roots supplied. The richness of the soil in which this splendid tree grew accounted for its extraordinary dimensions.

The fertility and beauty of the gardens belonging to Europeans at Saffi, and especially that belonging to Mr. Murdoch, showed what might be done by cultivation in this country. The great want is irrigation. Wherever that is carried out, the earth, otherwise parched and barren for a great part of the year, wears a perpetual robe of green.[4]

While I was at Saffi the Ramadan, or Mohammedan fast, commenced. It was ushered in at early dawn by firing of cannon, blowing of horns, and other great tumult in the streets. During this month of Ramadan, that in which Mohammed received his revelation, believers are

---

[1] Since the above was written, *The Garden*, an admirable weekly publication, has had an article on this subject. It says, "The groves of rose-trees and the flower farms of Marocco are said to exceed in extent and value those of Damascus, or even those of the valley of Mexico. The general climate of the country is very favourable to this kind of culture. Swept alternately by the breezes of the Atlantic and the Mediterranean, and tempered by the snows of the Atlas ranges, the degree of heat in Marocco is much lower than in Algeria, while the soil is exceedingly fertile. To the date-palm and to orange and lemon trees the climate appears to be especially suited, the dates of Tafilet having been famous even from Roman times. The orange plantations are of great extent in various parts of the country, while olives and almonds are also staples, and exported in large quantities. Seeing that this fertile land, lying within five days' steam of London, produces so much vegetable wealth under the most barbarous cultivation, it appears extraordinary that European enterprise does not, in such a climate seek profitable employment for its over-abundant capital in its application to the development of such vast resources so close at hand, instead of going so far afield as Australia or America."

forbidden to eat, drink, smoke, or bathe. Even to swallow the spittle between sunrise and sunset is a sin. This fast is particularly severe, when, as happened on this occasion, the month falls in the hot season. The Ramadan, owing to lunar months, varies greatly as to the period of its occurrence; in fact, it can fall at any time throughout the year.

CHAPTER XII.

AZAMOOR, AND A RIDE AT NIGHT.

Upon returning up the coast from Saffi, the vessel was delayed at Mazagan. I resolved, therefore, to take advantage of this circumstance, and ride on to Casa Blanca, and, thus preceding the vessel, to rejoin it there when it arrived. My object was to see the ancient town of Azamoor, and the country generally to the north of Mazagan. Mr. Scott, American Vice-consul at Tangier, and Mr. L. Ford, fellow-passengers, agreed to accompany me; and Messrs. Redmond and Spinney, of Mazagan, materially assisted in carrying out our purpose. We set out at two o'clock in the afternoon, mounted on mules and accompanied by a soldier and a guide. Our way lay close to the sea, over a smooth mass of delicate herbage, in many places interspersed with white flowers; the whole resembling a beautiful carpet of delicate embroidery. All the country around was very fertile, and much of it was cultivated after a manner. Here and there the plough was at work; and the deep-reddish coloured soil gave promise of rich returns.

We arrived at Azamoor in two hours and a quarter, but the town had been for some time previously in full view. It is situated on an eminence about a mile and a half from the sea, and on the southern bank of the Wad-Oumer-Rebiah, "River of Forty Mothers," so called from the water flowing from many sources. The Arabic words have been corrupted into Morbeya, the name by which the river is commonly known. The town was built by the Berbers, in whose language Azamoor means olives, which are produced in great abundance and perfection in the neighbourhood. Leo Africanus says that in his time it contained five thousand inhabitants, but one thousand would be nearer the number in the present day. Azamoor was taken, in 1513, by the Portuguese, under the command of the Duke of Braganza. He added greatly to the strength of its fortifications, but a century later it was abandoned as worthless.

The walls are in comparatively good repair, and the place seemed better built, cleaner, and busier than most Moorish towns. We were received by a Moor, with whom Mr. Ford had business relations; but though he was civil and showed us about the place, he gave us no encouragement to remain there. Indeed it was clear, from the glances of the people, that they owed us no goodwill; and the boys were, as usual, troublesome. Azamoor is, in fact, a most fanatical place, and no Christian is allowed to pass the night therein.

The river, as it flowed by the town, appeared to be about one hundred yards wide; but its stream is deep, sluggish, and muddy, and its mouth so obstructed by sand-banks as to be unnavigable, except by boats. The effects of the tide are felt a long distance inland. At certain times the river overflows its banks, and, like the Nile, increases the fertility of the adjacent country.

The prosperity of Azamoor is greatly owing to the vast quantities of shebbel, a species of shad, which the river yields. These, when dried, are in great demand throughout the country. The fishing season extends from October to the end of April.

While waiting for the embarkation of our mules in the ferry-boat, a matter of no little difficulty, I shot a gull, which, on falling, was eagerly examined by the Moors. It happened that it did not bleed, and that no wounds were visible. These results excited great astonishment, and the worthy fellows were disposed to assign the death of the bird to magic, or to some sinister influence possessed by the European.

The view of the place from the opposite side of the river was the most perfect thing of the kind I ever saw. The rock upon which the town is built rose almost perpendicularly from the river's brink; while a castellated wall with turrets was extended along the edge of the cliff. Numbers of square houses, with a minaret here and there, were perched one above another on the sloping sides of the hill, and some fine palm-trees, inclined in different directions, relieved the stiffness of the formal and monotonous architecture. The whole scene was enriched and lighted up by the red glare of the sun sinking in the sea. It would have been difficult to find a fairer or more peaceful scene, overhanging a fine river, and commanding a most fertile but neglected country, than this nest of fierce fanatics.

From the river we proceeded through a country overgrown with palmettoes. Night soon set in, and with it a drizzling rain, so that it became suddenly dark. After a ride of only three-quarters of an hour we were compelled to take refuge at the house of the governor of the province. What, in some respects, this place was like I do not know, as we arrived in the dark and left in the dark; but in one respect it was only too forcibly impressed upon our minds. The room assigned to us was a better one than usual, and was well carpeted. Kuskussoo was sent us; and then, the usual amount of doctoring despatched, we tried to sleep. But no sooner did we lie down than a whole army of fleas issued from the carpet, and, after a vigorous onslaught, took bodily possession of us. To contend against them by anything like attention to a particular attack was wholly useless. We were bitten and run over everywhere—in a word, fairly vanquished. A description has been already given of a combined assault by a variety of vicious insect tribes; but this was essentially an encounter with fleas, supported by what may be termed a light cavalry corps of mosquitoes, which made incessant attacks wherever there was a chance of drawing blood. It is astonishing how habit, aided probably by a thick cuticle, seems to reconcile the inhabitants of these countries to such pests. A Moor of the better class, who lay beside us, laughed heartily at our misfortunes, assuring us that fleas were perfectly innocent bed-fellows, which gave him no trouble whatever. At length in despair we resolved to continue the journey. But no trifling difficulties interfered with this purpose. The castle gate was locked, and the key, we were told, had, as customary, been sent to the governor. To awaken the great man was out of the question. It was not only a thing unheard of, but one which would involve us all in trouble, and bring swift retribution to the guards in the shape of the dreaded bastinado. The whole was probably a ruse, for after much discussion the key was obtained, but how or whence from we did not stop to inquire nor care to discover. The Moorish passion for money prevailed here as elsewhere, and a key of silver opened the gate.

When we had resumed our journey, it was a little after one o'clock a.m., and from that hour till six a.m., when we made a stop for breakfast, we plodded through the darkness, led by our guide with marvellous dexterity. To realize his skill, it must be borne in mind that the mere bridle-path or trackway we followed had not only no fence of any kind, but it often became quite invisible in the great spaces covered with palmettoes and dwarf shrubs. An attack by robbers was not much thought about, because our movements had not been known beforehand, and that part of the country was not of bad repute. At all events, we considered it better to run some risk than remain to be eaten up alive at the palace.

The ride from Mazagan to the governor's house, not including stoppages, occupied eleven hours and a quarter, which made the distance about forty-five miles. From the governor's house to Casa Blanca is, by this calculation, fifty-seven miles.

CHAPTER XIII.

THE COUNTRY AND THE PEOPLE.

In the preceding chapters a good deal has been incidentally said about the natural history and productions of Marocco; and of the government, religion, and general habits of the people. In the succeeding chapters we propose to give supplementary sketches of the same subject, so as to convey to the reader a general notion of the country in its present state.

The Sultanate, or Empire of Marocco, known to its inhabitants as Maghrib-el-Aksa, or the extreme west, a country much larger than Spain, is situated between 28° and 36° of north latitude. Its superficial extent is calculated to be about 220,000 square miles. The three former kingdoms of Fez, Marocco, and Tafilet are included within its limits. The country is traversed throughout its whole extent from north-east to south-west by the immense range of the Atlas Mountains, which also sends off many lesser branches both towards the ocean and towards the desert. The valleys and plains intervening between these numerous mountain chains are watered by many rivers and smaller affluents. The principal rivers, placed in order from north to south, all of which flow into the ocean, are the Lucos, the Sebou, the Buregreg, the Oum-er-Rebiah, the Tensift, the Suz, the Noon, and the Draa. Very little is known of those in the south, but it is believed that none of the rivers of Marocco are navigable to any extent.

The twenty provinces which formed the kingdoms of Fez and Marocco occupy the northern and middle regions. The southern provinces which formed the kingdom of Tafilet are very imperfectly known, and are inhabited by a rude and fanatical population which scarcely acknowledges the sovereignty of the Sultan. The coast line of Marocco extends about 800 miles, 550 being on the Atlantic and 250 on the Mediterranean. The climate of Tangier in the north, and that of Mogador in the south, have already been spoken of at some length. It is enough to say here that the climate of the coast is, as a rule, tempered and refreshed by winds cooled by sea-breezes, while the summer temperature of the interior reaches a tropical heat.

There are several cities or large towns, besides a great number of small towns and villages. The principal cities lie inland, namely, Marocco, Mequinez, Fez, El Kassar, Wazan, Terodant, and others hardly known to the outside world. The chief maritime towns are Tetuan, Tangier, Larache, Rabat Salli, Casa Blanca, Azamoor, Mazagan, Saffi, and Mogador.

It is extremely difficult to form an estimate, even approximately, of a population scattered so unequally over an extensive area. In fact, the estimates vary from four to fifteen millions, and therefore it is best to set the calculation down at something between these figures. It is believed that the population has materially diminished since the sixteenth century. In some of the seaports, however, the number of inhabitants increases slightly, especially that of the Jews, who depend on commerce.

Excluding the negroes and the Jews, the eye of the traveller soon detects well-marked differences in the outward aspect of the people. Brown of various tints is the usual colour of the skin, and that of some individuals greatly resembles the rich tone of a well-smoked meerschaum pipe. Others are as light-coloured as the inhabitants of southern Europe. Albinoes are now and then seen. One whom we met at Saffi was a well-grown young man. His beard resembled snow in colour, and his skin presented a peculiar flat whiteness.

The difference in features and build is more striking than that of the colour of the skin. For although, for convenience, we have called all the brown-coloured inhabitants Moors, yet, properly speaking, these form only a section of the whole. Three distinct races are usually included under the name of Moors, namely, the Arabs, the true Moors, and the Berbers.

The Arabs, who are tent-dwellers and camel-breeders, came originally from the Sahara, over whose boundless wastes a large proportion of their race still wanders. The primitive custom of living in tents made of goats' hair still remains with these Arabs of Marocco, who inhabit all the country west of the Atlas Mountains as far down as Mogador. They are agriculturists; but one of the obstacles to the development of the country is their restless and quarrelsome nature. These Arab tribes are continually at war with each other. It is unhappily the policy of the Government, on account of its own weakness, to encourage these dissensions, in order to preserve the empire from more serious danger. Hospitality even towards an enemy seeking an asylum is one of the patriarchal virtues which the Arab still retains.

The Moors, a mixed race between Arab and Spaniard, are essentially townsmen; they are the degenerate descendants of that section of the Arab race which, in the eighth century, after establishing the powerful kingdom of Fez, overran a large portion of Spain. There with varying fortunes they remained till the fifteenth century, when they were finally expelled, but, as is well known, not without having largely contributed to the advancement of science, literature, and art in the country of their adoption. The language of the Moors of Marocco still bears testimony to this brilliant and long connexion of their ancestry with Spain. Many Spanish words are interspersed in the Arab dialect they speak.

The Moors and Arabs, thus springing originally from one race, differ mainly from each other only so far as the inhabitants of town differ from those of the country. The Moors, as might be expected, are a fairer race. Both are tall, well made, and capable of great fatigue. They are pleasing in manner; and many of them appear to be men of ability. But, as a rule, they are boastful, faithless as regards promises, and apt to mistake courtesy of manner and much civility on the part of a stranger as indications of fear.

The Moors fill the places under the Government, and, notwithstanding a great inferiority in numbers, possess more power than any of the other races. They are also much given to commerce, and have a good deal of wealth among them.

The Berbers are the descendants of the old Gaetulian stock by which this part of Africa was once populated. One division of the Berbers inhabits the Atlas Mountains to the north of the city of Marocco. They live for the most part in tents, and support themselves by husbandry. They also collect much wax and honey from their bees, and are great hunters.

The Berbers of the Riff province, in the north-eastern part of the Atlas range, are of lighter complexion than the other sections of their race. They are of middle size, but they are well knit, active, and possess a great power of endurance. They are a turbulent and aggressive people, constantly at war with their neighbours or among themselves. This unsettled and warlike spirit gives great trouble to the Government. Formerly the Riffians were noted pirates, but the vigilance of the European powers has freed the shores of the Mediterranean from dangers arising from this source. The greatest insult one Riffian can offer to another is in saying, "Your father died in his bed." No further evidence is needed than this of the sanguinary nature of the people. The Shilluh is another division of the Berber race, about which less is known than of the others. They inhabit the southern ranges of the Atlas Mountains and the country south of Mogador generally. They live mainly by husbandry, and are of more settled habits than their brethren. Walled towns take the place among them of the douar, or circle of tents. Their food consists chiefly of barley prepared in various ways. In person the Shilluhs are dark-complexioned and tall, and their hands and feet struck us as being smaller and better formed than those of the other races. Generally speaking, Moors and Arabs are alike clumsy about the ankles and feet. A tradition exists that the Shilluhs are in part derived from an intermixture of Portuguese lineage from the ancient colonies which existed on the coast. What gives colour to the statement is the fact that in a remote region of the Atlas Mountains, near Deminet, the ruins of a church containing a Latin inscription are still to be observed. The superstition of the people and the fear of Jinny or evil spirits have been the means of preserving these ruins. But from what is known of the tendency of crossed races to resort to the predominating type, it is very improbable, even assuming the intermixture, that the Portuguese element is at present discernible.

The Shilluh is quite a match for his neighbours in cunning as well as in warlike propensities. In the province of Sus and other places this race yields an obedience to the Sultan which is little more than nominal. The Shilluh women accompany the men in their tribal fights, and not only urge them on, but often fight themselves with ferocious courage. The Berber language, although originally similar, is now distinct from Arabic; it is extremely harsh and

guttural. The Shilluhs speak a dialect peculiar to themselves.

The women of all these races possess fine figures. The female peasantry are content with scantier robes than the women of the towns; and there are many among them that might sit as models to the most fastidious artist. Close seclusion and muffling of the face limit observation, but the traveller sees enough to convince him that the gift of beauty has not been withheld from the women of Marocco. The appearance of their eyes is enhanced by darkening the lids with kohl. The women of Mequinez are proverbially the most beautiful in the country. *Mekenzezal* is a term applied to any handsome woman. All the people known collectively as Moors have remarkably fine teeth.

Although capable of enduring great fatigue when induced by a sufficient object, the Moors are essentially inert and lazy. Not one of them would take a walk for walking's sake. They have a proverb which well expresses their views on this subject:—

> "Never sit when you can lie,
> Never stand when you can sit,
> Never walk when you can stand,
> Never run when you can walk."

Everywhere numbers of individuals are to be observed in whom the features and other physical characteristics of the negro race prevail more or less. The Mussulman doctrine of equality leads to this result, and for the same reason no social disadvantage is incurred by those who in any way betray their alliance, whether more or less, to the negro type. The late Emperor showed evident traces of black blood.

The negro population of Marocco is considerable, and a great proportion of them slaves. But the subject of slavery will be again referred to. The negro of this country is more sightly, and seems more intelligent than the west coast black. He is brought when a boy—rarely or never as an adult—from the far interior. But many of the blacks are descendants of those who have inhabited Marocco for many generations. A large number of the free negroes are enrolled in the boklary—the Sultan's black body-guard. These men enjoy certain privileges, and many aspire to the highest offices. The negroes of Marocco speak a language of their own, called Guenaoui.

The Jews of Marocco, about whom we have already said a good deal, are descended from those of their race who, expelled at various periods from European countries, found in part an asylum in that country. They are, however, mainly derived from the Israelites who were expelled from Spain in 1492, and from Portugal in 1496, and form at present a large and important section of the population; yet, considering their number and position, it is difficult to conceive why they bow their necks so submissively to the yoke, for they are browbeaten, despised, and treated with habitual harshness. This anomaly is the stranger for the reason that, in a certain sense, they are a dominant and powerful race. Love of gain, cunning, and self-interest teach them how to be indispensable to the Moors. In Marocco, as elsewhere, the Jew is a master of finance, and turns his knowledge to the best account.

Some of the highest places of trust are held by Jews. They farm the taxes and negotiate many matters of public business with the outside world. They live principally in the towns, where, as usual, they give themselves up to trade. Some branches they almost monopolize. They are butchers, bakers, silversmiths, engravers, tailors, shoemakers, and leather-workers; but never masons, blacksmiths, potters, sadlers, or curriers. As a rule, the Jew is comparatively fair-complexioned, and, when dressed as a European, would readily pass for one.

In the southern province of Sus the Jew is regarded as so indispensable to the prosperity of the country that he is not allowed to leave it. If he gets permission to go to Mogador to trade, it is only on condition that he leaves his wife and family, or some relation to whom he is known to be attached, as surety for his return.

The Moorish Jews follow the Portuguese ritual in respect to religion and its services. They are, as a rule, extremely ignorant and superstitious, and observe to the letter the precepts of the Talmud as interpreted by their rabbis. Through the cosmopolitan charity of their brethren abroad, noble exertions are now being made to rectify this state of things by educating the rising generation of Israelites. The Board of Deputies in London, acting in concert with the "Alliance Universelle" at Paris, have established schools at Tetuan, Tangier, Saffi, and Mogador, and the best results appear already. The late philanthropist, Sir Moses Montefiore, took much interest in this good and needed work.

The renegades consist almost entirely of convicts who have escaped from the Spanish penal establishments on the northern coast of Marocco, of Ceuta, Melilla, and from some smaller stations. There are a few French and Italians among them, but no British subjects, so far as we could hear. Most of the renegades are employed in the army, but the total number is inconsiderable.

The few Europeans in Marocco are entirely confined to the seaports, and are found especially at Tangier and Mogador. At Azamoor, Agadir, and some other coast towns there are no European residents. In point of numbers, the various races of Marocco may be ranged as follows: Berbers, Arabs, Moors, Negroes, and Jews. The last number, it is believed, about 100,000 souls.

Arrogance, the invariable sign and accompaniment of ignorance, is a prominent characteristic of the Moor. He believes himself and his nation to be superior to all the world. He recognizes the inventions and improvements made by Europeans, but it is the recognition of disdain. Railroads and telegraphs may be necessary to Europeans, but they are not necessary to *his* wants. As his fathers lived and died, so he desires to do. Nevertheless, we cannot help thinking that the day is not distant when the Moor, like the Turk, will open his country to foreigners; and that one of the last strongholds of conservatism will give way before the advance of enlightened opinion. The chief thing indispensable for the commencement and facilitation of this much-needed intercourse is the removal of restrictive duties upon articles of commerce. This freedom would at once stimulate productive energy and create resources, instead of inflicting, as is ignorantly apprehended, injury on the country and its people. But on all such matters conservatism has been always slow not only in comprehending but in introducing innovation. The lever of all others, which may just now be expected to act upon the Moor, is his desire to get money. His covetousness is an ancient byword. Whenever it becomes clear to him that the Kaffir and the introduction of the Kaffir's arts will be a source of direct gain, the believer, like other men, will tolerate and at length welcome innovation.

It must be owned that though we met with undeserved rudeness when placed in an unofficial and almost unprotected position in the city of Marocco, we otherwise received much courtesy and politeness from the higher class of educated Moors. When they choose, or when they think it their interest to be so, they are polite and communicative, and show more of good breeding than might be looked for. They are hospitable in the sense taught by a religion that, with all its faults, has many redeeming qualities. As a rule, when you have eaten of his salt the Mussulman regards you as a friend.

The Moorish nature is cruel, and insensible to suffering not personally experienced. The tortures inflicted by those in power, in the name of law, but frequently out of revenge or to extract money, will be referred to hereafter. The Moors do not even comprehend how any one can be interested in the sufferings of the lower animals. The mules' backs often become terribly sore in travelling, from the carelessness of the men in charge, and should the traveller or spectator insist that something should be done to relieve this or other suffering, it is effected with reluctance or ill-concealed derision. It is a common thing to see fowls tied by the legs, and of course head downwards, to the saddle; in this way the wretched birds are taken long journeys. On our objecting to this cruel custom the Moors laughed outright at our folly.

The Moors are notably a sensual people. Not content with the legal number of four wives, which some who can afford it have, they indulge in the possession of concubines, who live under the same roof; and vices of a worse kind are far from uncommon among them.

We were often struck with the extraordinary vivacity and inexhaustible spirits of many of the lower classes of Moors with whom a visitor to Marocco comes in contact. They are the Irishmen of Africa. As in the case of the Irish Celt, ages of oppression, misrule, and poverty, from which as yet the Moor has not emerged, have been insufficient to crush out a keen sense of humour and a tendency to see things from their comic side. Some of the Moors are also inimitable mimics. We have seen a fellow imitate the manners, gestures, and tone of voice of another in a way that made laughter perfectly irresistible.

The fundamental political idea of republics, that all men are equal at birth, prevails in Marocco. Every free man may aspire to the highest offices in the State, and nothing except official employment bestows rank. The man who has been a slave may aspire to be a bashaw, and the bashaw descends to a private station and poverty with far less feeling of degradation than we can understand. It is true that ability is not the only test of fitness for promotion, nor integrity the best means of retaining power. He that subserves readily and fully to the supreme will of the Sultan, and contributes most to the Imperial coffers at the expense of his unhappy countrymen, prospers best.

Slavery is a delicate subject to touch upon, unless with the foregone conclusion that it is to be mentioned only to be condemned. Of slavery considered in the abstract, although favourably regarded by the Koran, not a fair word can be said. Yet it must be borne in mind that the iron yoke and barbarities which we associate with the unhappy lot of the slave belong to a condition for which so-called Christian men of England and of America are responsible. If the greed of gain had not sanctioned the systematic perpetration of a tyranny unknown to the Moslem, little interest would nowadays be excited by the subject of Moslem slavery. To say the truth, much philanthropy has been expended upon it to little purpose.

The problem which the so-called followers of Christ kept steadily in view was, how to get the largest amount of work out of the slave, or human machine, consistent with health, or in other words, by continued labour. The one foul, selfish consideration of the owner was, how to wring the most profit out of the perpetual toil of flesh and blood which he considered his. Contrast this course with that taken by the followers of Mohammed. With them the slave is adopted into the family, and lives much on an equality with its other members. So far, at least, as the duties of religion are concerned, he is educated; he is well fed and clothed; and it can scarcely be said that he is worse off, or that he is as low in the scale of life as he would have been if left wild in his native solitudes. Some of the highest-placed men in Marocco, not excepting the Sultan himself, have negro blood in their veins. The slave is obliged to work for his master, but it is not labour of the same severe description as that to be seen on the West Indian sugar-cane plantation or an American cotton-field. If he is hired out he is usually obliged to give up the greater part of his earnings to his owner, but he is sometimes allowed to retain them; or else he contrives to appropriate a portion with which to purchase his freedom. We should say, relying on our own observation, that it would be difficult to find a happier or more contented set of people. All observers, indeed, admit that slaves, as a rule, are well treated in Marocco. If a slave be illtreated he can demand by law to be resold, and in such a case it sometimes happens that he obtains his freedom by getting a friend to become his purchaser. In very many instances slaves are so much attached to their owners that they refuse to be liberated. If a slave runs away it is in the power of his master to beat or to imprison him. In the street the passer-by sees young runaway slaves with manacles on their feet, but generally speaking the runaway slave is an incorrigible scamp.

Married couples owned by the same master are seldom separated, unless he is compelled by necessity to sell his slaves. This separation is the cruellest part of the system. As for the sale of children, it comes practically to much the same thing as putting freeborn children out to apprenticeship or service.

As all negroes are supposed to be Mohammedans, Jews and Christians are not allowed to hold slaves, for to serve any but true believers would be a degradation greater than bonds. But the law in this respect is often broken: a Moorish friend buys, in his own name, the slave for the infidel.

In all places of exile, whether they be African or American, the negro shows his joyous nature. In Marocco, during festivals, the negroes parade the streets playing on instruments peculiar to themselves; and this discordant jargon, singular to say, exerts upon them an effect of intoxication.

The number of slaves in Marocco is very large. In the houses of governors, and other rich Moors, many of both sexes are always to be found; and there are few Moors above the lowest rank who do not possess one or more. Slaves are brought by caravans to Marocco, and sold in exchange for salt and other commodities. They have usually travelled from Timbuctoo, to which place they have been conveyed from Bambarra and other places in the Soudan. It is to be feared that the capture of these slaves is attended by the same outrages as in other parts of Africa. For these and like atrocities no palliation is offered; it is only suggested that, when settled in Marocco, the slave is probably better off than when a free man beyond its borders.

As previously said, almost all the slaves imported are children, who soon fall into the ways of their masters. In Marocco city there is a slave-market, but in most other places slaves are led through the streets for sale by auction. They are generally paraded in this way for days prior to sale, attended by a crier, who makes known the particular characteristics and qualifications of each individual. A healthy well-grown boy or girl brings about £20; but we were offered a girl of twelve years of age, who had scrofulous tumours in the neck, for £4.

In the matter of dress, the national colour of Marocco is white. Men as well as women appear in flowing robes of this colour. The dress of the men consists of a finely worked shirt (kumja) fastened down the breast by numerous small buttons and loops, and of very loose drawers. Over this is sometimes worn a coat with large sleeves (caftan), buttoned closely in front. For outdoor wear the haik is indispensable. This garment is a wide piece of thin cotton, woollen, or occasionally silk material, wound around the body and also the head in a series of artistic folds, which, in our own case, rendered dressing without assistance an utterly hopeless process. Stockings are not used, and the feet are thrust into a pair of loose-fitting yellow slippers, to walk in which without fatigue the wearer must be to the manner born. A red fez cap is worn on the head, and round this a turban made of a many-folded length of thin muslin.

In cold or rainy weather a cloak of thick woollen material (jalabiyah) is worn instead of the haik. This has a pointed hood, which, placed over the head, gives the figure a cone-like appearance. When not in use this hood hangs down the back. The jalabiyah has holes for the arms to pass through, and descends low enough to cover the knees. Many of the poorer classes always wear the jalabiyah. Sometimes, and especially in the north of Marocco, the jalabiyah is of a dark colour. In this part jackets and loose trousers of cherry, or some other coloured cloth, are also a good deal worn, and striped materials in various textures are favoured by the Moors. The dress of the women is much the same as that of the men; but the haik is arranged differently, and is employed in concealing the features when any of the opposite sex are present. The hair is carefully covered by a handkerchief of black silk, over which another of gay colours is coquettishly arranged. The women wear red slippers, and these are often handsomely embroidered in gold. The ladies are very partial to jewellery. The wealthy wear finger-rings and huge earrings of gold set with precious stones, necklaces of amber or coral, massive bracelets of gold, armlets and anklets of silver inlaid with gold.

Diamonds are not much worn; but rubies, emeralds, generally uncut, and pearls of inferior quality are often seen. The Moors consider that the risk of fraud by imitation is lessened by not having precious stones submitted to the art of the lapidary. The Moorish and Jewish ladies are much given to the fictitious improvement of their charms by the use of rouge. Both also stain their hands and feet with henna, and blacken their eyelids with kohl. Tattooing is practised by the Moors alone.

Throughout the provinces of Marocco are a few water-mills[1] of a most primitive kind, for grinding corn, and in the large towns are a considerable number of corn-mills, each one turned by a horse; but the labour of grinding corn and preparing meal falls mainly on the woman. A small quern, or hand-mill, is

---

[1] As old, probably, as the Roman period. Mills of similar construction, and set amid Roman remains, are found in Syria and the East.

to be found in almost every dwelling. Good bread in the form of flat cakes is made and sold in the towns, but the national dish of Marocco is kuskusu. This resembles granulated maccaroni, and is palatable as well as highly nutritious. It is often cooked with pieces of meat, and butter is usually added, but the latter is, generally speaking, so rancid as to make the mess unendurable to Europeans, unless under the pressure of hunger.

There must be considerable art in the manufacture of kuskusu. The women make it by dexterously passing their hands, previously wetted with water, over a layer of flour placed in a tray; moistened particles are thus formed, which by the action of the fingers become granulated masses. These are constantly removed as the operation progresses. The granules are afterwards sifted in a sieve made of a sheepskin pierced with holes, and the larger masses rejected. When dried in the sun the kuskusu is fit for use. The granules vary in size, but are generally about as large as a mustard seed.

The use of steam in cooking is comparatively a recent improvement among ourselves; but, in the preparation of their national dish, the Moors from a remote period have employed this method. They use a double pot: the lower one, containing water, is placed on the fire, and in this meat or poultry is boiled; the upper pot fits on this, and the bottom being pierced with holes, admits steam to the kuskusu it contains.[2]

The Moors, as a nation, are fairly well fed. Food is abundant except in famine years, when locusts or a drought destroys the crops. Many of them scarcely ever eat meat. Cakes of barley-meal are the staple food of the poorer classes; and if to these they are able to add butter-milk, they are considered fortunate. The Moor never puts aside the remnant of a meal,—it is given to his poorer neighbours; but except among the Jews there is little actual want. Maize is largely used, and wheat by those who can afford it. For some years previous to our visit, cows had not been killed on account of the scarcity of horned cattle. Mutton and fowls are the chief articles of animal food. Camels are killed and eaten only when the animals are hopelessly injured.

To be a guest at a Moorish dinner-party is somewhat trying to the uninitiated. There are no chairs, tables, knives, forks, nor spoons. The company sit in a circle, cross-legged, on the floor. Sometimes, indeed, an apology for a table, a few inches in height, is placed in the centre.

---

[2] See, on this subject, "Pillars of Hercules," by David Urquhart, vol. i. p. 398. London, 1850. A truly philosophical work.

Upon this, or on the floor, a huge case made of straw sewn together and decorated with coloured leather-work, is placed. A conical cover of the same material fits over the case, and when the former is removed, a wooden bowl or tub filled with kuskusu is displayed. Before eating, every one says grace for himself by exclaiming, "Bismallah!" "In the name of Allah!" Each person then thrusts the fingers of his right hand into the smoking mess, and, taking up a considerable quantity, forms it into a sort of ball or lump, and then by a clever jerk tosses it into his mouth, which the serving hand is not allowed to touch. The left hand is never used in eating. Once it happened that a Moor who dined in our company paid an attention which would gladly have been dispensed with. Taking a piece of mutton out of the kuskusu, and using but one hand, he slowly manipulated it between his fingers till fat and lean were separated. He then presented the delicate morsel to our mouth, which, though unwillingly, we had to take as a matter of politeness. It must, however, be borne in mind that the Moors wash their hands before beginning to eat, and do not touch the mouth in eating. From all this it will be seen that the etiquette of the Moorish dinner-table is quite as exacting as the corresponding etiquette among ourselves. After each meal, water and napkins are brought for the hands.

We have already described some of the amusements of the Moors. Military exercises, or powder play, on foot or on horseback, are popular. They have also games of leap-frog, leaping, and football, played by kicking up the ball without any reference to a goal. Mention has been made of the story-tellers and jugglers. Some of the best jugglers come from Sus, and it is curious to observe among a rude people the performance of tricks and artifices such as the best European masters of legerdemain could hardly equal.

The dances of the Moorish girls, who hire themselves out for exhibition, are similar to those which we had seen in Egypt and other parts of the East. They consist more in posture and movement of the feet without raising them, than in what is called dancing. To say the least, these performances are anything but decorous.

Every one knows that the Eastern nations prefer fatness to leanness. The Indian baboo adds to his corporeal development, as well as to his importance, by swallowing an unlimited quantity of glue. In Marocco, the taste for obesity principally affects the fair sex. Ladies must be fat, for such is the will and pleasure of their lords and masters. Mussulman and Jew are on this point alike unanimous. Both are great admirers of the female figure; but in their eyes the Venus de Medici, or the Venus of Milo, would have been far from perfect. They sigh for much fuller charms than even Rubens would have looked for in his models.

As soon as a young girl is engaged, it at once becomes her mamma's duty to fatten her if she is thin, and, if already plump, to increase this plumpness duly. A certain reticence is observed about all this; but the whole mystery was kindly revealed to us by a Jewish lady of Mogador, who was our patient. The system may be fairly called anti-Bantingism, as the food is made to consist largely of fat-producing elements. The crumb of large loaves, made expressly for the purpose, is moulded by the fingers into great pellets, rather thicker and nearly as long as the human thumb. These are called *harrabel*, and in shape they resemble conical cannon shot, except that they are double cones. From forty to fifty of these are swallowed, by the aid of a little tea or infusion of thyme, after the mid-day meal; and this process is repeated at bedtime. Literally speaking, the operation is one of cramming, differing only from that employed in fattening poultry by its being voluntary. The *modus operandi* consists in pressing the big solid mass down the gullet with the fingers as far as possible, so that the act of swallowing must necessarily follow. At first there is, as a general rule, great repugnance to the process, with subsequent feelings of indigestion. But it was stated to us that habit soon set both points

right, and no inconvenience was experienced.
Twenty days of cramming is considered a fair
course. By the end of this time, if the general
health is good, the increase of *embonpoint* is
very obvious. If necessary, the course is now
prolonged; and some women, whose tendency
is to fall away, have recourse to it at certain
intervals of time. El helba, *fenugreek* seeds, are
also much used by women for inducing fatness.
The high estimation in which obesity is held by
the men seems not only to have a great moral
effect upon the women, but to make them
disregard the trouble of the fattening process.
There is no subject about which they are more
jealous than that of fatness. If Mrs. A., although
an Israelite, partakes of the nature of Pharaoh's
lean kine, she regards with intense envy, and
consequently hatred, the broad expanse and duck-
like movements of Mrs. B. Now, since fatness
is a question of degree, and no woman *can* be
too fat, even one fairly well favoured in this
respect may be eclipsed and rendered wretched
by the knowledge that among her friends or
acquaintances is a monster of nature or art, or of
both combined. Thus, in Mogador there was a
lady of such immense proportions, that when
she took an outdoor walk—an event of rare
occurrence—it was necessary to have a strong
man on either side, so as to support her as she
moved, and to lift her when she wished to rise;

and a third man, carrying a chair, formed part of the procession. On this, in the open street, she sat down groaning at short intervals, and the difficulties attending the raising up and propelling onwards this cumbrous mass of human flesh were ludicrous in the extreme.

There was nothing in Marocco we tried more to avoid than the customary tea-parties, both on account of their effects and the loss of time. Tea is the dissipation of the country, and is indulged in at all times of the day. By this habit many of the Moors impair their health. Unfortunately, it is contrary to etiquette to refuse tea, as it used to be in England to refuse wine when your host called upon you to refill your glass. Tea has been known to the Moors for a long period, and it is curious to find this exotic beverage in such universal use. They are great connoisseurs, and will only drink fine green tea, which makes the practice all the more injurious to the nerves of a stranger. It is imported from England, and sells in Marocco at from four to six shillings a pound. The equipage in which it is served is often elegant and costly—the tea-pot among the wealthy being of silver; and the cups, which are always shaped like those used in England for coffee, are sometimes fine specimens of Oriental or European porcelain. Usually, however, tea is taken in small footless glasses adorned with gilding, and of German manufacture.

The tea is washed before it is infused, and a great quantity of sugar is put into the teapot. It is, in fact, a syrup; and it might be supposed that people so particular about flavours as are the Moors would find such excessive sweetness objectionable. Yet, what is more extraordinary still, they endeavour apparently to suppress the delicate tea flavour altogether. Tea has to be taken in regular course, impregnated with different flavours, which are all more or less disagreeable to the novice. The order may vary; but from the numerous opportunities we had of judging, the following seemed the rule in "the best circles." First there was a round of plain green tea with no addition but sugar. Milk or cream was never used. Then came a second course, in which spearmint was infused—a horrible compound. Third, an infusion of tea with wormwood, not quite so objectionable. Fourth, one flavoured with lemon verbena. Fifth, one with citron. Sixth, and more rarely, as being an expensive luxury and intended as a great compliment, tea with a little ambergris scraped into it, which could be seen floating like grease on the surface. Of this the flavour, if peculiar, was not disagreeable. Each course of tea was taken while very warm, and with a loud smacking noise of the lips; nothing, meanwhile, was eaten.

As time is of no value to the Moor, many hours are consumed at a sitting. The tea-party is frequently held in the open air, often in a garden under the shade of lofty trees. Here carpets are spread by the servants, who also light a fire and boil the water for tea. At these parties politics —as far as may be done with safety—are discussed, and the retail of gossip is an invariable and important business. Tea and gossip, proverbially associated, are supposed to belong exclusively to the fair sex, but in the country of the Moors the turbaned squatters seem equally masters of the situation.

We saw and heard less of the effects of kief than we had expected.[3] This intoxicating drug is prepared from hemp, which Marocco produces in greater perfection than any other country. Now and then a Moor may be seen drawing those few puffs from a miniature pipe which are sufficient to induce the dreamy condition, so plainly visible in his drooping, purposeless eyes. But as a rule this kind of smoking is done in private, and, as far as we could learn, the practice, as also that of eating hashish, a confection made with kief, are not injurious to health. We made trial of this confection, and can bear testimony to the remarkable mental phenomena it induces.

The Moors are not a nation of tobacco smokers, yet the practice is indulged in by many. A long pipe is used, but the nargily or water-pipe of the Turk is, we believe, unknown to them. In some

[3] See Appendix C.

parts Spanish cigarettes are largely smoked. Snuff-taking is also much in vogue. Some snuff which was made for us in the city of Marocco was of good quality. In making snuff powdered walnut-shells and the ashes of the broom plant are mixed with the tobacco. The Jews are very fond of mahaya, a weak, colourless spirit flavoured with aniseed. This spirit seems to be made from almost any fermentable material; for they use indifferent grapes, pomegranates, figs, or dates; and at Mogador and other places whence wax is exported, mahaya is largely made from water in which honeycombs have been boiled. The distillation of this spirit is conducted in the rudest manner, for we witnessed the process at Casa Blanca. The condenser consisted of an old gun-barrel, while the water into which the lower end was plunged, in order to cause condensation, was allowed to become too hot for the hand to bear. So much for the science and manufactories of Marocco. The Jews also make wine, but it does much injustice to the splendid grapes grown in the country. Their method is this: they boil down the fresh juice to about half its original bulk. This, after being kept for some days, is mixed with unboiled juice and allowed to ferment. The product is a dark sweet liquid, somewhat resembling inferior Malaga wine. Another kind is also made, which is not unlike poor claret.

The Jews will not drink sherry, and their sapient reason for this is that the Virgin is invoked to pour out her blessings on the Spanish vineyards.

CHAPTER XIV.

GOVERNMENT, LAW, AND MILITARY POWER.

The throne of Marocco has been long hereditary in a family of the Cherifs of the Fileli, as the inhabitants of Tafilet are called. But it is hereditary in a more extended sense than we understand by that term. The reigning Sultan may choose his successor, as indeed he generally does; nevertheless, not only a son, but a brother, uncle, or nephew of the sovereign may claim the throne, and success will depend on the claimant's popularity, and this, in turn, on his wealth, or rather on his power of disposing of his wealth. Thus a new Sultan is almost always obliged to squander his predecessor's hoarded treasure.

The title to the throne is, it is considered, established when the Sultan has been proclaimed as such at Fez by a council of the priests and principal personages of that city. Other communities then follow the example of the northern capital, by sending written acts of submission to the new order of things. But such distant and important centres as Marocco, Tafilet, and Terodant too often resist the decision of the Fez assembly, and the country becomes plunged in civil strife.

The late Sidi Mohammed Abderahman (our Lord Mohammed, son of Abderahman,) was the thirty-fourth lineal descendant of Ali, nephew and son-in-law of the prophet. He died September 17th, 1873, and was succeeded by his son Muley Hassan, who to the present hour has been engaged in establishing his rights to the throne by the sword.

The Sultan of Marocco is the recognized head of the Mohammedans of the West. But this temporal recognition is limited by his power of enforcing it. A very large proportion of the country nominally embraced within the empire, including all the Atlas Mountains and the province of Sus, is either almost or altogether independent of his authority.

We have little to say about the Court of Marocco, as we had no opportunity of visiting it. The Sultan gives audiences while on horseback, the persons presented to him standing at a respectful distance. There are some curious points of court etiquette, as, for instance, the word *death* must never be spoken, nor the subject referred to, in the Sultan's presence. Still more curious is the objection to the word *five;* every one must scrupulously abstain from uttering it in the Sultan's hearing; it is also considered to be a mark of ill-breeding to mention the objectionable word in the presence of any superior. To avoid doing so, the Moors say "four and one." The word *nine* is also objected to. We have spoken elsewhere of the cabalistic power attributed to five fingers rudely painted on doors, tombstones, etc. The Sultan resides alternately, for two or three years at a time, in Fez, the northern, and in Marocco, the southern capital. Thrice a day, with the exception of Friday, the Mussulman Sabbath, the Vizier or Prime Minister, secretaries, and other high functionaries, meet at the palace. All the affairs of state are then inquired into and decided upon by the Vizier in the Sultan's name. The power of this minister, acting for the Sultan, is apparently absolute; for in the councils held the inferior ministers offer no opinion unless invited to do so; their function being to execute decrees and carry out, with blind and passive obedience, the orders they receive. But although the Sultan's rule thus appears to be absolute, it is scarcely so in fact, as the ministers he chooses commonly obtain a share of power sufficient to control the source from which it is derived.

Besides these ministers at court, there is a Minister for Foreign Affairs, who lives at Tangier. He represents the Sultan's Government in dealing with the various representatives of foreign governments, all of whom reside in that town. There is also a commissioner, whose duty it is to visit, at stated times, the various ports, and there take cognizance of all commercial disputes between Europeans and natives. Next in rank to the officials who form the supreme Government follow the governors of provinces.

In many instances these men hold their posts by hereditary descent. But their tenure of power is, nevertheless, entirely at the will of the Sultan. Whenever the tribute money of a province is not considered sufficient, its unhappy governor is ordered to court. If his explanations relative to the presumed deficit are not considered to be satisfactory, he is imprisoned, and perhaps tortured, to force him to give up his concealed wealth. Meantime, his son or some near relative is appointed to govern in his place, and if money be not soon forthcoming it fares hard with the wretched prisoner, even if he is permitted to survive.

The governors of towns hold a lower position. They are generally chosen from the military class, and their pay is only nominal. They extract as much as they can out of the citizens, and are themselves expected to make presents to the Sultan. If these fail to be made, the governors are soon put out of office.

The sheikhs act under the governors of provinces and collect the taxes from the people, whom they screw as much as possible. In fact the whole system of collecting the public revenue brings forcibly to mind the nursery ditty about the "dog that worried the cat, that worried the rat," etc., etc. There are fixed imposts, but under various pretexts the scale is habitually set aside. Fines are levied at discretion, and under all sorts of pretences. If a quarrel arises and blood is shed, the aggressors are sometimes deprived of half their property for having broken the peace. If a robbery is committed, the whole *douar* is fined double the amount plundered, one half of which is given to the person who has been robbed, and the other half to the bashaw of the province. It must, however, be admitted that these exactions have their utilitarian aspect—that of tending to the security of life and property in such wild regions.

The sources of revenue are briefly as follows:— A tax of ten per cent. on corn and agricultural produce in general, and two per cent. on all domestic animals; the tax on shebbel, the fish which abound in the rivers, the monopoly of tobacco and hashish, and the poll-tax on the Jews. A duty of ten per cent. is also levied on all goods exported and imported. The gate duty is a tax levied on every camel-load of goods which enters any city or town. Moreover, the

Sultan is the legal claimant to the property of all his subjects who die without heirs. To this must be added the large amount received as tribute or presents. Every man who possesses considerable power is liable to be supplanted by the intrigues of others. The only safeguard lies in the frequency and extent of the additions made voluntarily to the imperial coffers.

The provincial governors have the law very much in their own hands. Nominally the Sultan retains the power of life and death, but practically this restriction is a dead letter. For though a governor cannot order decapitation, it is in his power to have as many strokes of the stick or leather thong inflicted as he thinks proper. There are frequently cases of persons who by this method are legally executed. Situated in most instances at a distance from the central Government, these arbitrary rulers indulge the promptings of revenge and cruelty with perfect impunity. The Sultan requires of them ample contributions to his treasury, and, provided these are made, their acts are not scrutinized. Certain laws are, however, well defined and rigorously enforced. One of these is the *lex talionis*, that which exacts an eye for an eye, a tooth for a tooth, a life for a life, unless the bodily injury to the person, or his death, is expiated by the payment of a fine to the nearest of kin. Instances have occurred in which Europeans have become involved in the action of this law. Many years ago, Mr. Leyton, an English merchant residing at Mogador, was accused by an old mendicant of having knocked out two of her teeth by striking her with his whip while out riding. Although she was known to be toothless, her complaint made so much noise in the town that the governor before whom it was brought was obliged to report it to the reigning Sultan, for Mr. Leyton steadily refused to pay any compensation. In consequence of this, the Sultan, by the hand of one of his ministers, wrote and requested him to yield; but not succeeding, the merchant was summoned to Marocco. Mr. Leyton obeyed, but on arriving there he still obstinately refused to pay any fine. Thereupon popular clamour increased to such a degree that, as a matter of state policy, a penalty had to be enforced, and Mr. Leyton submitted to the extraction of two of his teeth. But the injustice of his case was tacitly acknowledged, for on his return to Mogador he was, by order of the Sultan, presented with two shiploads of grain.

A few years ago the following result of the law of blood occurred at Mogador. A young man killed his brother under circumstances admitting of great palliation in Moorish eyes. The step-sister of the deceased, as next-of-kin, refused every offer of compensation, and demanded the life of the culprit, as she was entitled to do by the precepts of the Koran. Her relatives and friends made their entreaties in vain. The public authorities threw every possible obstacle in the way to prevent the accomplishment of this diabolical purpose. Years passed away, and yet the bloodthirsty, vindictive woman did not relent; at last she made her way to the presence of the Sultan, and he, in accordance with the law, but with reluctance, granted her request. The order went forth, and the unhappy man was seized and executed. The woman was present at the execution, and marked her triumph by dancing before her victim. According to a late treaty, Europeans are exempted from the operation of the law now described.[1]

The Koran is the source of all Mohammedan law. It is, therefore, hopeless to expect reforms so long as the law is administered by true believers. In this lies one great obstacle to national progress. A system of jurisprudence, adapted to the life and habits of the wild tribes of Arabia in the seventh century, is still rigidly adhered to. Yet owing to the small advance made in that long interval of

---

[1] I cannot personally complain of the exactions of the Moors on account of a bodily injury. It is true the one in question was slight—slighter, perhaps, in the estimation of the man injured than in my own. When shooting in the neighbourhood of Saffi, in company with Mr. Hunot, some shot glanced off the ground and struck a Moor who was riding in front. Two of the grains penetrated the lower lip. The wounds bled freely, yet the man took the matter good-humouredly, and was content to accept a dollar in full acquittance of all claims, present and to come.

time, and considering how closely the modern Arab resembles his ancestors in past ages, the result on the whole is not so unfavourable as might be expected. Let us look at home for what sacerdotal law might be among ourselves if enforced to the letter. Who, for instance, are the strongest and most persistent advocates of capital punishment, and desire to avenge blood by blood? It is doing the clergy no wrong when we say that they, as a body, maintain the enforcement of the Mosaic law. In like manner the followers of Mohammed can see no necessity for altering the law of capital punishment, so as to fit it to the visible results of lapse of time and change of circumstances. Thus, as usual, dogma and progress are unalterably opposed. In the application of their savage law to the punishment of crime, the Moors act consistently. Does it ever occur to the advocates of capital punishment that, if life is to be taken for life, by the same reasoning, and as a logical sequence, an eye should be blinded for the malicious destruction of an eye, or, in like manner, a limb be amputated for a limb? yet from such barbarities even the advocates of the scaffold would recoil.

The sanctuary, *zawizah*, is an extraordinary institution which, in bygone days, had its counterpart among ourselves. In Marocco a refuge of this character is to be found almost everywhere within easy reach. In some cases sanctuaries are included in cities; in others they form a part of large spaces outside the walls, yet adjoining them, as in the case of Saffi; and in the rural districts numerous saint-houses serve a like purpose. Yet, whatever be the size, description, or situation of the privileged place, the criminal who gains its precincts is, for a time, perfectly safe. The executive has no power therein; and the culprit, while there, is subject solely to its distinctive laws and rules.

If a man who has committed murder takes refuge in a sanctuary, he is unmolested as long as the negotiations between his friends and the prosecutor, who is always the next-of-kin, continue; but if the blood-money offered in recompense be considered insufficient, or if the friends of the murdered man will not accept it, a summary procedure is adopted. The prosecutor, exercising his right, demands that guards be placed over the criminal, and by these he is prevented from obtaining food or drink. A few days of such discipline compels the culprit to go outside the boundary, and there he is at once arrested.

In so despotic a country as Marocco sanctuaries serve a useful purpose in allowing leisure for the investigation of crimes. The protection they afford prevents hasty judgments and summary executions in numerous instances in which justice would be outraged. On the other hand, their powers are abused by the prevalent bribery and corruption.

Akin to the barbarous law of like for like, is that which punishes the bodily member for the crime of which it has been the instrument. Thus a common punishment for theft is the loss of the right hand. For this reason it is not uncommon to see one-handed Moors. The hand is chopped off at the wrist, and the bleeding stump plunged into boiling pitch to arrest bleeding. Prior to the plan introduced by the famous Ambrose Paré, of tying arteries after amputation, this was the method followed in Europe.

A severe punishment, on the same principle, is sometimes inflicted for libel. The lips and mouth of the offender are rubbed with capsicum pods, until an almost insupportable smarting, followed by inflammation, is produced. We knew a Moor at Mogador who was accused of speaking ill of a governor living in the neighbourhood. He was enticed some distance outside the town and there beset by his pretended friends, who so effectually peppered him that the wretched man suffered from the effects for several weeks.

Another instance of this kind of punishment occurred recently at Saffi. Two women, who enjoyed a reputation as vocalists, sang at the house of an official personage what might be called a topical song, in which the propensities of certain people in power were referred to. Another official who was present took offence at some expression it contained. Concealing his anger, he in turn invited the women to his house and requested them to repeat the song. They complied, with the result that they were at once seized, imprisoned, and bastinadoed. In addition, they were rubbed with capsicum pods as already described, from the effects of which atrocious acts the poor creatures suffered frightfully.

But the bastinado is the most common of all punishments. Every governor and every kadi has the power to order an unlimited number of stripes. The Turk says, "The stick is the gift of Heaven," and in this appreciation of its merits the Moor agrees entirely with him. No rank, not even that of governor of a province, gives exemption, if the Sultan orders the infliction. The punishment is so common as to leave no sense of degradation. The instrument in general use, which is attached by a loop to the wrist of the operator, is a double thong of twisted leather, about three feet long, and nearly as thick as the little finger. The culprit, placed face downwards on the ground, is held securely by four men, while the blows are inflicted on the back. When women are bastinadoed they are made to sit in a basket out of which the feet project. These are secured to a pole, and the soles receive the stripes. The punishment to either sex is very severe; but as there is no evil without some compensation, it is seriously affirmed in Marocco that the bastinado has a fattening effect; and that cases have been known of wretches who, having been previously thin, became very stout soon afterwards. Several instances were mentioned to us in which severe application of the bastinado had been followed by obesity. One remarkable case was that of a person of note known to us in the city of Marocco. From a lean man he became, soon after the infliction of this punishment, very stout. The bastinado is given not only as a punishment for crime, but as a means of extorting confession of guilt. For the same purpose, as also for extracting money, an infamous mode of torture is sometimes employed. It consists in placing the person in a box, called facetiously the "wooden jelabee," or cloak. It is only large enough to receive the prisoner in a sitting posture, and the four sides being stuck over with sharp nails, all rest is effectually prevented. Persons have been submitted for months to this cruel ordeal, and in some instances it has been continued until release has only come through death. Another torture, often employed, is that of keeping a man chained against a wall by means of an iron collar round his neck. His arms are secured in an extended position, so he is obliged to stand on tiptoe to avoid strangulation. Indeed, the variety and cruelty of the tortures appear to be solely limited by the ingenuity of the torturers; and the unhappy ex-governors of provinces who have amassed wealth are, as already said, frequent victims.

It is almost impossible to exaggerate the horrors of Moorish prisons. Their condition, in several instances, has been already described. In some cases they are dungeons excavated deeply in the earth; in others, vaulted spaces above ground; but in every instance they are unventilated, dark and most dismal chambers, devoid of needful accommodation, and, consequently, reeking with fetid odours. In some of them several hundred persons are confined together. They are heavily chained, and sleep on mats spread on the floor. The mortality in these prisons must be enormous. It is only surprising that prisoners and keepers are not invariably swept off altogether and at once, by that fatal sickness known as gaol fever, once so prevalent in this country, and the natural result, as in Marocco, of overcrowding, stagnant filth, and need of ventilation.

Prison life has also been described, while referring to the prisons in the city of Marocco. Many of the prisoners are supported by alms. Happily the Mohammedan religion inculcates charity, not only as a commendable virtue, but as necessary for salvation.

We were told by an English merchant that he once had a Moor imprisoned for debt. At the end of two months he visited him in prison, and was then so shocked at the miserable state of the wretch, who was not only emaciated, but covered with vermin, that he went immediately to the governor and obtained the prisoner's discharge. Yet, true to the Moorish character, the man neither thanked the merchant nor paid the debt.

The *shraa* or Mohammedan civil law is administered by the kadis assisted by the adools, who act as attorneys and public notaries. This *shraa* is derived from the Koran, and under it Europeans who have legal disputes with Moors are placed at a great disadvantage. The pleadings are conducted in writing, and certain fees are paid to officials. But no secret is made of the fact that sums of money, in proportion to the magnitude of the case, are bestowed on the kadis in order to influence their decisions. In a Moorish lawsuit the judicious use of a long purse is more influential in obtaining a desired verdict than the truth or justice of the cause. In civil suits in which Europeans are concerned various difficulties arise; for, in addition to the irreconcilable hatred entertained against them, Christians are generally debarred from bribing the kadis, through fear of exposure. To be known to have taken a bribe from a Kaffir would involve any kadi in certain ruin. Thus it happens that, being paid by one side only, he is advocate as well as judge; and, more frequently than not, he interferes in the drawing out of the documents, so as to make it impossible for the European to prove his case. Moreover, while in the adool, or notarial evidence, every facility is afforded to the believer, all sorts of restrictive rules are enforced in the case of Europeans.

What justice can be looked for in a country in which, with a single exception, that of the administrator of customs, no official, whether he be judicial or administrative, is paid, except it may be in a nominal way, by the State? for the judges must be corrupt, and the governors and other people in authority speculative and extortionate, in order to exist. Although the Jews are subject to the general laws of the country, they are allowed to settle their civil disputes according to their own *shraa*, which accords with the Mosaic law. In this they possess a great advantage; for, according to Mohammedan law, neither Christian nor Jew has, in legal matters, any *locus standi*. In taking evidence their oath is not received, and the presumption is always in favour of the true believer. The Jewish civil law is administered by the priests, acting in concert with the elders of the community. These find means to execute their decisions by threatening excommunication and other modes of degradation.

The day is gone by for ever when the mere lust of conquest or greed for territorial empire can, as regards England, cause uneasiness to the Moorish Government. At one time, it is certain, France contemplated adding Marocco to her adjacent Algerian possessions. But the difficulties which would attend conquest—first the nature of the country, and next the fierce fanaticism of the people—presented obstacles before which the ruler of France prudently recoiled. Spain would have gladly revived the glories of a past time, had that been possible, when she undertook to punish some affronts offered to her flag, with results hardly satisfactory. In that war the Moors made the fatal mistake of meeting the Spaniards in open field. Whenever this occurred, the precipitous valour of horse and foot was expended in vain against the serried ranks of the foe. The error of the Moors lay in the traditionary dash of cavalry against large masses of infantry, accompanied by wild cries and wilder firing. Their fire-arms were imperfect, and their want of artillery was another great cause of defeat. In relation to warfare, as in all else, the Moors have much to learn. They need modern weapons, and, still more, instruction, drill, and discipline. They have many qualities which go far towards making good soldiers; and if their cavalry could be regarded and used as mounted riflemen, a force of immense value, on account of its rapid movements, would be the result. In case of invasion, every ridge, hill, and defile with which the roads leading from the coast to the interior are flanked, could be lined by an array of men unseen by an advancing foe till too late. In such a case the result would not be favourable to the invaders. This, at least, is our conviction, after seeing much of a country admirably fitted by nature for a guerilla method of warfare. The material, as regards men, is excellent. They are patient and obedient, easily roused by religious enthusiasm, fond of fighting, and inured to hardship. But to ensure the integrity and permanence of the Moorish Empire, internal reforms, such as those connected with the levying of taxes, are greatly needed. Were these carried out, productive industry would be encouraged, instead of discouraged as at present. No race is more desirous of possessing property than this. But the numerous examples of calamities resulting from possession of wealth, beget indifference to industry. Under a wiser and healthier system of taxation, the immense resources of the country would be speedily developed, and population increased. As a natural result improvement would soon be shown in the returns to the Imperial Exchequer. Other reforms would be requisite, and might be expected to follow. The Government should abandon its policy of isolation, and, like the Japanese, boldly enter the comity of nations. Intercourse with the outer world, although attended by some drawbacks, would introduce new ideas, and the comforts and decencies of life would be accepted and regarded. If, in addition to this, the hot zeal of religion could be tempered by consideration for the temporal welfare of the people, even if to no greater extent than that at present seen in the governing policy of Turkey, the whole aspect of Moorish society would rapidly undergo a most beneficial change. The languishing, but not yet stamped out genius of the Moor, of which traces are still visible in many a ruin in his own country, and still more frequently in that neighbouring land which he so long held against all comers, would revive. Trade would rapidly increase on the removal of those restrictions by which it is at present oppressed, and the wealth of the people would augment proportionately.

These combined reforms would speedily render Marocco the strongest of existing Moslem states as regards the possibility of foreign invasion. For, beside those internal features of the country already mentioned, the great extent of coast without harbours, and the dangerous surf which fringes the land, form a natural barrier against the landing of troops. Under such physical conditions, no navy would be required for coast service, while such pier and harbour works as the development of trade might demand could be effectually fortified.

The isolated position of Marocco is another great feature in its favour. Its rugged hills and fertile plains, except in themselves, are of no value to the invader. Whenever these hills and plains have been traversed, the arid desert invariably stops the way. The country thus can never be a coveted highway to lands more favoured, regarding which the cupidity of nations might be excited, and it possesses no city which, by its position, might form the key to empire. Compact, self-contained, with ample space for development into a first-class power, Marocco has nothing to lose or to dread from the stranger, but everything to gain.

The army of Marocco is far from contemptible. As regards the number and quality of the men which form it something has been already said. It consists of the regular troops, almagazen, or the Sultan's soldiers, and the soldiers of the bashaws, or militia.

The almagazen are reckoned at about 16,000 men, of which half are cavalry. These troops are armed and clothed at the Sultan's expense, and when on service receive as pay about sixpence a day. When not actively employed, this stipend falls to about eight shillings a month. Besides this pay, they receive many favours at the hand of the sovereign, who counts especially on their fidelity. Whenever Europeans travel in Marocco, they are always accompanied by an escort drawn from these troops by the consul of the port at which the stranger has disembarked, or at which he has otherwise arrived. The escort is responsible for the safety of its charge, and, as previously explained, this makes travelling alone possible. For these services the soldiers are well paid by their employers. The Sultan attempted the organization of a body of troops on the European model. Four thousand men were drilled and equipped by the aid of European officers; but the system was so entirely opposed to the traditions and habits of the people, that the plan did not succeed.

The inhabitants of all large towns, with the exception of Jews and slaves, who are capable of bearing arms, are enrolled under the standard of their respective governors. These troops form the militia, or national guard, and their ordinary duties are confined to their own districts. It is thus easy to conceive that when these local troops in time of war are mobilized, a very considerable force can be thrown into the field. And notwithstanding all the disadvantages of want of discipline, efficient arms, and artillery, the Moors are capable of stout resistance, as the events of the short Spanish war of 1859-60 sufficiently proved. That campaign cost the Spaniards nearly three millions sterling, and, at the lowest estimate, the lives of 15,000 men from loss in battle and disease. Moreover, after the fall of Tetuan, an event which terminated the war, it was found that to make that town the base of future operations, and to hold the small addition of territory acquired, would require the presence in Marocco of 20,000 men. From such heavy responsibility Spain wisely withdrew. She contented herself with the exaction of a large sum towards payment of the expense of the war. To raise this, a loan was contracted in England, since which time the interest thereon has been punctually paid by the Sultan's governments. A good many of the artillerymen stationed in the batteries throughout the country are Spanish renegades. The Moorish vavy which in former years was respectable, both as to number and equipment of vessels, has now entirely disappeared. A few brigs and gunboats lie rotting at Salee, where the principal dockyard and arsenal were situated. But these relics of a maritime power which no longer exists are fast yielding to decay.

CHAPTER XV.

EDUCATION—RELIGION—SUPERSTITIONS—THE HEALING ART.

EDUCATION, such as it is amongst the Moors, belongs almost exclusively to the male sex. It is very rare to meet a woman who can even read.

Boys are sent to school very early, and by a liberal allowance of the stick are forced to learn the Koran by heart, and to write a little. The *taleb*, or schoolmaster, receives a *mozouna*, less than a halfpenny, every Thursday; and two *okeas*, or threepence a month, besides, from each pupil. Presents of corn or fowls are also usually given by the parents. When a certain amount of progress has been made, the pupil is mounted on a horse, led in triumph through the streets, and proclaimed Bachelor of the Koran. If he desires further instruction he is admitted into a *madrasah*, or college, where he learns the elements of arithmetic and geometry, of history and the theology of Sidi Khalil. When he has passed some years in the *madrasah*, he can go out *taleb*, a man of letters; after this he becomes '*àdil*, a lawyer; then *jàhil*, doctor; then *álim*, savant; and finally he becomes qualified for *kadi*, judge in matters civil and ecclesiastical.

There can be no doubt that some of the Moors are men of learning; but it is learning of the dogmatic kind, derived almost entirely from the Koran. It is this which stops the way of any progress.

The hours of the first daily prayer are announced by the muezzin from the towers of the mosques in the following order:—

Adhan es sebah—About three o'clock a.m.
1. El Foojar—At dawn.
2. El Oualy—At noon.
Dohoor—An hour and a half after noon.
3. El Aser—From a quarter to three to a quarter past three p.m., according to the season.
4. El Meghab—At sunset.
5. El Asha—An hour and a half after sunset.

A few of the wealthy Moors possess clocks and watches, but they are so accustomed to the division of time provided by the mosques as to regard them as superfluities, and rather as playthings than for use. From *el asha*, an hour and a half after sunset, till *el adhan*, about an hour before sunrise, the inhabitants of the city of Marocco and other places are required to keep within their homes under pain of imprisonment by the guards of the Maulú m'el Dour.

It is not our purpose to dwell upon ordinary

matters of religion. The Sultan is the head of the Moorish Church, which differs little in its rites from those of other Moslem countries. But what may be called the eccentricities of Mohammedanism, or the extraordinary ceremonies and customs of particular sects, such as those of the howling dervishes, are worthy of notice. These we had seen in our travels in Syria and Asia Minor; but in Marocco, as it appeared to us, the vagaries of religious zeal reach their climax.

Foremost among these singular religious bodies is the strange sect known as the Eysawi. Its members are adherents to the faith of a saint named Ibun Isa, whose tomb is at Fez.

This holy man, in order to prove his saintship, is said to have cast himself from the top of a high tower, and to have fallen without injury. His saintship thus attested, his followers profess to be equally invulnerable to physical injury. They assert that snakes, scorpions, and all other venomous creatures cannot injure them, and that they therefore can handle them with impunity. They also make it appear that they can eat and handle articles on fire, and in this kind of tricks they are very expert. On a certain day in the year they meet early in the morning, at the sanctuary of any town they inhabit. Here a fire is lighted, and the peculiar orgies of their festival commence. Taking hold of each other's hands, and rapidly tossing their heads backwards and forwards, they dance round the fire with wild shouts and increasing pace. It is said that the chief man among them throws into the fire a dried herb the fumes of which have an intoxicating effect. If this is so, the herb must be hemp, from which kyfe is prepared. But it seems doubtful that any marked effect could be thus produced in the open air; it is far more probable that religious frenzy is answerable for what soon follows. While the mad dance is still proceeding, a sudden rush is made from the sanctuary, and the dancers, like men delirious, speed away to a place where live goats are tethered in readiness. At sight of these animals the fury of the savage and excited crowd reaches its height. In a few minutes the wretched animals are cut, or rather torn to pieces, and an orgy takes place over the raw and quivering flesh.

When they seem satiated, the Makaddam, who is generally on horseback, and carries a long stick, forms a sort of procession, which is preceded by wild music, if such discordant sounds will bear the name. Words can do no justice to the frightful scene which now ensues. The naked savages—for on these occasions a scanty piece of cotton is all their clothing—with their long black hair, ordinarily worn in plaits, tossed about by the rapid to-and-fro movements of the head, with faces and hands reeking with blood, and uttering loud cries resembling the bleating of goats, again enter the town. The place is now at their mercy, and the people avoid them as much as possible by shutting themselves up in their houses. A Christian or a Jew would run great risk of losing his life if either were found in the street. Goats are pushed out from the doors, and these the fanatics tear immediately to pieces with their hands, and then dispute over the morsels of bleeding flesh, as though they were ravenous wolves instead of men. Snakes are also thrown to them as tests of their divine frenzy, and these share the fate of the goats. Sometimes a luckless dog, straying as dogs will stray in a tumult, is seized on. Then a layman, should one be at hand, will try to prevent the desecration of pious mouths. But the fanatics sometimes prevail, and the unclean animal, abhorred by the Mussulman, is torn to pieces and devoured, or pretended to be devoured, with indiscriminating rage.

Having traversed the principal streets of the town, it is the practice with the Eysawi to leave it by the gate opposite to that at which they entered. They are met at a short distance from the walls by a body of their country brethren. Here the previous orgies are renewed, and here we must leave them. On the day succeeding the Eysawi saturnalia the procession of another sect, that of the Hammatchas, takes place. The doings of these gentry, if not so dangerous to others as those of the Eysawi, are far more dangerous to themselves. Self-inflicted bodily injuries seem, in fact, the main object held in view. We should not, perhaps, criticize these barbarities too closely while self-discipline is the practice of a purer faith. But Mr. Whalley himself would stand aghast at the list of implements carried and used against themselves by the fanatic Hammatchas. These consist of choppers, clubs thickly studded with large nails, small cannon-balls, and iron rings which have five or six short thick sticks attached by one end to the ring. With these instruments they literally cut and thrash themselves, as they walk along, till they are covered with blood. They will then, by way of change, throw the cannon-balls into the air, so that they come down upon their heads. Occasionally they are for a time completely stunned by this proceeding; but on recovering they will again join the procession. Sometimes, however, fatal results follow. Lately, at Saffi, a man died speedily after an injury of this kind.

These sects are commonly recruited from the lowest classes. It is not uncommon, in a family more than usually ignorant and fanatic, to find one son brought up an Eysawi, another an Hammatcha; while a third may belong to the sect of the Durkouas.

The rites and processions just described have an allegorical meaning. The naked howling savages are intended to represent the state of human society before the civilizing influence of Mohammedanism was brought to bear upon it. The man on horseback, who is always very well dressed, and sedate in his conduct, typifies the proprieties of the present state of things. But the processions are now less numerously attended than formerly, as the late Sultan discouraged them. One of the functions of the Eysawi consists in the cure of the sick; and, in order to effect this, the patient lies on his face while his back is trampled on by the holy physician.

The doctrines of Dr. Cumming have their counterpart among the Moors. They have a current opinion that the end of the world is at hand. When in the city of Marocco, we were told that this event is to take place in the year 1300 of the Hegira, a date corresponding to A.D. 1883. The destruction of the world will, according to the best orthodox views, be preceded by wars and tumults, miracles and portents. The successful revolt against the powerful governor, Ben Dáúd, was regarded as the first sign of the times.

There is no end to the superstitions of the Moors, or, rather, the people of Marocco; for the people, as a whole, appear to be infected. Witchcraft is generally believed in, and its rites are largely practised. As might be expected, love charms are in great request. The Moorish priests sell them to men and women, and the ingredients are as heterogeneous as they are occasionally repulsive. Sometimes a piece of paper, upon which the charm is written, is soaked in water, which is given the victim to drink. Bits of the beloved object's clothes, hair, parings of nails, nay, even the earth he or she has trodden upon, are used in various ways for the specific purpose in view. But the oddest thing of all, in the way of a charm, came under our notice at Mogador. One now and then sees a fowl or pigeon with a little red bundle tied to its foot. This puzzled us greatly until, on inquiry, we found that the bundle contained a charm. It is believed that if the charm is kept in constant motion by the bird a corresponding ferment is excited in the mind of him or her against whom the charm is directed. This device is also employed in order to obtain the friendship or assistance of the great—such as governors of provinces, or even of the Sultan himself.

The bones of dead men pounded, as well as other disagreeable things, are administered in articles of food; but these are given for the purpose of causing injury to the victim. The brain of the hyena is another thing used for enchantments. The term *Ras el Dubbah*, applied to a person, means he has eaten the head of the hyena, and has become silly.

Written charms, sewn in small squares of silk, and suspended by silken strings, are worn as a protection against injury. The belief in the evil eye prevails in Marocco, as it does in all Eastern countries. Rough representations of the human hand, which appear to be regarded as a safeguard against witchcraft, are commonly painted on the doors of houses, and the same are rudely carved on gravestones. Guardian angels are supposed to be numerous, their protective powers extending not only to men, but even to the gates of towns and cities.

When a newly-built house is first inhabited barley-meal is mixed with oil, and portions of the mass are thrown into the four corners of the building, to propitiate the underground neighbours—in other words, the demons—with whom the residents have to come in contact. When a person falls by accident, it is thought proper to pour out a libation of oil on the spot, to satisfy the demons. Iron is considered a great protection against demons. When a person is ill in bed it is usual to put a knife or a dagger under his pillow; and before the reason for the custom was explained to us, we had been puzzled by it when prescribing for a patient.

It has been already said that the Jews are equally superstitious with the Moors; and some of the current stories are of such recent date, and are told so circumstantially, that they are half believed by some of the Europeans. Take the following one, which has about it the smack of a tale from the "Arabian Nights."

About six months before our visit a Jew of Wadnoon, well known to some of our English friends, happened to be at Mogador, and lodged in the house of one Moses Bassoon. A Moorish priest persuaded Moses to pay him a sum of money for a certain charm by means of which a fortune might be made within twelve months. In the meanwhile, in order to ensure the desired result, the priest enjoined him not to cut his hair, and to strictly attend to other details. In a short time Moses received a box from the priest, in which apparently were a number of pearls and emeralds, and other precious stones. These were offered for sale to the Wadnoon Jew, and after the usual careful examination they were bought for £600. For greater security, the purchaser took the box of gems at once to Wadnoon, intending to sell them to the sheikh; but when the box was opened in his presence it was found to be full of common pebbles instead of gems. The Jew returned to Mogador in great distress, only to be assured that when sold the gems were genuine. The Sheikh of Wadnoon represented the case to the Governor of Mogador, adding that he would stop the traffic between the two places, and prevent all debts from being paid by his people, unless justice were done. Subsequent investigation proved that the deception was caused by the charms of the Moorish priest. He was accordingly thrown into prison; but on the night of his arrest the Jew who bought the jewels was heard to scream. To account for this he declared that he had received a severe flogging from two black slaves, who appeared in his closed room. This flogging was repeated on the two following nights, and then the sufferer made such representations to the Governor of Mogador as led to the release of the Moorish priest. After this the Jew was not molested, but his £600 were irrecoverably lost; while his co-religionist, who had made the nefarious compact with the priest, was, according to its terms, a richer man by so much within a given time.

Among superstitions which affect the sovereign is the following. If he has occasion to pass through certain parts of his dominions he always walks. It is believed that his death would soon follow if he attempted to ride.

There are superstitions about salt in Marocco as there are in Europe. Salt is believed to be a safeguard against evil spirits, and is carried in the hand with that view when people have to go in the dark from one room to another.

Another strange instance of superstition occurred among the Moors while we were at Mogador. It was the more remarkable for the reason that an analogous circumstance had occurred in London no great while previously. A house in Lambeth was alleged to have been pelted with stones from an invisible source, and a statement to this effect going the round of the newspapers caused great excitement in certain quarters. In this case all the residents in Mogador heard of their swarthy fellow-townsman's misfortune and his persecution by malignant spirits. In company with our friend Mr. Brauer, who knew the owner well, we visited the haunted premises. The house was situated in a blind lane, or *cul-de-sac*, in a quarter of the town called the Medina. It consisted of three rooms on the ground floor, opening on a small *patio*, and one small first-floor room. In one corner of the *patio* was a heap of peccant stones which had been collected from the *patio* and the terraced roof. The man's story, so far undoubtedly true, was that daily and nightly large stones came through the air into his premises, causing imminent danger to himself and family, which consisted of his wife and a daughter about twelve years old. Mr. Brauer, who took great interest in the Moor, assured me that while in the upper room, a few days previously, two stones passed through the doorway and struck the opposite wall, and in the course of the hour he remained there several other stones dropped into the enclosure. The strange mendacity of the Moors was apparent. Seeing a stone that weighed several pounds in the middle of the *patio*, we inquired of the little girl how and when it came there, as it had the appearance of having been recently detached from some place where it had been partially imbedded; she replied, without hesitation, that when engaged a short time before our visit, about something in the *patio*, she observed the stone wriggling to-and-fro as if to loosen itself out of the lower part of the wall of the enclosure, and that it then apparently flung itself a distance of some yards out of its mortar bed into the position it occupied. We took up the stone, and found that it exactly fitted the cavity pointed out in the wall. It ought to be mentioned that our attention had not in any way been directed to this particular stone, and had we not inquired about it its strange story would not have been told. The readiness with which the girl put together this little fable was, therefore, truly amazing.

The Moor told us that he had brought a taleb or scribe to the house to write a charm which might relieve him of the persecution, but that when the scribe commenced the stones came so rapidly that he was obliged to desist. This attempt having failed, a holy man who had been to Mecca was solicited to visit the place, and he had been there the previous evening. The saint first directed the rooms to be cleaned; this done, he went through a form of incantation; next he took a nail and drove it into one of the walls, when, as my informant showed by word and action, a hissing noise accompanied each blow of the hammer. This, as the holy functionary said, was caused by the evil spirits taking their departure under this curious ejectment process. Since then no stones had come into the premises.

But our Moor's troubles were by no means ended. If his daughter's word was to be believed the foundation stones of his premises were in an unquiet state; and a few days after our visit the rain of stones from without was as bad as ever. The kaid of the town came in state to witness the

T

phenomenon, but could make nothing of it. Finally the man was reluctantly obliged to leave the house, in building which he had expended what was to him a considerable sum.

This account, given with some detail and exactly as things occurred, is placed at the disposal of all whom it may interest, to explain as best they can. Spiritualists may claim it as a manifestation of the powers of the unseen world. For ourselves, we believe that the Moor had enemies who took this method of persecuting him; while he, honest man, was not loth to supplement his real misfortunes by improbable lies, in the detail of which he was loyally supported by his family. The flat roofs of the Moorish houses are well adapted for inflicting the annoyance of missile-throwing. Unless we mistake, the Lambeth stone showers were at length traced to some practical jokers living in the neighbourhood of the assailed houses.

A very curious chapter might be written on the state of medicine among the Moors. The mantle of Avicenna or of Rhazes has not fallen on their modern representatives. Certain nondescript practitioners may be seen squatting in the streets. They dispense drugs and practise astrology, for this last is regarded as a most useful adjunct to the medical art. Most of the drugs in use are herbs, which are brought to market by women. Of these the greater number are well known and in common use in Europe.[1] But in Marocco greater faith is probably placed in written charms than in the most active drugs. The former are given in various diseases, and under various circumstances, as, for instance, when a person is about to undertake a journey or to transact business.

Certain surgical operations are practised, and the Moorish doctors even perform the operation of couching for cataract. There is a kali lah beyond Tafilet which is noted for its oculists. One of the applications to the eye is that of the doctor's tongue, which is drawn across the organ while it is held open. No doubt sand and other foreign bodies are thus effectively licked out. The application of a red-hot iron —the actual cautery—is held in high esteem. Cupping is managed by means of cuts made with a razor; the wide end of a cow's horn is then placed over them, and through a hole at the tip the operator draws blood by suction. Bleeding from the arm is also practised, and among the Jews women are always bled in the last month of pregnancy.

The grossest superstitions are mixed up with the Moor's conception of the healing art. But of this parallel instances might be cited nearer home. A few years ago a Moorish woman, who was called "Lallah Tasrout," or "Lady of the

[1] See Appendix C.

Stone," made a great sensation at Mogador. She was the fortunate possessor of a talking stone, from which she extracted what was better than sermons, namely, many valuable secrets, and, particularly, infallible methods for curing diseases, which she, of course, turned to her own good account.

The Jewesses of Mogador, by the advice of old women, practise the following method for the cure of certain diseases. They select the outlet of a sewer, and throw into the filthy liquid which flows from it seven eggs, broken up one by one. These are well mixed with the sewage. Prayers are then offered to demons, and the horrible mixture is swallowed seven times. It is difficult to understand how the patient survives the remedy. If ever there was a case in which a cure is worse than the disease, it is surely to be found in this treatment by liquid manure.

Cholera is attributed to evil spirits who gain possession of people. To avoid meeting them it is the custom, when the disease is prevalent, to keep as close as possible to walls when out of doors. For the same reason sand-hills are avoided, as they are considered to be a great resort of evil spirits.

Bezoars, from the *horrep*, or Sahara antelope, are held in great esteem. Signor Korkos, of the city of Marocco, showed me one the size of a small walnut, for which he paid twelve dollars.

It was a very smooth cream-coloured concretion, the interior of which showed the mode of formation in concentric circles. When used the bezoar is rubbed on a stone, and the powder thus obtained is swallowed. It was stated that it was always necessary that the patient who took it should observe strict regimen, and remain in the house for seven days. Bezoars are esteemed as sovereign remedies for diseases of the heart, liver, and other internal organs, as also for sore eyes, for rheumatism, and other ailments.

Gold dust is taken internally when it is desired to prevent offspring. Shot is swallowed with the same intention, and also scrapings from a rhinoceros's horn.

Ants are given to lethargic people as a remedy, on the principle, we may presume, of antithesis and pure allopathy. But, as it is held that eating lion's flesh makes a cowardly man brave, it would also seem that homœopathy is not despised. A chameleon split open alive is a common application to wounds and sores. The dried body of the animal is also employed. This is burned, and the noisome fumes arising therefrom are inhaled by the patient as a sovereign remedy for debility. I have before spoken of leprosy, which is one of the scourges of the country. But in some places, as at Mogador, it seems to be unknown, although it prevails in the province of Haha, in which the town is situated.

The fearful epidemic of plague, which cut off so many of the people in the last and beginning of the present century, has been entirely unknown for more than fifty years. It has certainly not been "stamped out" by precautions or improved sanitation. It is probably only in abeyance, in obedience to some unknown law.

CHAPTER XVI.

AGRICULTURE—DOMESTIC ANIMALS—MANUFACTURES—MONEY.

MAROCCO possesses no manufactures worthy of the name, its population depending in the main upon agriculture. The empire presents such variety and excellence of climate and soil in hill and valley, woodland and open plain, watered by rivers and numerous small streams, that almost every plant under the sun might be raised within its limits. Even by the application of ordinary industry, at least five times the present population might be supported. The change effected by rain, after the summer heats, is almost magical. Parched and apparently desert wastes burst out into one mass of green. Even the shifting sand-hills at this season show signs of life. Yet nothing strikes the eye of the stranger more forcibly than the absence of cultivation over great tracts of fertile country. No road is seen except the beaten tracks which are the highways of the country, or those which connect the widely-scattered villages together. Many hours may be passed in travelling without a house, a tent, or any sign of human life being met with, except possibly a camel or two and their drivers on their way to the coast with a small quantity of produce, or returning back empty. Around the villages the traveller sees a set of lazy, yet stalwart Arabs, rolled up in their rags, and sleeping in the shade. Ask one of these fellows why he does not till the ground, and grow corn for sale as well as for his family, he will probably point to a plot of barley or wheat near at hand, and reply, "If it pleases God to send rain, there will be enough for myself and my family." And he will almost certainly add, "What is the use of planting more? The sheikh will only come and take it from me if I have an extra quantity; and if I do manage to get it to the coast, there will be no price given for it if the year happens to be a fruitful one." Such are the specious arguments for an indolence which might seem inexcusable. The Sultan obtained, by treaty with foreign powers, the right to prevent the exportation of any article he pleased, and he at once prohibited the export of wheat and barley. Meanwhile his people are impoverished, and European nations deprived of an excellent market.

Except in the neighbourhood of towns, land is of no value. In many of the best grain-growing provinces, as in Abda, Doqualla, and Stooka, thousands of fertile acres lie waste and ownerless. Manure is never used, and when the soil is exhausted, the farmer moves to another locality. Almost the entire surface of the land, except that of the mountains, is covered with a rich soil, often of surprising depth. In some places, as in Bled-Ahmar (the red country), this soil is of a reddish colour, the dust of which, in the dry season, gives the face of the country, and everything in it, the same appearance. The great requisite of the Moorish farmer is water. Unless in the districts through which rivers flow, neither himself nor his cattle could exist through the long rainless summers except by the aid of wells. Some of these are of great depth, and the water is drawn from them after the most clumsy fashion. A bar is placed across the well's mouth, and to this bar a long rope is fastened, having a bucket, or rather bag, made of cow-skin, attached to it. The wells are not private property, but belong to the tribe; and it is the constant occupation of three or four men to draw up water for the use of the farmers. The stranger must obtain permission to get water for his animals, or even for his own use. The irrigating wheel, so common in the East, is sometimes seen.

The first thing to be done when the farmer settles on a plot of ground is to erect a hut. In the northern provinces this consists of low *tabia* walls covered with thatch; but in the south, where the population is more nomadic, the hut, or *novella*, is formed of reeds, in the shape of a bee-hive. Whatever its shape, it is generally surrounded with an impenetrable fence of cut thorn-bushes. Within this a sufficient space is enclosed to house his cattle at night, and for himself and family protection is afforded against surprise and injury. As a further security, the huts are arranged in clusters so as to form villages; and the authority of one individual as headman is always acknowledged. An isolated hut is never seen throughout the country, and the migration of a whole village is not uncommon. But in the remote parts of the country, where the population is still more nomadic, the Arabs live in tents made of goats' hair. The black sloping roofs may be seen clustered in groups in the vicinity of water.

If the land selected for agricultural purposes is overgrown with brushwood, it is cleared by fire. At the commencement of the rainy season, which is generally October, the land is ploughed. The plough consists of a log of tough wood about three feet long, roughly squared and pointed at one end. A handle is inserted into the other end, while another shaft projects from about the centre of the log. To this shaft a pair of bullocks is yoked by means of a rope. Sometimes a pair of mares, or a mare and a donkey, are employed. But the Moor is by no means particular as to his motive power. A camel and a donkey are occasionally used; and, as in Ireland, a woman may sometimes be seen joined to the fortunes of a donkey in this useful but lowly toil. It unfortunately too often happens that the oxen have been seized by the revenue officers of the Sultan, or rather of the governor, who acts for the Sultan.

Adam, driven by necessity, could not have devised a more primitive or ruder implement than this Arab plough. The furrows it makes are most irregular, and consist of a mere scratching of the earth to the depth of a few inches. For heavy soils, such as the plains of Marocco and Abda, the plough is sometimes tipped with iron. Another implement used is the hoe. This consists of a piece of flat iron, having an eye on one side, into which a short handle is inserted at a right angle. This serves the purpose of a spade. It is used in digging canals and wells, and is also the special tool of gardeners. The plough, thorn-bush, or hoe, *hadge*, or native sickle, and dagger, comprise the whole of the implements used by the Arab farmer. Yet, as already said, the results of his farming are often astonishing.

Barley and wheat are sown broadcast; but maize, beans, and peas are placed in the earth by means of the fingers, or in holes made with a pointed stick. A large thorn-bush, upon which a few stones are placed to give it weight, is then drawn over the surface to cover the seed, and the planting operations are complete. Yet, such are the advantages of climate and soil, that the crops are often splendid. Sufficient rain is the one thing requisite, and if this is forthcoming the rapidity and luxuriance of growth are marvellous.

Corn is reaped with little sickles, which make the work very tedious and imperfect. Not more than half the straw is cut, and one reason for this seems to be the interference of rank weeds. Maize and beans, having thick stems, are cut with the large curved daggers worn by the Moors.

Harvest along the coast usually commences at the latter end of March, when barley begins to be reaped. Beans are harvested in May, and wheat in June and July. Harvesting in the interior begins somewhat earlier than on the coast.

The corn, when cut, is tied in small bundles, which are collected first into small heaps, and afterwards into one large heap close to the threshing floor. This is made of clay, well beaten down, and enclosed by thorn-bushes. Into this enclosure cattle are put, which are constantly driven round, while the corn is thrown under their feet by women and children. After the grain has in this manner been trodden out, it is cleaned by tossing in the air. When sufficiently dry it is stowed away in excavations made in the ground, and plastered with *tabia*. As the mouth of the cavity is hermetically sealed, grain will remain perfectly sound in these receptacles for many years.

Farming to the north of Mogador consists mainly in the cultivation of maize, beans, and peas; these articles of ordinary agricultural produce are alone allowed to be exported, and at times even these are prohibited. Saffi, Mazagan, and Casa Blanca are the ports for these articles.

A considerable amount of wheat and barley is grown on the magnificent plain of Marocco; yet, so vast is its expanse, that, to those passing over it, it seems hardly cultivated at all. There is ample room for a great development of remunerative industry. The ground has a gentle slope from the Atlas Mountains; and, water being abundant, a perfect system of irrigation might be established. Here the steam plough might run for miles without interruption, and cotton might be grown to perfection. The cost of production, with labour at from 6d. to 8d. per day, and with transit, even by camel, at the rate of two dollars, 8s., per load of four quintals, about 480 lbs., for the journey of sixty or eighty miles to Mogador, are all circumstances highly favourable to the introduction of capital and scientific agriculture. The late Sultan planted cotton on a large scale, and encouraged some of his governors to follow his example. But the want of a proper system of irrigation, the absence of method in picking and cleaning, added to the fact that much of the cotton was stolen when ripe, led to the abandonment of its cultivation.

Notwithstanding all the advantages of this favoured land, famines, caused by the failure of crops from drought, are not unfrequent. These famines are generally local, and under a better system of government would be hardly felt. It has already been explained why the Arab, as a rule, grows only corn enough for his immediate wants. When a famine occurs in a district the stock in hand is soon consumed; and in places where the whole population might exist for years on the production of a single harvest, numbers of people perish from hunger. As the case stands, the starving people flock to the seaports, attracted by the grain collected by traders for export.

The olive gardens of the south form picturesque groves of great extent; their produce constitutes the principal wealth of the provinces of Haha and Sus. But the oil, probably from the imperfect methods of preparing it, is greatly inferior to that of Spain and Italy. It is, however, exported from Mogador in large quantities.

The tree next in importance to the olive is the almond. It is grown largely in the provinces of Shedma and Haha, and in the country about Marocco. Immense quantities of almonds are also grown in Sus, but they are of inferior quality. The mulberry-tree flourishes, and the silk-worm is reared in the city of Marocco and in some other places. But, though the silk is of superior quality, very little is made. The vine grows well, but is only to be seen about towns, where it is trained upon trees as in Italy. Through want of cultivation the grapes are deficient in flavour, and the badly fermented, heavy wine prepared by the Jews is in all respects inferior.

The forests of the south yield a large quantity of argan oil, which throughout Marocco is employed in the preparation of almost every dish. In the north a good deal of oil is extracted from mastic-berries. This is used chiefly for burning, and it forms also an article of food among the poorer classes. Tobacco is grown in some places; but its flavour is strong and its quality altogether bad.

Every large town we visited, with the exception of Mogador, was surrounded by fields and gardens extending a considerable distance. These were fenced in by hedges of mastic or prickly pear, or, at Marocco, by *tabia* walls. The gardens, according to locality, are filled with orange, citron, lemon, pomegranate, fig, date, and other fruit-trees. In good seasons the respective fruits are so plentiful as to be scarcely worth gathering; but, with the exception of dates, for which Tafilet is celebrated, and citrons, none of these are exported.

Truffles—Arabic *tarfas*—grow in the country around Saffi, and in wet seasons are very abundant.

Dr. Hooker, who, as previously stated, travelled in Marocco in 1871, and ascended the Atlas range, made a large collection of plants, many of which have been since figured and described in Curtis's "Magazine of Botany."

Vegetables might be raised in great perfection,

but their cultivation is much neglected. Most of the ordinary kinds are grown near towns by the Jews. The Moors take little trouble to raise them. Cabbages grow to an enormous size, and I saw radishes in the city of Marocco which might have been mistaken for large carrots.

The burden-camel—*jamal*—is the most important of the domesticated animals. By its means the products of distant provinces are interchanged, and commerce is carried on with places like Timbuctoo, in the heart of Africa. The strength and enduring qualities of the camel alone make such journeys possible. Day after day, from sunrise to sunset, this patient animal will plod through a desert at the rate of about two miles an hour while carrying a load of four hundredweight, or even more. To sustain all this patient toil a meal of grain, or even of straw, with water at intervals of days, will suffice. In the north, where the camel is larger and food can be procured on a journey, it will carry as much as six hundredweight.

But the camel is also valuable to the Arab for its milk, which is much esteemed, and for its flesh, which he eats with great relish. Among the Moors, camel's milk has the same reputation for curing consumption as ass's milk has with us. The male camel is extremely vicious at a certain season. The Moors say that a camel keeps spite for a year, and that a man who has done

one of these beasts an injury is in great danger if he approaches the injured animal at this particular time. The camel first knocks his victim down, then kneels on his chest, and (they say) listens to ascertain whether he still breathes before getting up. We have seen a camel rush frantically about until he succeeded in throwing his rider, to the imminent risk of his neck. Camels also bite savagely. The ordinary price of one is about £10. The riding or running camel —or *Heah'ri*—bears the same relation to the burden-camel as our thorough-bred horse does to a cart-horse. The form of the dromedary is more slender and elegant, and his special characteristic is his speed. The statements made with respect to this, and also as to his powers of endurance, seem almost fabulous. The camels of this breed vary greatly in excellence, and one of first-rate quality is valued at a very large sum of money.

The affection of the Arab for his horse is proverbial; and in Marocco the horse has the place of honour among animals. It is not used as a beast of burden, but bears its master only. When it dies it is not skinned, as this would be profanation of the noble creature.

When the Arab rises in the morning he lays his hand on his horse's head, at the same time saying, "In the name of Allah." He then kisses his hand to it, because of the favour in which the horse was held by Mohammed. Horses are carefully tended, and frequently washed. Their food is crushed straw and barley; the last being given in a nose-bag, and only at sunset. They are sent to grass every spring for a period of forty days.

The imaginative powers of the Arab are greatly exercised in the matter of their horses. They attribute different qualities to different coloured animals. A black horse is at its best at night, and a chestnut at sunrise. A white horse is more on the alert than one of any colour; while the grey horse, above all others—and there is much truth in the observation—is remarkable for soundness and endurance of hoof. The plains of Abda, to the eastward of Saffi, are renowned for their fine breed of horses.

The desert horse, which is employed in hunting ostriches to the south of Wadnoon, is a wonderful animal. It is trained to live on camel's milk and dates, but sometimes, as it appears, on milk altogether; and the effect of this diet is to impart extraordinary speed and endurance. If the desert horse is brought north into Marocco, and is put on ordinary provender, its spare, grey, hound-like frame soon fills out, and much of its great speed is lost. But these swift horses, unlike the swift camels, require much attention. They cannot, in fact, travel without their nurses. Each horse requires a pair of camels to supply it with milk. Here is a hint for Newmarket! Let a thorough-bred horse, from the time of weaning, be fed entirely on cow's milk in default of camel's milk, and let it contend for the prize with its oat and bean-fed brethren! Other desert horses live like their owners when travelling — almost entirely on dates.

But the ordinary horse of Marocco has nothing wonderful about it. It is small and not always a well-bred animal. It has endurance and fair speed, and its performances in the Moorish cavalry exercises prove it to be docile. As might be expected, the veterinary art among the Moors is in a barbarous state, but they shoe horses skilfully. The shoe has a bar across the frog. The average price of a horse is from £10 to £15. All the horses are stallions, and mares are seldom ridden; usually they are kept solely for breeding.

The mules of Marocco excel even those of Spain. Some of them are as large as a full-sized horse. Plodding, patient, sure-footed, and docile, they carry the traveller at the rate of four miles an hour through a long day, with few halts and little sustenance. The mule in Marocco holds the place of the stage-coach or railway train in more advanced countries. The price of a mule ranges between £20 and £40.

An ass with the driver mounted on it is commonly seen preceding a drove of camels. The price of donkeys varies from £1 to £5.

The horned cattle of the country are small but not unsightly animals, and they resemble more or less the Alderney breed imported into England. The flesh is good, but the animals are generally in poor condition from want of attention. Bullocks, as already said, are used generally for ploughing. The price of a good cow is about £6, and of a bullock about £4.

Sheep are reared extensively for the sake of their wool. This is in general of inferior quality. The best wool comes from the province of Tedla, and is largely used in the manufacture of the far-famed Fez caps. The mutton is poor, and tastes woolly, but improves considerably in the rainy season. The mountain sheep of the province of Sus, which feed on aromatic herbs, are however noted for their fine flavour. The price of a sheep is about 10s.

Goats are very numerous, especially in the south. Shedma and Haha are famed for them. In those provinces they take the place of sheep. In Haha goats are often seen in the top of the argan-trees; and a good climber, which can therefore support itself on the argan berries, brings a higher price than one that is not so active. Goats are valued for their skins, which yield the well-known Marocco leather. The price of one is about 8s.

The domestic fowl is very common in all parts of the country; on it the traveller in the main depends for animal food. He will often be obliged to go for many days without meeting with anything that he can eat except the rooster, slain for his dinner and cooked with oil. Ducks are common only at Mazagan, and turkeys are unknown except in Marocco City. The want of better means of communication between distant places is the cause of many curious anomalies of the kind.

The primitive art of weaving is carried to considerable perfection in Marocco. The loom is of the rudest kind, and is probably the same that has been in use for thousands of years. Fez is the chief seat of silk-weaving, while Rabat and Marocco contain a great many looms for wool. No one can look at the beautiful carpets which the weavers turn out, without feeling that the rude designs and mixture of colours are guided by a taste which, although peculiar, has much in it to be admired. Weaving is an occupation confined to the poorer classes, and is in no way indebted to patronage or capital. Mineral dyes are hardly used; but madder, pomegranate peel, henna, logwood, cochineal, and indigo supply the ordinary colours. Of these, the three last are imported. As far as we could learn, mordants are unknown.

The potter's art receives a good deal of attention; and the coarse glazed ware, which is seen on all sides, is often creditably ornamented. The principal manufactories are at Fez; but the best specimens of ware are now scarce, as the two best designers died from cholera some years ago.

Some of the Moorish metal-work deserves commendation. There are goldsmiths and coppersmiths in all the large towns. We have often wondered at the precision with which the artificer forms elaborate decorations on brass trays with his graver alone, without pattern or sketch of any kind. The whole thing is evolved from the depths of his inner consciousness in a remarkable manner. The best gun-makers are found at Tetuan.

The world at large is more familiar with the name of Marocco applied to leather prepared from goat-skin than with the country itself, or anything which concerns it. But the tanners of Europe have learned to excel the Moors themselves in the art of preparing this kind of leather. In Marocco it is made only in four colours; bright yellow, which is largely used for men's slippers, white and red for women's slippers, and brownish-red, which is employed for other purposes.

The Moorish ladies are very clever at embroidery. Some of their work is very fine and most beautiful.

Churning, like all domestic work, falls to the lot of the women. The churn is a bag made of goat-skin. This, when nearly filled with milk, is closed by tying the mouth tightly. The bag is then rolled about and kneaded till butter is formed.

The Moor will never part with money if he can

by any means avoid it. In a country where there are no banks or other places of security, every man must be his own banker. To bury money in the earth, or otherwise hide it, is the common practice. The amount of money hoarded in the country must thus be very large, and the treasury of the late Sultan was known to be rich. The European steamers are constantly conveying large amounts to Marocco in return for produce, while the exportation of specie is very trifling.

Much of this money must be hidden away. If a man gets the reputation of being wealthy his position is perilous. He is sure to be soon arraigned before the governor of his province, who, on one pretext or another, demands the money. If it is refused, the unhappy owner is imprisoned or bastinadoed to make him disgorge. Yet such is his avarice, that not unfrequently he yields his life rather than disclose the amount or show the hiding-place of his gold. It must thus often happen that hoarded wealth is lost, and hidden treasure is not uncommonly found; but the law of treasure-trove in Marocco is inflexible. Woe to the wretch whose ill stars have placed temptation in his way, in case the matter reaches his governor's ear. Not only is the finder of money compelled to give it all up, but, in proportion to his means, he is heavily fined as a punishment for concealment.

The following story, *à propos* of the pains taken

to conceal money, incredible as it may seem, is strictly true. To the axiom known and often acted upon among ourselves, "Get money, if you can honestly, but get it at all events," the Moor adds another: "Hide money, by fair means or foul." Some years ago a certain governor, who lived near Saffi, employed two masons to build a strong-room or vault on his premises. As long as the work was in progress the men were treated as prisoners, and not allowed to communicate with anyone, for even the materials used were conveyed only to an outside door, whence they obtained them. The object of all this was to prevent the exact situation of the vault from becoming known. In this, when finished, a large amount of treasure was placed, and the opening to the vault was then built up. The men were then paid for their work and dismissed. But they had only proceeded a short distance before they were waylaid and killed by three slaves sent after them by the governor. The secret of the vault was by this atrocious means confined to his own breast.

It sometimes happens that when a governor gets into irretrievable disgrace with the Sultan, his house is utterly razed for the purpose of discovering hidden treasure.

CHAPTER XVII.

NATURAL HISTORY AND SPORT.

THE wild boar, *El Halúf*, is found in all parts of the empire of Marocco, but abounds more particularly in the southern provinces. Wild boars are numerous in the neighbourhood of Mogador, as also in the argan forest near the Haha mountains. Here various roots and berries supply these animals with abundant food, and the argan-tree gives them its nutritious fruit, on which, when ripe, they fatten.

The supposed affinity between devils and swine is not unknown to Christians; but with the Moslems this belief has a practical application. In nearly all the stables of governors and wealthy Moors a young wild boar is kept, in order that evil spirits may be diverted from the horses and enter into the pig. So artful and mischievous is the young boar, that it is no wonder he bears this bad reputation. If he has not made good his escape to his native wilds by the time he is six months old, he has generally become so fierce as to make it necessary to despatch him and supply his place. A tame pig, as affording more permanent quarters for the evil spirits, is occasionally substituted.

The traveller sometimes sees in the retinue of a governor a slave carrying a small deer-skin. This the great man kneels upon when he says his prayers, which he must do, no matter where he is, at stated times in the day. The skin is that of a small antelope—*El Horreh*—about the same size and shape as the gazelle. But the colour of the back is reddish, while that of the belly is a very delicate white, and the Arabs say that the animal through fear of soiling this part never lies down. On this account the creature is regarded as an emblem of purity, and its skin is much prized for use as a praying-rug. The bezoar-stone, already described, and so highly prized, is obtained from this animal. The horreh is an inhabitant of the Sahara.

The *Audéd*, or wild sheep, inhabits the most inaccessible parts of the southern Atlas. It has strong horns about a foot long, curved backwards, and a long tufted growth of hair attached to the under part of the beard and the front of the chest, which gives it a noble appearance. It is seldom caught alive, but a fine specimen was in the possession of Mr. Yule at Mogador, and others have been brought to Europe. Every one has heard of the mónkeys on the rock of

Gibraltar, the only spot in Europe they at present inhabit.[1] Some years ago they were in danger of extermination; but they are now so rigidly preserved, that it is the duty of a look-out man to note in his book the number of apes seen daily. It is curious that the opposite mountain, called commonly the Pillar of Hercules, and Ceuta on the African coast,[2] are frequented by the same tailless species. This latter mountain is called "Apes' Hill," and it was formerly believed, on account of the varying number of the animals observed within short periods at Gibraltar, that a passage known only to the monkeys existed beneath the sea between the two places.

These tailless monkeys are also found near Tetuan, in the neighbouring mountains of the North Atlas chain. But strangely enough they are not met with in the southern provinces, where abound various fruits and berries that might supply them with food. We had not the good fortune to see, during our travels in Marocco, a monkey in the wild state.

We heard nothing about lions in Marocco, except that they exist in the Atlas range, and are neither

---

[1] Cæsar, in his History, mentions their appearance on this rock. Mr. King, in his "History of Antique Gems," refers to the passage.

[2] Mr. Boyd Dawkins, in his learned work, "Cave Hunting," shows that in the pre-glacial ages Europe and Africa were formerly united at this point by an isthmus. The former continent then stretched far west into the Atlantic.

numerous nor dangerous The spotted leopard, which attains a large size, is a more ferocious beast. He is met with in the southern provinces, and is not unfrequently taken in pitfalls, and then dispatched by shooting. The lynx, *Felis caracal*, is found in wooded districts, and is sometimes brought alive to Mogador.

The striped hyena, *Dubbah*, is common in the mountains. He is not dangerous to man, but commits great ravages among sheep and goats. The vacant stare of the hyena has gained him the reputation of being the most stupid of animals. If an Arab wishes to express that anyone is extremely dull of comprehension, it is common for him to say, " He has eaten the brains of a hyena." In connexion with the following superstition, the Arabs entertain a grudge against the hyena, and, considering him to be a dangerous pest, destroy him whenever possible. It is believed, that if a woman should meet a hyena she instantly becomes quite stupid. What is more, should a woman find a dead hyena, and, having obtained a portion of its brains, administer the same to her husband, he would become stupid, and her ascendency over him would be complete. In order to prevent these and other calamities, whenever a hyena is slain, his head is always cut off and burned.

When leaving Mogador for England we had for fellow-passengers two fine hyenas. They were confined on deck, as it was supposed, quite securely.

But after we had been a short time at sea the brutes contrived to escape unobserved during the night, by gnawing away the bars of their wooden cage. They must have jumped overboard, as, although well searched for, they were never seen afterwards. This assumption as to the way they had disposed of themselves was by no means satisfactory to a Mogador gentleman who, with ourselves, occupied the cabin. He could not divest himself of the idea—nor, to say the truth, did his companion try to help him—that the savage beasts lurked in some corner of the vessel, and that in the dark hours an attack, something worse than that of nightmare, might be expected. So, in spite of heat and want of ventilation, he took special care every night to close and bolt the door of his private cabin.

Jackals are numerous in Shedma and Haha. We often saw them by day, and heard their melancholy wails by night. *Deeb* is the Moorish name for jackal. The red fox, *Saleb*, apparently the same as the northern fox, is common. For the ornithologist, Marocco is a fertile and little explored field. In some of the wooded districts birds are very numerous, but where there are no trees the traveller may go miles without perceiving any signs of feathered life. Almost all our own familiar birds, in addition to many unknown in northern climates, inhabit Marocco. The raven, rook, jackdaw, blackbird, nightingale, goldfinch, linnet, greenfinch, robin, wagtail, skylark, are all common. The crested lark is seen in all parts of the country, and is so tame that it barely keeps clear of the mules' feet as travellers pass on. Sometimes this pretty little bird merely backs out of the way, raising its crest and shaking its feathers in a coquettish and amusing manner. The tree-lark is also met with.

In the city of Marocco a beautiful little bird called the *Tabib*, or doctor, is plentiful. It is of a brownish colour, about the size of a sparrow, but of a more slender and elegant form, and its habits and manners are altogether more engaging. When "at home" we were constantly visited by two or three of these little birds, which, descending through the opening in the roof, were on the most familiar terms with us. They would hop, peer about, and pick up crumbs in so gentle a manner that it was pleasant to see them in such a turbulent place. It seemed, in fact, that they alone gave us a welcome to the city, and we always felt grateful to our little friends. The tabib has a local distribution. It was not known in any other part of the country we visited except Mogador; and it was introduced into that town many years previously by an English merchant.

But what particularly strikes the traveller are the number and variety of the hawk tribe. They are of every intermediate size between the majestic eagle and a small hawk about the size of a thrush.

This little bird is common in the city of Marocco, where it wheels gracefully in the air above the houses, on which also it frequently perches. Falcons, prized for hawking, are procured in the country; and, as previously said, the island at Mogador is famed for them. In the argan forest, on the road to the city of Marocco, as also mentioned before, a beautiful species, *Melierax polyzonus*, stated to be unknown on the coast, was procured. Vultures are not uncommon. In some places starlings are seen on the wing in countless thousands, giving the appearance of a great moving cloud ever changing its shape and dimensions. The starlings which we were able to examine were the black variety, *Sturnus unicolor*.

As in other Mohammedan countries, the stork lives unmolested in the midst of towns, where he mars the proportions of the minarets by overshadowing them with his ungainly nest. The turtle-dove is very common about villages and wherever there is cultivation. In certain places the blue rock pigeon is extremely abundant.

In the winter, when the rains have filled the rivers and covered the marshes, waterfowl and other birds in great variety resort to them. Flamingoes, herons, curlews, snipe, green-plovers, red-shanks, many other waders, and ducks of various species are then more or less plentiful.

The bustard is found in some localities, and the lesser bustard is widely diffused. The Barbary partridge is found almost everywhere, and the desert partridge of several varieties is common in the south.

The ostrich is met with only in the south, about Wadnoon and the borders of the Sahara. Birds of the largest size and finest plumage are found in this district.[3] The ostrich is hunted by Arabs mounted on the desert horse already described. The party advance cautiously against the wind, and with long intervals between each horseman, until marks of the birds' feet are observed. These are followed up until the birds themselves are discovered by the hunters. A dash at full speed is then made after the game until the ostriches turn and face their pursuers. They do this because their pace, which is accomplished by a combination of flying and running, is interfered with by the action of the wind upon their wings. The gauntlet has then to be run among the armed sportsmen, who either shoot the birds or maim them by throwing at their legs a short, thick stick formed of hard-grained and heavy wood. In the use of this implement the Arabs are extremely dexterous. When secured, the throats of the birds are cut, and the feathers plucked off. These and the flesh, which, although coarse, is eaten, are then divided among the hunters.[4]

[3] Quoted in "Ostriches and Ostrich Farming," by Mosenthal and Harting (Trübner, 1876), page 44; also at page 21, in a note.

[4] The feathers are brought to Mogador from Tindoof, Teezoon, and Wadnoon.

The chameleon is often met with, especially in gardens, leisurely stalking along the ground, or clinging to a vine, its favourite haunt. Although, when disturbed, its pace is quickened, it is easily captured. The change of hue, for the obvious purpose of escaping detection, which the skin of the chameleon undergoes according to the colour of surrounding objects, as well as the rolling of its eyes in opposite directions, both excite the stranger's wonder. Although perfectly innocuous, the Arabs declare that the chameleon is a snake-destroyer, and that it kills it by dropping a portion of its glutinous saliva on the head of the sleeping reptile. But the Arabs are famous for libelling the beasts of the field as well as their fellow-men. The dried body of the chameleon forms part of the native *materia medica*, and in this state it is sold in the bazaars.

Lizards of many varieties and sizes, some of them presenting beautiful colours, are seen basking in the sun, particularly in places where there are rocks and large stones beneath which they can shelter. Their quick and nimble motions give them a grace all their own.

Marocco possesses many varieties of snakes, and two species are extremely venomous. The hooded viper, called by the Arab *buskah*, is a frightful reptile. It is from six to eight feet long, of moderate thickness, and of a black colour. When about to attack, it raises its neck straight up a foot or more out of the coils which it forms with its body, while at the same time its head expands to several times its ordinary size. In this position its hideous form, coupled with the idea of the deadly nature of its bite, gives it a truly demoniacal aspect. By means of the muscles of its body it then springs a distance of several feet and bites with fatal precision. This is the species upon which the *isowa*, and serpent-charmers, chiefly practise. We have seen them pulling the reptiles about, and apparently acting in the most reckless manner. It is supposed by many persons that their poison-fangs have been extracted, so that there is no risk whatever in handling them. But this is certainly not always the case. At Saffi, sometime before our visit, a snake-charmer, during his performance, was bitten in the forehead by a hooded snake, and expired in a quarter of an hour. Fortunately the *buskah* is not common; being, as it seems, confined to the country southward of Mogador.

El Effah, translated the viper, is the name given to another snake, sometimes exhibited by the snake-charmers. It is not more than two feet long, but is very thick in proportion. The colour of its skin is yellow, with brown and black marks. *El Effah* is brought from Sus, where it lives in holes in the earth. Its bite is extremely venomous. A species of viper about a foot long, thin in the body, and black, is not uncommon; but its bite, although dangerous, cannot be compared with that of either of the snakes just described.

In the city of Marocco and some other places a snake about four feet in length, handsomely marked in yellow and black, frequents houses, and is never molested. These snakes may be seen crawling about the ceilings, and emerging from holes in the floors. They do the duty of a cat in killing rats and mice. But, in addition to this claim to recognition for services, it is considered highly injudicious to incur their displeasure, for these domestic snakes are believed to bring good luck to the house, as also to harbour resentment towards those who injure them, or for whom they entertain a dislike.

Frogs abound in almost every tank and pool, and some are of very large size. When evening sets in they may be heard at a considerable distance, and the cry of one variety closely resembles that of the partridge.

Of late years, in London, small tortoises have been common on the barrows of costermongers. These creatures are sold for sixpence each as pets for children. Yet few people know the native country of the reptiles, or the cruel treatment they undergo on the voyage to England. Among the minor exports from Marocco is that of tortoises. They abound about Mogador and Saffi, where they are met with, when the sun is out, dragging their unwieldy bodies along, and, when interfered with, defying danger by retiring within their impregnable armour. These tortoises are collected by the country people, and bought up by the Jews, who pack them closely in barrels for exportation. Cold-blooded and abstinent although they are, they must suffer much during the long voyage from deprivation of food and power of locomotion.

Foremost among insect pests is the domestic fly, our own familiar friend, which with us is a well-mannered, unassuming creature compared with the same insect in Marocco. In the city of Marocco flies are bred by millions in the vegetable offal which everywhere abounds. The things on which they alight present a black appearance by reason of their numbers. It is uncomfortable to know that at one moment they are diving into all sorts of nastiness, and at the next are alighting on your face. There cannot be a doubt that some diseases are propagated by direct contagion conveyed by the feet and proboscis of flies. Notably this must be the case with regard to ophthalmia. We have often seen swollen and exuding eyelids thickly surrounded by flies, which the sufferers allowed to have their own way rather than be at the trouble of a worrying contest with them. These insects would certainly convey disease by passing from unhealthy to healthy eyes.

Mosquitoes are in some places very troublesome, and a mosquito curtain is an indispensable article in the bedroom. In the neighbourhood of certain lakes, these pests, and a species of sand-fly, make the adjoining country uninhabitable.

Fleas thrive so greatly that if a room be shut up for some time they literally swarm. An ingenious mode of disposing of them is then adopted. A sheep is confined in the room, and the bloodsuckers are thus induced to collect upon the fleecy victim, which is presently driven out with its cargo of live stock. Many of the houses are infested with the filthy insects which are associated in our ideas with dirt and neglect. Still worse, the majority of the people harbour on their persons some noisome pests.

Locusts are every year more or less present, but Marocco is subject, at long but uncertain intervals, to the sudden appearance of immense hosts of them, which cover the face of the country, destroying in their progress every vestige of vegetation. These hosts come invariably from the south, where, in the vast wastes of the Sahara, they are bred. But when they have once migrated they are apt to remain in force and to multiply for some years. They travel in such well-defined masses that, while the face of one portion of the country has been suddenly changed by them from that of spring to autumn, an adjoining portion, perhaps only separated by a stream, will remain entirely unattacked. The Arabs attribute this to discipline, and declare that the movements of the insects are regulated by an individual locust which they term the sultan.

Sometimes the farmers make feeble attempts to protect their crops by lighting fires around their fields. But there is some compensation in the circumstance that although the locusts devour the food of man, they are also themselves a source of food. They are collected in sacks by night, boiled in salt and water, and then fried. Only the body is eaten (head, legs, and wings are pulled off), much as we eat shrimps, which they resemble in taste. They are considered to be wholesome food, and in perfection as soon as the insects can fly.

Nevertheless, the total loss of crops is too often followed by calamitous famines. These hosts of locusts, rising high in the air, are carried by the winds out to sea, in which they perish. Their decomposing bodies, in countless millions, are afterwards cast up on the shores, and there give out an intolerable stench.

The sea around the coast of Marocco contains the majority of our northern fishes, together with many not known in our latitudes. Mackerel and herrings arrive at certain seasons, and are caught in great numbers. Turbot, soles, mullet (grey and red), dog-fish, and conger-eels abound. The tunny fishery on the coast employs many vessels, which belong chiefly to Spain and the Canary Islands. The Spanish and Portuguese fishing vessels go in considerable numbers as far south as Rabat in search of fish. Three steamers are employed in carrying the fish. Sardines are also caught in large quantities.

The shores about Mogador are particularly rich in fish, probably because the northerly current which flows along the coast finds its limit here, and is diverted thence towards the Canary Islands. This part is visited every few years by shoals of a fish measuring from five to six feet in length, of excellent flavour, and called by the Moors *tusergelt*. It is fished for with a long rod and wire instead of line, and is so voracious that a piece of rag is sufficient bait. Lobsters, crayfish, shrimps, oysters, and mussels are abundant in many places. But the fish which claims special attention is the shebbel, a species of shad. On account of its flavour, this is regarded as the salmon of Barbary; indeed, by some Europeans it is preferred to the salmon. It leaves the sea in spring, and ascending all the rivers of any magnitude, is then abundant. In some places, as at Azamoor, in the description of which place this fish was referred to, at Larache, and at Aghadir in the south, the shebbel forms a staple article of trade. Salted and dried, it is carried far into the interior.

In the bay of Tangier, where there is a shelving sandy bottom, a curious mode of fishing for soles is practised. The fisherman wades into the water till it reaches his waist or beyond, and as he proceeds he carefully examines the bottom. But as the least ripple on the surface greatly interferes with his vision, he pours upon the water, when necessary, a very small quantity of oil from a bottle which he carries. This makes the surface for some distance around perfectly smooth, and enables him to see the fish, which he then strikes with a single barbed spear, and rarely misses his aim. The cachelot, or sperm whale, is not unfrequently cast up on the southern coasts, and considerable quantities of ambergris are in this way obtained. The Moors maintain that it was on the coast of Sus that the prophet Jonah was cast out of the belly of the whale. A temple has been erected in his honour, and it is appropriately fashioned out of the ribs and other bones of whales obtained on the shore.

Partridge shooting in Marocco is a very different thing from the easy-going sport in England. It begins about the same time in both countries, but the fierce glare of a September sun in Africa is not like his mild rays on the cultivated fields of Kent or Surrey. For this reason it is necessary to be afield before daybreak, so as to be on the shooting-ground when the dawn appears. At Tangier we made many excursions in company with Mr. Martin, who is a keen sportsman. The first thing necessary to be arranged on the previous night was to have the town-gate opened before the usual time. This was accomplished by the payment of half-a-dollar to the guard; and as it was then necessary for a stranger to go beyond the twelve-mile radius before looking for game, we were obliged to be on our horses as early as three or four a.m. This restriction, as may be well supposed, was not directed against the native population, but was intended as a preventive against undue destruction of game by the numerous visitors to Tangier. It was greatly objected to by the officers of the garrison of Gibraltar, and has recently been altogether removed.

Our way lay generally for some miles on the smooth sands along the shores of the bay, and the ride in the cool calm night compensated for such early rising. The phosphorescent light from the rippling waves was singularly striking. There was more sea than usual, and as each wave came grandly tumbling in upon the shore a nearly perpendicular wall of light was formed, illuminating the beach so that each pebble and shell could be distinctly seen. This was the more remarkable because the water beyond the well-defined crest of the wave was quite dark. It was only when stimulated by the breaking of the wave that the light-producing creatures shed their lustre.

One morning early we came upon a lonely fisherman, seated in the dark, upon a rock. He had caught some large fish of the bream kind, which afterwards made a welcome addition to our breakfast.

The shooting ground was, for the most part, a succession of dry stony hills, studded over with palmettoes. There were occasional patches of durrha, or millet, and here and there a few trees.

As soon as light permitted we commenced operations, which were continued until nine or ten o'clock. Then the shade of some trees was sought. The servants lighted a fire; and, as everything necessary was conveyed on our baggage-mule, we breakfasted with a zest that only such early rising and exercise can impart. Afterwards we continued our efforts until about noon, when we again sought shade, and generally slept stretched on the ground for a couple of hours. This *siesta* was not only necessary on account of the heat, but it would have been useless to continue shooting, because the birds at this time of day also avoid the heat by stowing themselves away in the closest coverts. We seldom left our ground until it was too dark to shoot.

We shall never forget a ludicrous but unfortunate incident that occurred in one of our excursions. We always took with us two attendants, and, on the occasion in question, Mogunnum, a black man, rode the mule with the pack-saddle that contained all our good things in the way of eating and drinking, as well as a new breech-loading gun belonging to Mr. Martin. We came to an almost perpendicular ridge of ground overgrown with stout shrubs, which any one else even on foot would have avoided by going around in search of an easier passage; but Mogunnum was not to be deterred by trifles. He was a little in advance, and faced the mule fairly at the obstacle. Up went the

docile animal, and on went Mogunnum and his load,
in spite of his master's unsparing and well-deserved
maledictions. But Mogunnum soon paid dearly for
his rashness. The *swerry*, or panniers, caught by the
shrubs, caused the mule, which pushed gallantly on
as long as it could go, to topple straight backwards, crushing poor Mogunnum badly, injuring
his head, smashing the new gun, and dissipating pleasurable anticipations of certain reviving
draughts after a hot walk. For the time this
incident spoiled all harmony; but it had its comic
side; and to this hour the sight of the poor heedless fellow, making his equestrian somersault, rises
before us.

The Barbary partridge appears to be a larger
bird than the European red-legged, or French
partridge, from which it also differs in plumage.
Three brace—all, with one exception, young birds
—weighed six pounds. The Barbary partridge is,
however, an indifferent bird for the table; it is
dry, wants flavour, and requires skilful cooking
to make it good eating. Its habits are, in some
respects, very different from those of other varieties
of the partridge. It frequents thick trees, such as
the olive, for the sake of shade; and it is always
necessary to throw stones into their foliage when
beating for it during the heat of the day. In
general only one bird is found in the same tree.
Coveys vary in size from four or five to fifteen or
twenty birds. The best place to find birds, in

the morning and evening, was the durrha or millet fields, the soft grains of this plant affording them tempting food. We constantly found a covey wherever there was a stream, and the sheltered sides of the hills were always preferred by the bird. We had a steady pointer, but dogs are of little use before the rains begin; the scent will not lie, and the want of water in some districts is a fatal drawback; we were, in fact, obliged to carry water for the dog as well as for ourselves. On this account spaniels are useless in Barbary, except in the rainy season. Our plan was to hire three or four villagers to walk in a line with us as beaters. These fellows beat the palmetto tufts and threw stones into the trees as we advanced. It was astounding with what pertinacity single birds would cling to a tuft of covert under our feet; but, on the other hand, the coveys, except in the millet-fields, were apt to get up out of shot. Everywhere the provoking tendency of the red-legged partridge to run, instead of to rise on the wing, gave much trouble, and was an additional reason why dogs were of little use. A few quails were met with, and the lesser bustard was sometimes seen, but we never succeeded in getting near them. The bustard is not unfrequent on the southern plains. But this fine bird is very difficult of approach, and requires to be regularly stalked for one to obtain a shot.

Rabbits are fairly numerous in the neighbourhood of Tangier; and it is a curious fact that they disappear so entirely in the south that the Arabs there do not know what they are. It is said that the river at Rabat is the line of demarcation beyond which not a single rabbit can be found. There are no snipes till November; numbers of them then arrive, and shooting then begins.

It must not be supposed that such a laborious day as I have described was ever attended by the same results as a good day's partridge-shooting in England. From eight to ten brace would be regarded in Marocco as good sport for a couple of guns. The birds, although numerous, do not lie as at home; and they are apt to get up in places where shots cannot be obtained. If in trees, they will rush out at the wrong side for a shot; and in the millet-fields the height of the plant is a great obstacle to obtaining a good view of them.

The royal sport of falconry is much practised by the Moors, and they are very expert in training hawks. The late Sultan did not care much for hawking, but his father was devoted to the sport. Good hawks are greatly prized; they are taught to fly at partridges, bustards, wild ducks, wild geese, and hares.

The Arabs are fond of coursing, and some of their greyhounds are fine animals. They resemble the rough Scotch greyhound, but seem smaller and more strongly built. In our sense of the word the Arab is not a sportsman; he is, in fact, a pot-hunter. If a hare, even when chased by dogs, comes near him, he will, if possible, knock it over with the short stick he always carries, and which he throws with great dexterity. The number of dogs sent after a hare is not limited; sometimes as many as ten may be noticed. The hares are very fast and cunning, and if the ground is not open they are seldom caught. Arabs mounted on mares without saddles or bits, the place of the latter being supplied by pieces of cord in the mouth, commonly attend the dogs. They keep a look-out, and try to turn the hares into the open country. Horses are seldom ridden on these occasions, because they are far less manageable than mares. These swift and docile animals will often run down a hare, and it is alleged that they hunt by sight like the greyhound; hence, perhaps, the absence of the bits. The mode of riding calls to mind that of the reinless Numidians.

We frequently saw on the plain of Marocco small herds of gazelles gracefully bounding along. This beautiful animal is a great favourite with the Moors. They keep it in confinement as a pet, and sing its praises in their songs. It is hunted with greyhounds, accompanied by men on swift horses. The gazelle is also hawked in a peculiar manner; the bird swoops over the head of the animal, whose speed is thus slackened, and the greyhounds overtake it. The flesh of the gazelle is held in great esteem.

The jackal is also hunted with greyhounds. Such a hunt is the occasion of a great gathering of Moors, mounted and on foot. It is usual to commence proceedings with prayer, ending with the pious adjuration, "May God curse the devil." The dogs are ranged in the open, while a number of beaters advance towards them through a covert supposed to contain the game. As they advance the beaters keep up a frantic noise by shouting, screaming, and firing guns. When the jackal is started the dogs are unloosened. In speed the jackal is no match for the dog, and in the open country is soon run down. But this is a small part of the performance, for the jackal has still to be caught, and only some greyhounds will undertake to catch him. It is a fine sight to witness the precaution of the dog in seizing his savage prey. If he gets a chance the jackal is sure to make his long fangs sorely felt. The dog, therefore, watches the opportunity until he can seize the jackal by the neck, close to the ears. Having effected this, the brute is pinned to the ground and soon despatched. The Barbary jackal is a large and fierce variety.

The porcupine is common in the rocky hills of the south. It is hunted by moonlight with dogs. The flesh is considered good eating by the Moors, but is rather too luscious for the European palate. Live porcupines are often brought to Mogador, and the quills of the animal form a small article of export.

Boar-hunting, however, may be regarded as the

national sport. Hunts on a very extensive scale are periodically organized by the governors. Mounted men in a long line take up their places on one side of the thicket known to contain boars, while a crowd of beaters drive the game towards the horsemen. The uproar and imprecations showered on the unclean animal baffle description, and when a boar is started the excitement reaches the highest pitch. The boar is hunted by strong dogs of the greyhound kind, which boldly attack the savage animal; and a dog having once made good its hold will not quit it. But it is no uncommon thing for a dog to be ripped up by the boar's tusks. When a shot can be obtained, the opportunity is taken advantage of. If the boar is only wounded without being disabled, he will inevitably charge his assailant, who, if on foot, then stands in great danger unless the ferocious brute has his attention diverted by the dogs, or is brought down by another shot.

Boar-hunting in the neighbourhood of Tangier is carried on after the Indian fashion. The boars are pursued and speared from horseback.

Although the Moors regard the boar as an unclean animal, many of them make no scruple of eating the flesh.

APPENDIX.

A.[1]

THE SITE OF THE ROMAN CITY OF VOLUBILIS.

THE identification of an ancient city is always a matter of great interest, and with this object in view I carefully examined the remarkable ruins called Cassar Pharaon (Pharaoh's Castle), situated about twelve miles north-east from Mequinez, and about twenty-eight miles north-west from Fez. The ruins lie out of the direct road to either of these places; but the fact that they have been so seldom visited by Europeans is due not so much to this circumstance as to the extreme jealousy with which the adjacent Zaouia or sanctuary of Muley Edris is guarded.

Rohlfs, who travelled as a Mussulman, and was thus able to enter the sanctuary, makes no mention of the ruins. He says, in connection with his visit, that he was "always looked upon with distrust—to ask directly about any place would not do at all, I should have been at once denounced as a spy."[2] Following Leo Africanus, he supposes the town of Muley Edris to occupy the site of Volubilis. I shall have more to say on this subject hereafter.

This Muley Edris was the father of him of the same name by whom the city of Fez was founded. The town in connection with the sanctuary is placed on the southern declivities of two cone-shaped elevations of a mountain called Zarhoun. The ruins are situated at a distance of about two miles from the town upon a level platform, in part sup-

---

[1] This description appeared in the *Academy* of June 29, 1878.
[2] "Adventures in Morocco," pp. 120, 199. By Dr. Gerhard Rohlfs. (London, 1874.)

ported by a wall, beyond which the ground slopes abruptly towards the south. To the west of the ruins, blocks of hewn stone are scattered over a considerable space, with here and there Roman carved work in scrolls, and egg and tongue patterns, &c. All these stones, as well as those of the standing portions of the buildings and of the tombs, are of the same material—namely, grey limestone.

The ruins appear to belong to the late Roman period.

One of them consists of the remains of a building which measured externally thirty-six yards in length by twenty yards in breadth. Two large archways still exist in the portions of the walls that formed the ends of the structure, as seen in the reproduction of a photograph taken by myself. The southern wall, of which most remains, is about forty feet in height. It is interesting to find that Windus—who visited the place 156 years previously, under the same circumstances, having accompanied an embassy—gives a

APPENDIX. 323

drawing and a short description of the ruins.³ He describes the ruin now under consideration as the "good part of the front of a large square building .... parts of the four corners are yet standing, but very little remains, except these, of the front." Since Windus wrote, the whole of the front and the corresponding wall at the back have entirely disappeared, except so much of them as is almost on a level with the ground. No cement appears to have been used, and the stones in the standing walls in some places show spaces

of an inch or two in the perpendicular joinings. In other cases, the blocks are in such positions as to threaten to fall out of the edges of the walls. It is plain that these effects could only have been produced by a rocking movement in definite directions. It is almost certain, therefore, that a succession of earthquake shocks acting in the direction of north and south have prostrated the front wall described

---

[3] "A Journey to Mequinez, &c.; on the Occasion of Commodore Stewart's Embassy thither for the Redemption of the British Captives in the year 1721" (London, 1725), p. 85.

by Windus, and at the same time shaken the stones of the end walls loose in the manner above described.

At a distance of 100 yards towards the north on the same platform, and facing in the same direction, but at a slightly diverging angle, stand the remains of an arch. The archway was twenty feet wide, and from the massiveness of the structure (as shown in the above view, also from a photograph taken by me), and from the circumstance that its back and front were alike, it was probably a triumphal arch. This was the opinion of Windus, whose drawing of it represents the arch as unbroken. Underneath it, he found six fragments of stones that contained portions of inscriptions (also figured by him), which he says, " were fixed higher [on the arch] than any part now standing." A portion of one of these fragments was identified by me. The remainder probably lie buried in the *débris* of the fallen arch.[4] A mutilated bust in bas-relief, figured by Windus, is also still to be seen. Many pieces of pilasters, pillars, and Corinthian capitals are strewn about the platform. Besides fragments of buildings,

---

[4] The fragment I saw contained slender-shaped letters about six inches in length. All the portions of inscriptions figured by Windus were too fragmentary for anything to be made out of them, and he made no attempt of the kind. Sebaste, the Greek rendering of Augustus, appeared on one of them, and the repetition of the letters M Λ X indicated that the inscriptions were connected with something imperial, probably the record of a triumph. Windus says of the ruins: "Which the Moors call Cassar Pharaon (*i.e.* Pharaoh's Castle), who they told us was a Christian, but could not give any further account thereof. A draught of which, with the Inscriptions of several stones found in the ruins, I have taken, for the consideration of the curious." I have found another view of the ruins, in the same state as when drawn by Windus, in a work entitled, "Several Voyages to Barbary" (2nd ed., London, 1736, p. 141). The only reference to the plate is contained in the following passage. Speaking of slaves at Mequinez, it is stated:—"One of them, Capt. Henry Boyd (since deceased), having taken a plan of that place, with some sketch of the slaves' employment there, we thought fit to insert it, together with three other draughts of his, viz., a coast chart, some Roman ruins, and a plan of Alcasar, which possibly may be acceptable to the curious, tho' not immediately relating to the present subject."

APPENDIX.

the abrupt slope previously mentioned has upon it several tombs, apparently still intact. Two of these bear inscriptions of which Windus makes no mention. The larger one is covered by a slab almost on a level with the soil. Before describing this, I have to make a few observations.

It was a curious coincidence that the inscription on this slab, copied into a German journal, reached the *Academy* at the same time (August 4th) that a letter of mine, stating that I was about to make a communication about Volubilis and its inscriptions, was already in type for insertion in that journal. Circumstances prove that the long-neglected inscription in question was copied independently within a very few days by members of the German Embassy to the Sultan and by myself, assisted by the Portuguese Ambassador and Mr. C. Murdoch.

The thick slab in question is about five feet long by three feet wide, and is badly fractured longitudinally. The inscription is contained within a border of scroll-work ornament. Here is an exact copy of that made with much care by myself. The lines are numbered for convenience of reference :—

1. QCAECILIOQFILIO
2. DOMITIANOCLVDIA
3. VOLVBILIIANODICV
4. RIONIMUNICIPII
5. VOLVBILIIANIAN
6. NORVMX QCAE
7. CIIIVSS   ACRA
8. CIIISIICM
9. ANTONIANI
10. IISIIIIOIII
11.   IOS

Note, in lines 7, 8, and 10, the repetition of the letter I occurs because what is chiefly apparent in most cases is that the letters possessed upright lines. It is easy, however, in the majority of the cases to make out the letters to which these lines undoubtedly belonged. The reading of this by Prof. Mommsen, as given in the *Academy*, August 4th, is:—

"Q(uinto) Cæcilio Q(uinti) filio Domitiano Claudia Volubiliano, decurioni municipii Volubiliani, annorum XX, Q(uintus) Cæcilius . . . . . (et) Antonia N(ata)lis filio pii(ssimo) posueru(nt)."

This agrees with my reading and interpretation, with the following exceptions. It is, however, to be observed that the exact copy of the inscription sent to this eminent authority is not before us.

Line 3. A letter is omitted: it is "Volubiliiano," or "Volubilliano," not "Volubiliano."

Line 5. The same omission occurs.

Line 6. I could not decipher the letter which succeeded X, owing to the fracture of the stone. The hiatus is filled in the German copy by a second X.

Line 7. In my copy, after "Caecilius," S occurs, and with a hiatus of two or three letters, owing to the increased damage from the fracture; the letters "acra" are quite readable. This portion of the inscription is not included in the reading by Mommsen given above. But he says: "I cannot decipher the cognomen and position of the father; perhaps there stood something like 'Gracilis leg[ionis] I.'" Evidently these words were conjectured by reading the antepenultimate letter of line 7 as G, and making up the remainder from the letters and portions of letters in line 8, except the last letter; this is plainly M.

Line 9. Both copies agree with the exception of the last letter, which I make I, and Prof. Mommsen conjecturally A.

Line 10. The letters are very imperfect, but from their arrangement and general appearance, and comparison with other inscriptions, no doubt can be entertained that the words "Filio piissimo" were inscribed.

Line 11. The same remarks apply to IOS, which is certainly to be read "posuerunt."

The circumstance that the monument is in memory of a native of Volubilis, and one of its municipal officers, affords strong presumptive evidence that it was placed at Volubilis.

The other monumental inscription is on the perpendicular face of a block of stone about two feet square. There are two holes in the top of the stone, which seem to have been intended for attaching something to it, possibly a statue. The inscription is as follows:—

```
    M F A B I O L I I L C I
    R O G A T O A N X V I I
    L E A B I V S C R I S P V S
          P A T E R
    F I L I O P I I S S I M O
            P O S
```

"M(arco) Fabio . . . . Rogato An(norum) XVII Leabius (sic) Crispus Pater Filio piissimo pos(uit)."

That Volubilis was an important place may be judged from the ruins described—assuming, as I believe, that they belonged to that city—and from the mention of it by many ancient authors. Pliny says:[5]

"Ab Lixo XL. M. in Mediterraneo altera Augusti colonia est Babba, Julia Campestris appellata; et tertia Banasa, LXXV. M., Valentia cognominata. Ab ea XXXV. M. pass. Volubilis oppidum tantundem a mari utroque distans."

There can be no doubt that the Lixus river of Pliny is identical with the modern El Kus or Lucos river. But as the positions of Babba and Banasa are open to doubt, the distances given here can help us little in fixing the position of Volubilis. But the distance of the sanctuary of Muley Edris from either sea—that is, from the Mediterranean and

[5] "Natural History," B. v. c. 1.

the Atlantic—as shown on the best map of Marocco,[6] accords well with Pliny's statement. The map shows that Volubilis was somewhat nearer to the Atlantic than to the Mediterranean, if we place it close to Muley Edris. But if it be assigned to the site of the modern city of Fez it would be considerably nearer to the Mediterranean than to the Atlantic. Ptolemy mentions Οὐολουβιλίς in his tables of the positions of places,[7] but it is impossible in this case also to fix that of this city by his aid.

In one edition of Pomponius Mela, Volubilis is mentioned as one of the principal cities of Mauretania Tingitana;[8] in another edition the word Dubritania is substituted.[9]

The question arises whether the site of Volubilis was not that of the modern city of Fez, as alleged by some authors. If the distances given in the *Itinerarium Antonini* could be trusted, Fez must be adopted as the site. He states that Volubilis was "*Mill. pass.* xvi." from Aquae Dacicae.[10] Hot springs were known to have existed here, and at about the distance mentioned from Fez is the hot sulphurous water of Ain Sidi Yussuf, which is unquestionably identical with Aquae Dacicae. But from the many known errors with regard to distances in this author, it would be rash to accept his statement as a proof.

Hemso says:—

"Volubilis, o Volobilis, da molti creduta Fas, ma piu precisamente la Tiulit, e Gualili dei secoli di mezzo, e la Zauiat Mula-Driss dei nostri giorni."[10]

In all that concerns Marocco, no author is so much quoted as Leo, who wrote in the sixteenth century; and his state-

---

[6] "Carte de l'Empire de Maroc. Reduite et gravée au Dépôt Général de la Guerre" (Paris, 1848).
[7] "Geography," Book iv. c. 1.
[8] "Chorographia." Edit. Vossii (Frankerae, 1700).
[9] "Chorographia." Edit. Gustav Parthey (Berolini, 1867).
[10] "Specchio geografico e statistico dell' imperio di Marocco, dell' avliere conte Jacopo Graberg di Hemso" (Geneva, 1834).

ments may in general be relied on. He asserts that the town which contained the sepulchre of Muley Edris on Mount Zarhoun, was called Gualili, and was built by the Romans. Some author, struck perhaps by the possible transmutation of Volubilis (not mentioned by Leo) into Gualili, concluded that the modern town had succeeded to the ancient one. This statement has been often repeated without question. But a reference to Leo's work[11] will show that he also speaks "of a certaine towne called the Palace of Pharao," as being also founded by the Romans, and about eight miles from Gualili. The distance here given, even supposing the miles to be of the shortest description, makes it improbable that Leo visited the place. After combating the idea that the town was built by Pharaoh, King of Egypt, he says: "I am rather of opinion, by the Latine letters which are engraven on the walles, that the Romans built this towne."

My inquiries lead me to believe that the name Gualili is not known in connection with Muley Edris at the present time. And while I think it highly improbable that an important city like Volubilis would be placed on the steep declivity of a mountain, it seems to me reasonable to suppose that from the proximity of the two places the now obsolete name Gualili, assuming it to be derived from Volubilis, would easily be transferred by mistake or otherwise from one place to the other.

The position of the ruins is one admirably adapted for an important city. It commands a fine view over an extensive and fertile plain. It is central as regards the northern portion of Marocco, and on the direct road to many of the remoter parts. The ruins and inscriptions are of particular interest, because they are the most westerly remains of the far-extending Roman Empire.

[11] "A Geographical Historie of Africa," by John Leo a More. Translated by John Pory (London, 1600).

B.

I VENTURED to test the influence I had gained at the Moorish court by my connection with the Embassy, as well as by the turn of events, by asking certain favours. I was aware that the high officials were by no means conciliatory to strangers, and that a gentleman who had approached the chief minister a short time previously with an introduction from the best possible quarter was not even granted an audience. I asked Sid Moosa to obtain from the Sultan a document which should act as a safe conduct for a journey to Timbuctoo, or at all events as far as the Sultan's power extended. Not that I had formed a definite plan for so perilous a journey, but it seemed to me that as the greater includes the less, I might obtain a passport of great value for a future journey in the remoter parts of Marocco. Contrary to the opinion of my friends, which was that the Moorish Government would not issue a document which might be a cause of embarrassment to them, the request was received favourably. Sid Moosa had a paper drawn up, which, though short, is of great power. Here is its *fac-simile* :—

TRANSLATION.

"Praise to the One God.

"There is no strength nor power but in God Almighty the Most High.

"We have granted permission to the bearer, the English Doctor, to travel in our Dominions protected by God, and to visit the tribes who are under the control of the Government, but he is not to expose (his life) in parts where they are not under control. We order our governors and obedient tribes to take care of him, and give him assistance, and to receive him with kindness and attention, so that no injury may befall him from any one.

"Peace.

"12 Jumad the Second, 1294.
"(25th June, 1877.)"

It is in the seal, which is that of the Sultan himself, that the virtue of this edict resides. If handed to one of his subjects, it is first reverently applied to his forehead and then kissed devoutly. Such a passport, bearing the ministerial seal, is now and then issued, but one bearing the Imperial talisman does not appear to have been given to any previous traveller. As if to show still more good faith in the matter, the paper was forwarded through the hands of His Excellency Sir John Drummond Hay, at Tangier, whose popularity with the Moorish Government is very great. It was accompanied by a letter to him from Sid Moosa, pointing out the danger of an attempt to reach Timbuctoo. The fate that befel my application to examine the libraries at Fez has been elsewhere detailed.

C.

THE DRUGS IN USE AMONGST THE MOORS.

THE Moors employ a large number of drugs medicinally; and as very little was known about them, I made an extensive collection of specimens. The information obtained by this means was communicated to the Pharmaceutical Society in a paper read before that body, and published in their journal. The list of these drugs and, when possible, of the plants from which they were derived, together with the scientific names of the plants, is reproduced here revised and extended. I was assisted in the work of revision by Mr. E. M. Holmes, the able Curator of the Pharmaceutical Society's Museum. Care has been taken to give the native names as correctly as possible in English. These names appear to be in the great majority of cases peculiar to Marocco, and many are derived from the Shluh language. Very few of them correspond with the Arabic names of the same drugs as given in books.

The collection was made at the coast towns visited, and also at the city of Marocco, but chiefly at Mogador. Here I was mainly indebted for additions to my collection, as well as for much information about them, to Signor Yusef Elmaleh, Jewish High Priest, and to his son, Signor Reuben Elmaleh. In every case possible the leaves and flowers of the respective vegetable productions were obtained for the purpose of identification. In the instances in which these were not available, it was impossible to refer the drugs to their natural orders and species. It is believed that what has been done will prove interesting to the scientific reader, and useful to future inquirers in the same field.

LEAVES, FLOWERS, AND PLANTS.
MALVACEÆ.

KHUBBAIZAH.—*Malva parviflora*, L. The whole herb. The name Khubbaizah appears also to include other species of the *Malvaceæ*, as the specimen also contained *Lavatera hispida*, Desf. Khubbaizah is used as a demulcent in catarrh.

RUTACEÆ.

RUTA.—*Ruta angustifolia*, Pers.—Rue. Carried about the person as a safeguard against infection. Given for nervousness, &c. *R. bracteosa*, D.C., is also used under this name.

LEGUMINOSÆ.

SENAHARAM.—*Cassia elongata*, Lémaire Lisancourt.—Senna. Stated to be brought to Marocco by the pilgrims returning from Mecca. This is confirmed by the fact that the specimen is identical with Mecca senna, imported *viâ* India into this country. Used as a purgative.

ARTIM.—*Retama Rætam*, Webb.—This shrub forms a feature of the landscape. In many places it covers thousands of acres of sandy soil, to the exclusion of almost every other plant. Its white flowers in spring diffuse a strong and agreeable odour. At Mogador, the name "Artim" appears to be restricted to this species, but some dried flowers from Tangier, under the same name, include also *Genista candicans*, L., and *G. linifolia*, L.

"Artim" is probably, therefore, a generic name for several leguminous plants used as food for cattle.

The bitter roots of *Retama Rætam* are said to be used by the Arabs for internal pains, and the shoots macerated in water are applied to wounds. The shoots much resemble in appearance those of *Sarothamnus scoparius*, but are slenderer, more branched, and the branchlets are longer.

CRASSULACEÆ.

GHASSOUL.—The structure of the fruit, which is mixed up with the stalks and leaves, is evidently that of some calycifloral plant, with a half-inferior ovary, nearly allied to the genus *Mesembryanthemum*, but we have not yet succeeded in identifying the species. Although evidently it is nearly related to *M. cordifolium*, L., apparently other plants are employed under the same name, since a species of *Silene* was received as Ghassoul or Tegaghust. Used instead of soap for cleaning woollen clothes.

ILLECEBRACEÆ.

HAYDORLEY.—*Paronychia argentea*, D. C.—Flowers used as a diaphoretic, and also for abdominal pain.

MYRTACEÆ.

RAHAN.—*Myrtus communis*, L.—Myrtle leaves. The infusion is used for diarrhœa. The leaves are also employed by the Jews in their ceremonies.

COMPOSITÆ.

SHECH.—*Artemisia Aragonensis*, Lam.—Tops. Barbary worm-seed. Used in infusions for colds, and also in fumigation for small-pox, &c. It is exported to Holland to make "bitters." Barbary worm-seed was considered by Guibourt to be the produce of *Artemisia glomerata*, Sieber.[1]

SHIBAH EL AGOOZ. (Trans. Old man's beard).—*Artemisia*

[1] Pereira's Mat. Med. Art. Artemisia.

arborescens, L.—Wormwood. Used in dyspepsia, and also for giving flavour to green tea.

Babinoose.—*Matricaria Chamomilla*, L.—A species of Chamomile. Used as a stomachic.

Asbardo.—*Kleinia pteroneura*, D. C.—The green stem. These curious cactus-like stems belong to a composite plant nearly allied to the common groundsel.

The stem is about the thickness of the fore-finger, leafless, except at the top, where there is a rosette of leaves, furrowed externally, and has a large discoid pith; the branches are nearly equal in size, quite erect, and parallel with the stem, and remind one of a candelabrum with a number of candles in it.

It is used externally for "pains in the hands and feet" (rheumatism?).

Gentianaceæ.

Cust el heeah, or, Noar Muley Ali. (Trans. Muley Ali's Flower.)—*Erythræa ramosissima*, Pers.—Tops, &c. Closely allied to gentian. Used for indigestion.

Labiatæ.

Helhal.—*Lavandula Stœchas*, L.—Tops, &c. Used as a stomachic.

Murroot.—*Marrubium vulgare*, L.—Common Horehound. Variety, β. *lanatum*.—Tops. Used as an external application in small-pox and in hæmorrhoids.

Flayu.—*Mentha Pulegium*, L.—Penny-royal. Flowers, &c. The infusion is used for flatulence and abdominal pain.

Timzah or Menta.—*Mentha rotundifolia*, L.—Round-leafed mint. Tops. Used for diarrhœa.

Zater.—*Origanum compactum*, Bth.—Marjoram. Flowers. The infusion is used to promote digestion. It was formerly exported to Holland in large quantities. It is also much used by the Moors for flavouring tea.

AZEER.—*Rosmarinus officinalis*, L.—Rosemary. Whole plant. Used for fumigation in small-pox, &c.

MURROOT YURB.—*Salvia triloba*, L.—A kind of sage. Leaves. This plant probably owes its Moorish name to its resemblance (having a woolly stem and leaves) to *Marrubium vulgare*. It is used as an application to wounds.

SADEEAH.—*Teucrium Polium*, L.—Tops. Used in colic, &c. A nearly-allied species, *Teucrum montanum*, L., known under the name of Poly-mountain, appeared in the London Pharmacopœia as late as 1763.

TASERKENNAH.—*Thymus vulgaris*, L.—A variety which has the leaves more tapering towards the base than in the form which occurs in this country. Tops. Used as a stomachic.

URTICACEÆ.

HEBIKA.—*Parietaria officinalis*, L.—Pellitory.

CANNABINACEÆ.

KIEF.—*Cannabis sativa*, W.—Hemp. Whole plant. It is grown largely in the provinces of Haha and Shedma. The right of dealing in it and in tobacco is monopolized by the Emperor. These monopolies are farmed to Jews, who buy at a price fixed by law, and sell at an enormously-advanced price. The plants are pulled up when the seed is ripe or nearly so; and the leaves, when dried and coarsely powdered, constitute kief. This is smoked in very small pipes, and a few inhalations exhaust the contents of the bowl. The smoke is taken into the lungs, and produces a powerfully narcotizing effect; but, unlike the preparations of the plant, which are swallowed, the effect soon passes away. Some smokers indulge their propensity frequently during the day; yet I have been assured by them that, after twenty or thirty years, they have not suffered from the practice.

Hashish, the preparation which is eaten, is too well known, from recent descriptions, to require much to be said about it. It is made by mixing the powdered leaves with butter, and also as a conserve with honey, to which opium is added.

ARISTOLOCHIACEÆ.

IRIFFA. — *Aristolochia species.* — Leaves, applied when pounded to wounds and bruises.

FRUITS AND SEEDS.

RANUNCULACEÆ.

HUBRAS. — *Delphinium Staphisagria*, L. — Stavesacre. Seeds used to destroy vermin.

SANOUS.—*Nigella sativa*, L.—Seed. It is supposed to be the fitches mentioned by Isaiah. Used as a diaphoretic.

RUTACEÆ.

HARMEL. —*Peganum Harmala*, L.—Seed. Used in fumigation as a disinfectant, and also against the effects of the evil eye.

RHAMNACEÆ.

NABU.—*Zizyphus orthacanthus*, D. C. — Jujube berries. The fruit of the sidra-tree. This tree varies in size from that of a small tree to a small shrub, depending upon the soil in which it is found. It is widely diffused. The berries are eaten, and are commonly sold in the markets of Marocco. The oil of the kernel is used as a perfume.

LEGUMINOSÆ.

HULBAH. — *Trigonella fœnum-Græcum*, L. — Fenugreek. Taken by women to induce fatness, and also given with barley to horses. When first taken it purges.

CUCURBITACEÆ.

EL HEDJA.—*Cucumis colocynthis*, L.—Fruit. Colocynth is

an article of export from Mogador. I got a specimen in the
city of Marocco, which, instead of being of a yellow colour,
was of bright green with numerous yellow streaks made up
of more or less irregular patches, which marked it into
segments. It was probably only a variety. Colocynth is
used as a purgative by the Moors. They also keep the
broken gourd amongst their woollen clothes when put
away, to keep off moths.

Umbelliferæ.

Carwia.—*Carum Carvi*, L.—Caraway seed. It is grown
largely in the neighbourhood of Larache, and is shipped at
Tangier in sugar casks and serons, but chiefly in bags to
England and America. It is also produced round the city
of Marocco. At Mogador, where it is rarely shipped, it is
called Fez caraway seed. One cannot help being surprised at finding this cold climate plant a product of
Marocco.

Cumin.—*Cuminum Cyminum*, L.—Cumin seed. This
is grown largely in the interior provinces of Ahmar and
Rahamna. The Jews mix it in their bread. It is exported to America, and also to the Canary Islands, where
it is used in preserving tunny fish.

Naffa.—*Fœniculum dulce*, C. Bauh. junior.—Fennel
seed. This is used for flavouring mahaya, a spirit obtained
from the water in which honeycombs are boiled in preparing bees' wax, and from other sources, as previously
described (p. 237).

Sapotaceæ.

Argan.—*Argania Sideroxylon*, Rœm. et Sch.—Seed. The
oil expressed from the nuts is in general use for cooking.
Fowls and other articles of diet are served up soaked in this
oil, which is preferred by some Europeans to olive oil. But

such greasy food is very distasteful to most stomachs. It is customary to allow it to simmer over a fire with a piece of bread in it to remove its pungent taste, and this process is also believed to obviate a supposed tendency of the oil to cause leprosy.

Goats, sheep, and cows eat the fleshy part of the argan fruit freely, and the nuts are then laboriously broken with stones in order to extract the kernels. These are first partially roasted and then ground in a handmill. The oil is extracted from the meal by working it with the hands, and water is added to the mass as seems necessary.[2]

PLANTAGINACEÆ.

ZURKTONAH.—*Plantago Psyllium*, L.—Seed. Used as a demulcent in fevers and in colds.

EUPHORBIACEÆ.

HABTMLEK.—*Croton Tiglium*, W.—Croton oil seed. The Moors use the seeds as a strong purgative, and I found that they are well known in the interior of the country. But I was not able to satisfy myself that *Croton Tiglium* grows in Marocco. The seeds were stated by the Moor who gave them to me to be *Romi*, i.e., European.

CASTOR.—*Ricinus communis*, L.—Castor oil seed. The plant is abundant about Saffi, and attains to the dimensions of a small tree. The oil is not expressed by the Moors, but the seed itself appears to be used as a purgative.

SCITAMINEÆ.

GOOZA SAHRAWEEA.—(Trans. Nutmeg of the desert.)—*Amomum Melaguetа*, Roscoe.—Grains of Paradise. The drug is brought to Marocco by the caravans from the interior. The

[2] See p. 93.

Grain Coast of Western Africa takes its name from the profusion of *Amomum Melagueta* which it produces. It is used as a sexual stimulant and also as a spice with meat, and mixed in bread.

ROOTS.

CISTACEÆ.

IPHERSCUL.—*Cistus salvifolius*, L.—It has an earthy and slightly aromatic taste. It is given for palpitation of the heart and nervousness.

LEGUMINOSÆ.

ARK SUS.—(Trans. The root of Sus.)—*Glycyrrhiza species*.—Liquorice. Used for coughs and chest affections. Grows in great abundance in the southern province of Sus.

FUÊLY.—*Astragalus eriophaca*, Ball.—Identified by Dr. Ball, who has been lately engaged in examining the flora of Marocco. The taste of the root is saltish; it is used when pounded as an application to wounds.

COMPOSITÆ.

ADAD.—This is a large, somewhat cylindrical root, more than a foot long, and about two inches in diameter. It has a crown consisting of several stems, springing from the contracted upper portion of the root. The radical leaves show beyond a doubt that Adad is the root of some species of the Composite order. The transverse section of the root is white and starchy, but nevertheless hard and tough, and shows about six ill-defined concentric rings, marked with horny-looking radiating lines, which, under a lens, are seen to consist of vessels containing matter resembling caoutchouc. This material has exuded from several parts of the root, where it was apparently injured in the fresh state. The smell and taste of the root are aromatic. Leo Africanus says of Adad:—" The herbe thereof is bitter, and the root is so venomous that one drop of the water distilled thereout will kill a man within the space of an hower, which is commonly knowen even to the women of Africa.' The drug does not appear to be so poisonous as here stated. It is taken for debility and low spirits. It is *Atractylis gummifera*, L.

ILLECEBRACEÆ.

TAUSERGHINT.—*Corrigiola telephiifolia*, Pourr.—Externally the root is pale brown and twisted, rather knotty at the top, more or less fusiform, from a quarter to half an inch in diameter, and from two to four inches long. Its internal appearance is very characteristic. The transverse section is of a yellowish-white colour, with 3-5 concentric rings, which have a horny and translucent appearance. The taste is acrid, causing a tingling sensation like that produced by Senega. The grated root is mixed in bread to induce fatness. Leo Africanus says concerning "Tauzarghente:" "This root, growing in the westerne part of Africa upon the Ocean seashore, yeeldeth a fragrant and odoriferous smell, and the merchants of Mauritania carry the same into the land of Negros, where the people use it for a most excellent perfume, and yet they neither burne it nor put any fire at all thereto; for being kept only in an house, it yeeldeth a naturalle sent of itselfe. In Mauritania they sell a bunche of these rootes for halfe a ducate, which being carried to the land of Negros is sold again for eightie or one hundred ducates, and sometimes for more." The root received is not so powerfully odorous as represented by Leo Africanus; it has a very faint odour, like that of orris-root.

RUBIACEÆ.

FOOAH.—*Rubia species.*—A kind of madder root. Infusion used for diarrhœa, and as an emmenagogue. It is also applied to sore eyes.

PLUMBAGINACEÆ.

TAFRIFA.—*Statice mucronata*, L.—A sea lavender. The

taste of the root is saltish and pungent. It is supposed to strengthen the nerves.

SCROPHULARICEÆ.

EMSLEH-EN-DER.—*Verbascum sinuatum*, L.—The root is ground very fine, and placed under the eyelids as a cure for ophthalmia.

EUPHORBIACEÆ.

WASKEEZA.—*Euphorbia terracina*, L.—A spurge. This root is used as an emetic.

ZINGIBERACEÆ.

KEDILSHAM.—*Alpinia officinarum*, Hance.—Galanga. Infusion of the root used in urethral discharges.

LILIACEÆ.

ABLALUZ.—*Asphodelus ramosus*.—Mœnch.

B'SELT-DEEB.—(Trans. Jackal's Onion.)—*Urginea maritima*, Baher, or *Urginea Indica*, Kunth.—This, when boiled in oil, is highly esteemed as an aphrodisiac.

IRIDACEÆ.

AMBER-EL-DOR.—*Iris Germanica*, L.—Orris root. It comes in large quantities from the city of Marocco to Mogador, whence it is shipped to England and France, and of late far more extensively than formerly. It bears little more than half the price of Florentine orris root.

AROIDEÆ.

IRENE.—*Arisarum vulgare*, Hook.—The interest which belongs to this plant lies in the circumstance that it yields a useful starch. In times of famine, which occasionally happen from drought or from a visitation of locusts, the tubers are dug up, washed, dried in the sun, and ground between hand mill-stones. Without further preparation the meal is then cooked by steam, like kuskussoo, the national dish, made of granulated wheaten flour. As happens in the case of the allied plant, *Arum maculatum*, which yields Portland arrowroot, Irene tubers contain an acrid poisonous principle which should be removed by repeated washings. As this is neglected by the Moors, it is not surprising that people who live entirely upon such food suffer severely from abdominal pain, and that many of them die. When travelling between Saffi and Mazagan in the early part of November the ground was in many places studded all over with the single leaf of this plant, which had then just appeared above ground. I succeeded in bringing home some growing plants, which are now flourishing in Kew Gardens. The plant has been figured and described from these specimens by Dr. Hooker, in Curtis's "Botanical Magazine" for March, 1878.

Not identified.

TASECRA.—This is a large, somewhat woody root, twelve or eighteen inches long, two inches or more in diameter at the top, much branched, and tapering to half-an-inch in the smaller branches. The cortical portion is brown, spongy, and rather thin in proportion, being on the average not more than a line in thickness. The meditullium is of a yellowish colour, with the concentric rings not visible, and in many of the pieces the medullary rays are of an ash-grey colour (perhaps from imperfect drying), which gives a distinctly radiate appearance to the meditullium. The root is almost tasteless; attached to it are portions of leaves which appear to belong to some species of *Carlina* or *Carduus*. It is taken to mitigate thirst.

BOCBOOKAH.—This root occurs in pieces varying from one-third to half-an-inch in diameter, and several inches in length. It is dark brown externally, with numerous closely-placed annular ridges and numerous small warts, and is sometimes branched in the upper part like dandelion-root. The meditullium is large, white, and starchy, occupying about two-thirds of the diameter of the root. The cortical portion is white internally, and has a ring of resinous-looking rays next to the meditullium. The taste is insipid. It is used for "pains in the bones" (rheumatism?).

OUDEN EL HELLOOF.—This consists of a short prostrate rhizome, terminating in a hairy bud, and giving off below a tuft of straight unbranched roots, of a reddish-brown colour, about the size of a crow-quill, and finely striated longitudinally. The odour resembles that of arnica, and the taste is aromatic and somewhat acrid. It is taken for strangury.

BERSMOOS.—This root has a thick, brown, spongy, cortical portion, and a white, soft, radiate meditullium. It tastes somewhat like turnip, but without any pungency. The infusion is given in fever.

BARKS.

ANACARDIACEÆ.

DRO.—*Pistacia Lentiscus*, L.—Used in fumigation and also for tanning.

JUGLANDACEÆ.

SWAK.—*Juglans regia*, L.—Walnut bark. Used by the Moorish women for staining the lips black.

EXUDATIONS.

UMBELLIFERÆ.

FASHOOK. — *Ferula species*. — Gum ammoniac. Called Fasoy by the European merchants and Kelth by the Moors. It is abundant in Woled Bu Sba, two days' journey from Mogador, on the road to the city of Marocco. It grows very quickly after the first autumnal rain. A stalk obtained at Mogador was one inch and a quarter in diameter. Before parting with it the Moor broke off a portion, intending it, as he said, to fumigate his sore eyes. Some roots procured by Signor R. Elmalch were of the size and shape of carrots, of a blackish-brown colour, and studded over with numerous warty projections. When broken they exuded drops of milky juice which formed yellowish-white opaque tears. The taste of this gum resin was slightly bitter with considerable acridity. A single fennel-like leaf accompanied the roots; it was evidently the leaf of an umbelliferous plant. It was found that the taste of this gum resin differed from that of a specimen of African ammoniacum in the museum of the Pharmaceutical Society; the latter had no taste at first; but after a time a burning, acrid taste was developed, which lasted longer than in the case of the gum resin obtained direct from the root. It seems probable, therefore, that African ammoniacum is produced by more than one species; some of the roots procured are planted both at Kew and at the Royal Botanical Gardens, London, so that one may hope to be soon able to identify the plant with certainty. On account of its adhesiveness the gum is used by the Moors as a depilatory. The seed, when heated over a fire until it becomes glutinous, is used as an application in skin diseases. Very little ammoniacum is sent to Europe. But a great deal is carried by pilgrims to Egypt and Arabia, where it is used for incense. It is chiefly shipped from Mazagan to Gibraltar for reshipment to Alexandria; a little is sent from Mogador, and none from the other ports. Pereira was of opinion that the Greeks and Romans were unacquainted with Persian ammoniacum (the produce of *Dorema ammoniacum*, Don.). The name ammoniacum is stated by Pliny (b. xii. chap. 49) to be derived, like that of the oracle of Jupiter Ammon, near which the gum was produced, from ἄμμος (sand), in reference to the surrounding sandy country. This would indicate that it was brought from Lybia, the modern Tripoli. The Arabian physician, Serapion, writing at the commencement of the ninth century, mentions two kinds of ammoniacum, the best sort of which was produced from the root of a plant found in Crete; and an inferior kind, of which he says, " Sed illud quod continet terram et lapides, nominat chironia et defertur a terrâ quæ dicitur Monacon et est succus plantæ, similis plantæ galbani in similitudine sui et nascit ibi." This description agrees with the present Marocco product, and Monacon may be an early name for that country. It is observable that Serapion calls ammoniacum "raxach;" and that "assach," "ushak," and "oshac,' are severally employed by Arabian and Persian writers to designate the gum. These approach "fasogh" and "fashook," the modern Moorish names.

EUPHORBIACEÆ.

PHORMIUM.—*Euphorbia resinifera*, Berg.—Euphorbium gum. I have little to add about this substance to what is already known. It is produced in the inland provinces of Deminet and Antife, but the plant is found in other places. A plant which grows freely in the neighbourhood of Mogador was pointed out to me as that yielding the gum, but it proved to be *Kleinia pteroneura*. A kind of honey from the province of Haha is sold in the Mogador market. This when eaten causes a burning sensation in the mouth and throat. It is on this account regarded as of a heating nature, and like the squill is valued as an aphrodisiac. I was assured that these properties are due to the euphorbium flowers, from whence bees obtain the honey. It calls to mind the intoxicating effects of honey, as experienced by some of the ten thousand Greeks in their retreat under Xenophon, effects attributed to the *Azalea Pontica*. But poisonous honey is found in various countries, and the poison seems due to many different plants. The people who pack euphorbium at Mogador wear veils to protect themselves from the dust, which is so irritating to the eyes and nostrils. Pliny tells us (b. xxv. c. 28) that persons engaged in collecting the juice of the euphorbium plant were, on account of its acrid nature, obliged to stand at a distance and pierce it with a pole shod with iron, and that the juice flowed into kid-leather receivers placed beneath. Serapion makes the same statement, except that the stomachs of animals were employed as receivers.[3] Avicenna says that euphorbium loses its virtues after three or four years. But, he adds, some think these may be restored by placing the gum for some time in a vessel containing decorticated beans."[4]

Not identified.

ALK EL EBTUM.—This resin occurs in small, yellowish, rather dirty tears, in colour and taste resembling American frankincense. It is probably the product of some coniferous plants. Its Spanish name, "Gomma di Pinezia," gives probability to this suggestion, indicating as it does that it is derived from a species of fir. The resin is used in urinary complaints, accompanied by pains in the loins and deposits in the urine. It is administered mixed with bitters and honey.

MISCELLANEA.

PAPAVERACEÆ.

BEN NAAMAN.—*Papaver dubium*, L.—A poppy. Capsules, &c. Used as a diaphoretic.

TAMARICACEÆ.

TACOOT.—*Tamarix articulata*, Vahl. — Galls. Used for tanning, and shipped for this purpose to Algiers.

ANACARDIACEÆ.

ILLEG.—*Pistacia atlantica*, Desf.—Pistachia galls. Produced in Showia. Used for diarrhœa, and also as a cosmetic.

---

[3] "Serapionis Medici Arabis celeberrimi Practica," Venetiis, apud juntas, 1500, p. 179.

[4] Avicenna, Venetiis, apud juntas, 1595, b. ii., p. 313.

AURANTIACEÆ.

MA-DEL-LETCHIN.—*Citrus species?*—Orange-flower water. This, the quality of which is good, was brought from Terodant, a town south of Mogador, unvisited by Europeans on account of the fanatic nature of its inhabitants. Rosewater is brought from the same place, and both articles are largely used by the Moorish ladies. Vessels like that here represented, which was kindly given to me at Mogador by Mr. Alfred Jordan, are used to convey these waters. They are made of hammered copper, tinned over, and are of the shape of half an egg. The top part, to which a handle is attached, is depressed. 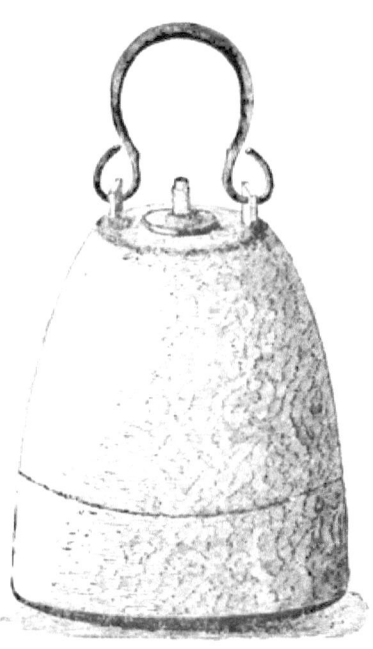 These vessels are eight and a half inches in height by seven and a half inches in diameter at the base, and contain about a gallon. It is curious to find such peculiarly-shaped and well-made vessels, probably formed of native copper, employed in this way in this rude country.

ANIMAL SUBSTANCE.

AMBER EL HOR.—*Ambergris.*—Strangely enough, this substance is brought to Mogador in considerable quantities by the Timbuctoo caravans from the interior of Africa. It probably finds its way there from the west coast. It is also obtained from sperm whales, which drift in dead on the Marocco coast. One of these whales has been thus procured at Casa Blanca in each of three years lately passed. All contained ambergris, and the last an unusually large quantity. It was purchased by a Jew, who, it is said, sold it for £3,000. Much of it was exported to London. At Mogador it sells for about £20 per pound. Leo, speaking of the town of Messa in Sus, says: "Here may you find upon the sea-shore great store of amber, which the Portugal and Fezzan merchants fetch from thence for a very meane price, for they scarcely pay a ducat for a whole ounce of most choice and excellent amber." Most of the well-off Moors have ambergris in their houses. They use it in green tea as a flavour, and one of the greatest compliments paid to a guest is to present him with a cup of this curious mixture. Ambergris is also used as an application for the sting of a scorpion, when a knife made red-hot is also placed over the wound.

Out of the foregoing list of sixty-six articles, more than half of them proved to be derived from plants identical with those of Europe, or else from plants so closely allied to European species as to possess practically the same properties. A few, as Argan oil, Fashook, and Phorbium, are peculiar to Marocco, while others, as Adad, Ouden el Haloof, Tauserghint, &c., appear to possess active qualities which deserve careful trials of their therapeutic powers.

INDEX.

AGRICULTURE, 166, 280.
Aguidel, the garden of, 131.
Ain O'must, 104.
Al Buyda, 113.
Ambergris, 349.
Amusements, 231.
Arar wood, 96.
Architecture, 89.
　In City of Morocco, 156.
Argan-tree, 92, 339.
Army, 258.
Art, 90.
Artim, 99.
Audéd, 298.
Azamoor, 202.

BASTINADO, 76, 250.
Baths, 75, 162.
Batteries, 13, 87, 194.
Ben Daoud, 125.
Berbers, 213.
Bezoars, 277.
Birds, 301.
Boar hunting, 319.
Bu Bekr Sid, 122, 130, 119, 147, 149.
　Visit to his house, 129.
Busellam Boisha, 42.
Butter, 191, 102.

CAMEL, THE, 204, 288.
Casa Blanca, 60.
　Surf at, 53.
　Unhealthiness of, 55.
　Exports of, 57.
Cattle, 292.
Chameleon, the, 305.
Character of the Moors, 220.
Cherif, the Grand, of Wazan, 24, 126.
Circumcision, the ceremony of, 74.
Citron wood, Pliny's account of, 94.
Climate, 22, 55, 69, 107, 110, 117, 119.
Consumption, exemption of Mogador from, 73.
Costume, 225.
Coudiat Ardhous, 115.
Coursing, 317.
Court etiquette, 240.

DINNER ETIQUETTE, 230.
Diseases, 88.
Dogs, 88.
Drugs used by the Moors, 333.

EDUCATION, 261.
El Geroui, 130.
El Horreh, 298.
Emshras, 183.

Euphorbium gum, 347.
Evil eye, 91, 172, 268.
Eysawi, 266.

FAMINES, 285.
Fashook gum, 345.
Fatness, method of inducing, 232.
    Induced by bastinado, 250.
Fish, 310.
Fishing, 44, 65, 85, 108, 311.
French war with Morocco, 87.
Funeral, Moorish, 98.

GAME, 92, 189.
Gibraltar, 2, 5.
Government officials, 250
Governor's castle, 187.
    Another, 207.

HAMMATCHA SECT, 265.
Harrabel, 232.
Hashish, 236.
Hawks, variety of, 302.
    Edible, 86.
    For sport, 89.
    Rare specimen, 100.
Hooker, Dr., Pres. R. Soc., ascent of the Atlas, 152.
Horse, the, 290.
Huts, conical-shaped, 63.
Hyena, the, 300.

INFANTS' FOOD, 92.
Insects, plague of, 112, 206, 308.
Inzella, what, 101.
    El Youdy, 116.
Irene roots, 343.
Iron mountains, 100.

JACKAL-HUNTING, 318.
Jewellery, 227.
Jew of Wadnoon, story about, 269

Jews in City of Morocco, 169
Jews in the empire, 216.
Justice, 163.

KADDUR, 4.
    His conversation, 48.
Kief, 236.
Kil'atu l'Hassan, 105.
Kuskussoo, 230.

LANDSCAPE, 99.
Law, 244.
Leper village, 145.
Lighthouse, 51.
Locusts, 309.

MAHAYA, 237.
Manufactures, 167, 227, 236, 293.
Marocco, geography of, 212.
    Population of, 210.
Marocco City, journey to, 97.
    Plain of, 118.
    Gardens of, 119, 123.
    First impressions of city, 121.
    Our house in, 123.
    Disturbed state of, 126.
    Gates of, 126.
    Visit to Jews' quarter, 127.
    Apathy of inhabitants, 129.
    Insults offered to us in, 132, 141.
    Prison in, 134.
    Life in the house, 136.
    Arbitrary tribunal in, 136.
    News in, 137.
    Food in, 138.
    Fine views from, 140, 156.
    Attempt to poison us in, 145.
    Motives for this, 149
    History and general description of, 154.
    Markets, 166.

INDEX. 353

Marocco City—
   Local taxes, 166.
   Manufactures, 167.
   Palace, 167.
   Sanctuary, 168.
   Fountains, 169.
   Jews' quarter, 169.
   Inhabitants, 178.
   Government, 179.
   Thieves, 180.
Marocco leather, 72, 167, 294.
Mazagan, history of, 59.
   Fine cistern at, 63.
   Danger of roadstead, 64.
   Trade, 64.
   Climate, 64.
Medicine in Marocco, 73, 273.
Mills, 56.
Millstone quarry, 52.
Mogador, 66.
   Mr. Perry's house at, 67.
   Climate, 68.
   Description of, 70.
   Trade of, 71.
   Jews at, 72.
   The High Priest of, 74.
   The Governor of, 76.
   Peculiar lingo at, 77.
   The island at, 80.
   Danger of the port, 81.
   Visit to the island, 83.
Mohammedanism, 104, 263.
Money, 294.
Monkeys, 298.
Montefiore, Sir M., 72, 174, 218.
Moorish costume, 132.
   Feast, 120.
   Incapacity, 99—155, note.
Moors, the race of, 211.
Mosques, 46 47, 86, 160.
   The Katoubia, 132, 161.
Mountain, The, 38.

Mshra, 116.
Muley Ali's gardens, 147.
Muley Hassan, 126.
Murders, 49, 103, 116, 180.
Mzoudia, 114.

NARCISSUS BROUSSONETII, 198.
Negro race, 216.
Nifys River, 116.

OLEANDER, 107.
Olive tree, large, at Saffi, 197.
Ostrich hunting, 304.
Owl, small species, 105.

PAPER NAUTILUS, 52.
Partridge-shooting, 315.
Pigeons, wild, 84.
Plough, 282.
Powder play, 28.
Prayer, hours of, 262.
Prisons, 14, 134, 162, 188, 251.
Proverbs, Arab, 175, 215.
Punishments, 249.

QUARANTINE, 83.

RABBITS, 316.
Reforms urgently required, 256.
Renegades, 218.
Revenue, 243.

SAFFI, 192.
   Sanctuary at, 193.
   Surf at, 197.
   Large olive-tree near, 198.
Saint houses, 56.
Salt, Lake of, 189, 190.
Sanatorium, site for, 39.
Sanctuaries, 248.
Schools, 17
Science, 161.
Scorpions, 16.

Scorpions, charm against, in City of Marocco, 173.
Seshoua, 107.
Shebbel, 44, 204, 207.
Shluh race, 214.
  Village, 88.
Shooting, 46, 65, 84, 92, 100, 183, 313.
Shraa, 253.
Sidi Moktar Sanctuary, 102. 106.
Slavery, 225.
Snake charmers, 141.
Snakes, 305.
  In houses, 129.
Soldier guards, necessity for, 150.
Spy, a, 100.
Squirrels, 106.
Starlings, immense flocks of, 85.
Stone-throwing, story of supernatural, 271.
Sultan, the, 27, 57, 120, 128, 240.
Superstitions, 267.

Tabia, 159.
Tabib, the, 302.
Tagharcet, what, 35.
Taiefer 'l Aras, what, 33.
Tangier, 2.
  Disembarking at, 3.
  Lord Sandwich's journal concerning, 6.
  Pepys' mention of, 7.
  Given up by the English, 9.
  Town described, 11.
  Batteries, 13.

Tangier—
  Citadel, 13.
  Hotels, 15.
  Amusements, 16.
  Antiquities, 18.
  Gardens, 19.
  Coffee-houses, 20.
  Prices at, 21.
  Institutions, 21.
  Climate, 22, 23.
Tax collection, 42.
Tea-drinking, 120, 234.
Tensift River, 108, 182.
  Bridge over, 147.
Threshing, 284.
Tortoises, 307.
  Taking bait, 108.
Tortures, 251.
Treasure, hidden, 295.
Truffles, 287.
Turkeys, 140.

Vegetation, curious distribution of, 117.
Voyage, 1.

Wages, 21, 289.
Water, effects of, on animals, 106.
  On vegetation, 107, 283, 285.
Wedding, a Moorish, 30.
  A Jewish, 30.
Wheat crop, 285.
Wild boar, 297.

Yezid, Sultan, story of, 195.

www.ingramcontent.com/pod-product-compliance
Lightning Source LLC
Chambersburg PA
CBHW032013220426
43664CB00006B/234